PEOPLE OF THE SEA

A MARITIME HISTORY OF BEARA

MARC O'SULLIVAN VALLIG

BEARA TOURISM

CONTENTS

FOREWORD

About thirty years ago, I first discussed the possibility of producing a book on the fishing community in Beara with Jim O'Sullivan and John Murphy of Beara Tourism. For various reasons, we did not get around to it back then, which is a source of regret when one considers how many local legends associated with the fishing industry we have lost in the meantime. However, I am grateful indeed to have had the opportunity to interview so many fishermen, boat owners, agents, dealers, search and rescue personnel and others associated with the sea at this point in time, and to have produced a record of the maritime community in Beara as it stands today.

Those who are familiar with the fishing industry will know that it has always been in flux. Good times have followed bad, just as bad times have followed good. My own family fished out of Garnish for generations; hardly anyone fishes there today, but I have vivid memories of when it was an absolute hive of activity in the late 1960s and '70s. The men in their yellow oilskins; the boats bobbing in the water; the crates of fish stacked up on the slip, awaiting collection. My father Frank still sometimes fished with his brothers in the summer, and it was a thrill indeed when we kids were allowed go with them.

The home place at Lehanmore was similarly busy. I remember my uncle Cormac mending lobster pots in the garden, and the fishing nets spread out on the lawn. Uncle John L had two Volkswagens in those days: the good one for driving east, and the rusty banger for driving west to the pier. Aran sweaters and woollen caps – inspired by the Clancy Brothers, no doubt - were all the rage. Stories were told of salmon fishermen disguising themselves with more elaborate headgear – balaclavas, and even saucepans – when they were being pursued by the Navy at sea.

I had no sense in those days that this boom in inshore fishing was a recent phenomenon, the latest in a series of booms that had occurred at intervals throughout the 20th century. That last boom lasted for ten or twelve years, but by the time I finished school in 1982 it was already over; the mackerel were gone, and so too was any notion I might have had of becoming an inshore fisherman. By then, we had a punt of our own at Ballycrovane, but the only fishing I ever did was for my dinner.

Later on, I spent several summers painting trawlers on Dinish Island. I've never envied anyone who worked, ate and slept in conditions as cramped as those I encountered on the boats. When I wasn't banging my head off pulleys and poles, I was tripping over ropes and nets, and that was when the vessels were on land; I couldn't begin to imagine how much more hazardous it would have been at sea.

The dangers associated with fishing for a living were brought home to me on New Year's Day 1973, when my uncle Cormac was drowned in Cobh. Like so many other such incidents, it occurred not at sea but at the quayside, when Cormac was casting off the ropes and fell between the trawler and the pier. What I remember most vividly of his funeral is the line of cars that seemed to stretch for miles behind us as we drove over Cousane Gap; so many friends and neighbours had come to meet the hearse along the way, to bring our Cormac home.

Cormac's is one of seventy-two names inscribed on the plaque on Barry Linnane's *Twilight Haul* monument erected by Mná na Mara on Dinish Island in 2010, to commemorate those who have perished at sea. Everybody in Beara will have known someone among them.

Thankfully, the recent establishment of RNLI and Coast Guard stations in Castletownbere, manned mostly by volunteers, has made search and rescue vastly more efficient, and helped reduce fatalities.

In the past few decades, the fishing industry has changed immeasurably. The days when a bunch of young fellows would leave school to go fishing are long gone. So too is the ready spending of cash that seemed easily earned; there is no longer that buzz around Beara that was so long associated with the comings and goings of the local fleet and the twice-weekly fish auctions. These times, many skippers have given up on finding crewmen in the area, and you are as likely to encounter a Filipino or an Eastern European as a local lad on a trawler in Castletownbere.

There is no doubt that joining the EU was detrimental to Irish fishing, as we relinquished too much control of our waters to Europe. Advances in technology, overfishing and pollution continue to impact hugely on the industry here, and it seems the very real concerns there are about all three have yet to be properly addressed.

The very nature of maritime industry has changed as well. Mussel and salmon farms are now common features in the harbours around Beara, and it is surely only a matter of time before wind farms and wave farms become just as familiar a sight. Leisure activities such as kayaking, diving and pleasure boating are readily available, and it is to be expected that they will all expand as tourism develops. Whatever happens, it is a given that the fortunes of the Beara community will continue to depend on the bounty of the sea.

For practical purposes, this book is divided into two sections: the first a series of essays on the maritime history of Beara; the second a series of interviews with twenty-three local people associated with the sea.

My thanks to everyone who agreed to be interviewed: to Jim O'Sullivan, PRO of Beara Tourism, who participated in most of the interviews and directed this project from beginning to end; to Dorothy Brophy and Penny Durell, who proofread the manuscript; to Beara Historical Society, Máiréad O'Driscoll, Richard McCormick, Aoife O'Sullivan, Noelie O'Sullivan, Mick FitzGerald and Martin O'Shea, all of whom provided photographs; to Anne Marie Cronin, who edited the images; to Frank Kelly and Pádraig O'Sullivan, who provided invaluable local historical information; to John Dwyer, our designer; to Aidan Hegarty, who provided my accommodation; to John Murphy, Chairman of Beara Tourism, who facilitated the publication of this book; and to our sponsors, Bord Iascaigh Mhara.

Marc O'Sullivan Vallig
Beara
July 2020

In memory of

Cormac O'Sullivan, Lehanmore

1945 - 73

PART 1: BEARA'S MARITIME HISTORY

JCTION

The Beara peninsula straddles counties Cork and Kerry and extends some thirty miles into the Atlantic. Beara is dominated by two mountain ranges, the Caha Mountains and the Slieve Miskish Mountains, and is bounded on the north by Kenmare Bay and on the south by Bantry Bay.

The Irish for 'peninsula' is *leathinis*, a half-island: an accurate description when one considers that, throughout history, Beara has more often been accessible by sea than by land. The peninsula is believed to have been settled as early as 3,000 BC, and is rich in sites of archaeological interest, such as ringforts, fulachta fiadh, wedge graves, dolmens and stone circles.

Beara today has a population of about five thousand, but it may have supported more than thirty thousand before the devastation of the Famine in the mid-nineteenth century. Traditionally, the local economy has depended on fishing and farming, and evidence of both can be seen almost everywhere, from the piers and fishing palaces along the coast to the sheep trails and stone walls which crisscross the hillslopes and mountainsides.

Given its exposure to the wild Atlantic, it is no surprise that much of the mythology and history of the Beara peninsula is associated with the sea.

1

THE MYTHOLOGY OF BEARA

The Song of Amergin

According to the medieval *Lebor Gabála Érenn (The Book of Invasions)*, the earliest Gaels to settle in Ireland were the Milesians, who arrived from Spain around 1,000 BC.

In Beara, the Milesians are believed to have landed their ships at Garnish, at the western tip of the peninsula. From here, they set off for Tara to do battle with the country's rulers, the Tuath Dé Danann.

The Tuatha Dé Danann insisted they were not prepared for combat, and asked that the Milesians withdraw their fleet of ships a distance of nine waves from the shore and wait three days before challenging them again.

The Milesians withdrew as asked, but then the Tuatha Dé Danann summoned a magic wind which drove their ships far out to sea. One of their leaders, Donn, drowned and was buried on the Bull Rock, known thereafter in Irish as An Teach Duinn. It was here that the souls of the dead were said to gather before departing for the otherworld.

The Milesians eventually made landfall again, on the stony beach at Garnish. The Tuatha Dé Danann - knowing they could not defeat the newcomers in battle - agreed to surrender to them the kingdom of Ireland, provided they themselves could live on underground, where they became the Sídhe, or the fairies.

One of the first Milesians to set foot in this country was the poet Amergin, who claimed it for his people through the utterance of these immortal lines, translated from the Gaelic by the first President of Ireland, Douglas Hyde:

"I am the wind which breathes upon the sea,
I am the wave of the ocean,
I am the murmur of the billows,
I am the ox of the seven combats,
I am the vulture upon the rocks,
I am a beam of the sun,
I am the fairest of plants,
I am a wild boar in valour,
I am a salmon in the water,
I am a lake in the plain,
I am a word of science,
I am the point of the lance of battle,
I am the God who created in the head the fire.
Who is it who throws light into the meeting on the mountain?
Who announces the ages of the moon?
Who teaches the place where couches the sun if not I?"

The Children of Lir

The legend of the Children of Lir is one of the most famous of all Irish folktales, and again, it has a significant association with the Beara peninsula.

The story begins with the election of Bodhbh Dearg to the position of King of the Tuatha Dé Danann. This was greatly resented by another chieftain, named Lir, who fancied the position for himself. Rather than quarrel with him, Bodhbh Dearg offered Lir his daughter Aoibh in marriage.

Lir agreed to the match, and Aoibh bore him four beautiful children: a son named Aodh, a daughter named Fionnuala, and then twin boys, Fiachra and Conn.

The family's happiness was shattered when Aoibh died suddenly. Bodhbh Dearg sought to comfort them by offering Lir his second daughter Aoife in marriage. Lir again agreed to the proposal; it made perfect sense that his late wife's sister should help rear their children.

At first, Lir and Aoife were happy too. But then she grew jealous of the children, whom Lir loved above all else. One day, she offered her bodyguards rich gifts to murder them. The bodyguards refused to harm the children, and Aoife became enraged; she took the four to a lake and cast a terrible spell, turning them into swans. She allowed them to retain one aspect of their human nature, the gift of speech.

Fionnuala demanded that the spell be limited to a specific period of time, and Aoife agreed, declaring that the four should live as swans for three hundred years at Loch Dairbhreach (on the River Inny, that flows into the Shannon), three hundred years on Sruth na Maoile (the Straits of Moyle, between Northern Ireland and Scotland), and three hundred more on the wild Atlantic.

At the end of that time, after many misadventures, the Children of Lir came ashore at Allihies, lured by the sound of a bell rung by a Christian monk. They regained their human form, but they were terribly aged and already on the brink of death. The monk baptised them, and when they died, he buried the four side by side and placed the rock over their grave which can still be seen today, by the roadside near Allihies village.

The Princess Beara

According to legend, the King of Ireland, Owen Mór, was gravely injured while battling the warrior Conn Céad Cathach – Con of the

Hundred Battles –at Cloch Barraige. Owen's men carried him away to Inis Greaghraighte, as Bere Island was then called, where the fairy Éadaoin tended to his wounds in her bower at Grianán until he was well again.

Owen sailed for Spain, where he won the hand of Beara, daughter of the King of Castille. Accompanied by a large army, he brought her back to Ireland. They landed at Grianán, and Owen took his new bride to the top of the highest hill on the island, showing her the extent of the peninsula he then named Beara in her honour.

A number of places on the mainland, including Rosmacowen and Kilmacowen, are believed to be named after Owen.

In 2009, the Beara Historical Society erected a plaque to mark the spot where Princess Beara was buried, in Ballard Commons, between Maulin and Knocknagree Mountains.

From 1901 to 1948, people and goods were transported back and forth between Castletownbere and Bantry on a steamship called the *Princess Beara*.

The Cailleach Bhéara

The Cailleach Bhéara – or Baoi, as she was sometimes known – was one of the most important figures in early Irish mythology. In Beara, she is remembered for having lived for nine hundred years before being turned to stone, and it is in this form she may still be seen, overlooking the sea in Kilcatherine, in the parish of Eyeries.

The author Frank O'Connor described the Cailleach as "the Mary Magdalene of Irish mythology." Some storytellers credit her with the ability to change her condition from that of a hag to a young woman at will.

Lugh, the god of arts and crafts, was among her many husbands. Another was the druid Dinioch. It was he who intervened when Corc and Cormac, twin brothers fathered by the Munster chieftain Cairbre Musc with his own daughter Duben, were judged to have been born in a state of sin and were sentenced to be burned to death. Cormac perished, but Corc was fostered by Dinioch and Baoi and reared on Dursey Island.

Each morning Baoi would set the child on a bull's back and wash his sin into the beast. Little by little, the bull assumed Corc's guilt, and when at last the child was fully cleansed, the bull leapt into the sea, followed by a cow and a calf. These then became the Bull, Cow and Calf Rocks as they are known today, while Corc himself grew up to be the king from whom the Corca Dhuibhne would later claim descent.

The Cailleach had several places in and around the Beara peninsula named in her honour. Dursey itself was given its present appellation by the Vikings, who, in the ninth century, used it as a posting station for captives. The island had previously been known as Oileán Baoi. Similarly, Bantry Bay was once known as Cuan Baoi, while the ruins of the O'Sullivan Bere stronghold at Dunboy – or Dún Baoi – bear a derivation of the Cailleach's name to this day.

A short distance from this historic site is the Glebe or Church of Ireland rectory in which the writer Standish O'Grady was born. O'Grady is best known as one of the leading lights of the Celtic Renaissance, a movement which revived general interest in Irish mythology.

Among his contemporaries was Douglas Hyde, who, in a book called *Legends of Saints and Scholars,* refers to a Connacht proverb that lists the three longest lives in the world as those of the yew tree, the eagle and the Cailleach Bhéara.

Hyde also mentions a folktale which describes how a visitor to the Cailleach asks her what age she is. She instructs him to count the skulls of all the cattle around her home, each of which represents a year. He counts five hundred.

Accounts vary as to the Cailleach's ultimate fate. An Old Irish lament in which, having entered a convent, she contrasts her life as a pitiful crone with that of her glorious youth, has been translated by several writers, though the version by Frank O'Connor in *Kings, Lords and Commons* remains the most stirring. O'Connor believed the poem to the surviving fragments of a dialogue between the Goddess of Munster and St Cummine. It begins:

> "I, the old woman of Beare,
> Once a shining shift would wear,
> Now and since my beauty's fall
> I have scarce a shift at all.
>
> Plump no more I sigh for these
> Bones bare beyond belief;
> Ebbtide is all my grief,
> I am ebbing like the seas."

In Beara, some claim an angry clergyman turned her to stone when she refused to convert to Christianity. Others say she transformed herself to avoid conversion. At any rate, it is in the form of a rough-surfaced rock that the Cailleach Bhéara may still be seen today, overlooking the sea in Kilcatherine.

The Cailleach Bhéara

2

DÓNAL CAM O'SULLIVAN BEARE

Dónal Cam O'Sullivan Beare, born in 1561, was the last chieftain of Dunboy. The sea could be said to have been both the making of his fortune, and ultimately, his undoing.

Dónal lived at a time when the old Gaelic order was finally being swept aside by English laws and customs, and for a time he took advantage of that. His father died when he was still an infant, and his uncle Owen became clan chieftain under the Gaelic Tanistry system. Owen was canny enough to have his title recognised under English law; he was knighted by Elizabeth I and became Lord of Bantry and Beara. But when Dónal came of age, he challenged Owen for the chieftaincy, insisting he should be recognised as his father's heir under the English primogeniture system. His claim found favour with the authorities, who recognised him as the O'Sullivan Beare and awarded him lordship of the Beara peninsula, leaving his uncle Owen with just Bantry and Whiddy Island. This naturally resulted in a split in the clan; when Owen died a year later, his son, also called Owen, became one of Dónal's bitterest enemies.

Dónal Cam's income was mostly derived from the sea, as he charged vessels entering Berehaven harbour a range of fees for berthing, landing fish and taking on supplies, and he claimed ownership of any cargo taken from vessels wrecked along the coast. Known to many as O'Sullivan of the Slender Ships, he was almost certainly engaged in smuggling wine and brandy from France and Spain. It is said that Dónal earned £40 per annum from his land holdings in Beara, a sum he gave to his wife to cover her expenses, and at least £500 from his maritime enterprises.

In Dónal Cam's day, Ireland was in an almost constant state of rebellion against English rule. The alliance of the Northern chieftains Hugh O'Neill of Tyrone and Red Hugh O'Donnell of Tyrconnell saw them lead a significant insurgency against the English, and victories such as the defeat of Sir Henry Bagenal at the Battle of the Yellow Ford in August 1598 raised hopes throughout the country that Ireland could reclaim its independence.

O'Neill and O'Donnell won the support of the Catholic King Philip III of Spain, who promised an army to bolster their forces. In 1601, Philip sent six thousand men on thirty-two ships to Ireland. Had they made it to their favoured destinations, Limerick or Galway, they might have swept east and taken Dublin. But the weather was against them, the fleet was split, and four of the ships, carrying two thousand of the more experienced soldiers, returned to Spain.

On the 21st of September, the twenty-eight remaining ships and three thousand two hundred soldiers, under Don Juan del Aguila, landed at Kinsale, almost as far from the Northern chieftains as could be imagined. The English, under the command of the Lord Deputy of Ireland, Charles Mountjoy, rushed to lay siege to the town. O'Neill and O'Donnell, after dithering for some weeks, eventually led their armies south to encircle them. Dónal Cam, sensing victory for the combined Irish and Spanish forces, wrote to Philip III to pledge his allegiance, and soon joined O'Neill and O'Donnell with an army of one thousand men. He must have cut a charismatic figure; in spite of his lack of experience in warfare, he was appointed leader of the Munster forces.

After weeks of siege, the English were weakened by hunger and disease, and the Irish and Spanish, attacking from both sides, might have laid them to waste, but luck was against them. On the 3rd of January 1602, the morning the Irish were to attack, the English seemed to have been forewarned of their intentions and met them head on. The Irish forces were routed, and del Aguila, realising the game was up, surrendered Kinsale. O'Neill fled back up north, while O'Donnell handed his command to his brother and went directly to Spain to plead for further assistance from Philip III.

Dónal Cam returned to Beara an outlaw. He was regarded by the English as the most dangerous of the rebel chieftains in the south, and his stronghold at Dunboy was targeted for destruction. George Carew, the Lord President of Munster, was dispatched to deal with him.

The Beara terrain was notoriously unforgiving, and Carew knew better than to attempt an assault on Dunboy Castle by land, but he believed it could be taken by sea. In early March 1602, he sent the Earl of Thomond ahead from Cork, setting up camp at Bantry Abbey and Whiddy Island with a force of four thousand men. Carew followed a few weeks later, and set himself up at Donemark Castle, which he renamed Carew Castle. At the end of May, he marched his army down the Sheep's Head peninsula, and in the early days of June, they crossed to the eastern end of Bere Island.

The chief defender of the O'Sullivan Beare stronghold at that time was not the chieftain himself, but Captain Richard MacGeoghegan, who held the title of Constable of Dunboy. MacGeoghegan sailed across the harbour to parley with the Earl of Thomond, who is said to have offered him favourable terms to change sides in the conflict. But MacGeoghegan would have none of it; the O'Sullivan Beare camp was convinced that a large party of Spanish reinforcements would arrive by ship at any moment, and the southern chieftains would drive the English out of Ireland for good.

Sadly, this belief proved to be ill-founded. A single Spanish ship, the *Santiguillo*, arrived at Ardea Castle, another O'Sullivan Beare stronghold, on the north side of the peninsula, and Dónal went to meet it. On board were two Irish priests, Bishop MacEgan and Father Archer, who still insisted that an army of fourteen thousand Spaniards was coming to their aid. This, had it happened, might very well have changed the course of history. But King Philip III of Spain had wearied of conducting a war in Ireland, and while he did indeed fit out some ships to send to Dónal's aid, he soon decided against the venture. So nobody came, and it was left to MacGeoghegan and a party of one hundred and forty to defend Dunboy against Carew's cannons.

There has always been considerable disagreement as to why Dónal Cam did not himself take charge of the defence of Dunboy. Some will argue that he knew well the defence was a suicide mission, and left braver men to die in his stead, while others insist he was simply waiting on the reinforcements promised from Spain before going to their assistance.

Among the men in MacGeoghegan's command were three Spanish artillery experts, who advised the erection of a sod bank - up to eighteen feet thick - against the castle walls to withstand bombardment by the English.

Carew soon brought his cannons over from Bere Island, landing two on Dinish Island as a ruse, and conveying the rest to a sheltered beach on the mainland and then dragging them to a vantage point northwest of the castle. It took weeks to get them into position, and in the meantime Carew sent John Bostock to attack another O'Sullivan Beare castle, a fortress built by Dónal Cam's uncle Dermot on Dursey Island.

Bostock, accompanied by Dónal's cousin Owen, arrived at the Dursey Sound on the 12th of June. The Dursey stronghold was defended by Conor O'Driscoll of Baltimore and forty men, equipped with three Spanish cannon. Given its relative inaccessibility, Dónal had earmarked it as his last line of defence in the case of Dunboy falling to the enemy. The Dursey Sound was, and is, notoriously difficult to cross, but Bostock's party were gifted with a calm tide and took the fortress by surprise. Notoriously, they took no prisoners, rounding up almost every soul on the island – many had fled there from the mainland, seeking refuge – and put them to the sword or tossed them off the cliffs to their deaths on the rocks below.

Meanwhile, around 4am on the 17th of June, Carew gave orders for his cannons to commence firing on the O'Sullivan Beare stronghold at Dunboy. He estimated it would take several days to destroy it. Not so; it fell within twenty-four hours. The sod bank proved to be largely detrimental to the defenders, as it blocked the windows and prevented them from shooting out, and it was only in the late stage of the battle, when the castle wall was breached and the English stormed in, that the Spanish cannon proved to be of any use. Even then, it was too late; the castle was taken, and the defenders beaten back into the basement, where they remained until morning, when most surrendered without terms.

MacGeoghan, already badly wounded, must have had some intimation of what would happen them, as he was discovered crawling towards a barrel of gunpowder with a lighted torch, intent on blowing himself, the enemy and what remained of the castle to pieces. He was killed before he could do so.

Carew showed no mercy to the survivors, not even those who'd surrendered. He immediately hanged fifty-eight of them, and the sixteen others were only spared for a time, with some being hanged in Cork, and one, Brother Dominic Collins, in his native Youghal.

The destruction of Dunboy Castle and the deaths of its defenders must have shaken Dónal very badly indeed. For the rest of the year, he moved his army about the hills of Beara, conducting a guerilla campaign against the English, but as the weeks and months went by, and winter came, it became more and more apparent that no reinforcements were coming from Spain. In December, the English seized his cattle and sheep in a valley outside Glengarriff, and the chieftain knew the game was up. Without their herds, his people simply could not survive the winter. At the end of the year, he led a party of four hundred soldiers and six hundred civilians on what is now remembered as the Long March to Leitrim. Along the way, they were attacked by both the English settlers and the native Irish; they risked starvation, many died, and others slipped away. Only thirty-five of the party arrived at the castle of the O'Rourkes in Leitrim.

Dónal Cam was all for fighting on, and raised a small army with the money he'd received from Spain. But the struggle was already nearly over. In 1603, O'Neill signed the Treaty of Mellifont, which brought an end to the Nine Years War and also effectively brought an end to the old Gaelic order. Over the next few years, most of the dissenting Irish chieftains fled to Europe, in what became known as the Flight of the Earls.

Dónal Cam sought but was refused a pardon by the English crown, and had no option but to go into exile as well. He found refuge in Spain, where he settled first in Santiago de Compostela, and later in Madrid, where he became de facto leader of the Irish community. The city had recently become the centre of the Spanish court, and he continued to press for a Spanish army to liberate Ireland from the English. He found favour with the king, who awarded him a generous pension and the title Count of Berehaven, but it seems unlikely that Spain would ever again have attempted an invasion of Ireland.

Dónal Cam never returned to Beara. On the 16th of July 1618 he was coming from Mass in Plaza de Santo Domingo in Madrid when he saw his nephew Philip O'Sullivan engaged in a swordfight with a man named John Bathe, who is often remembered as being English, but had actually grown up in Drumcondra. Dónal Cam went to break up the fight, and Bathe slashed at him with his weapon, cutting his throat. He died on the spot.

Ironically for a man so much associated with the sea, Dónal Cam O'Sullivan Beare was buried two hundred miles distant from it, in a church that was later demolished, so that there is not even a grave for his Irish relatives to visit.

Dónal Cam O'Sullivan Beare

The ruins of the O'Sullivan Beare stronghold at Dunboy

3

MURTAÍ ÓG O'SULLIVAN

Murtaí Óg O'Sullivan was a controversial character, a man who appears to have been loved and loathed in equal measure. He was not just a minor landlord and a smuggler, but also an officer in the French army, and a recruitment agent who is reputed to have press-ganged local youths into service in the Irish Brigade.

Murtaí was born in Eyeriesbeg, a short distance from the present village of Eyeries, around 1710. Locally, it was believed that Dónal Cam O'Sullivan Beare was fostered out to relatives and reared in the same place for at least part of his childhood. This was a common practice for centuries; Murtaí himself was fostered by a woman on Dursey Island named Muireann Ní Shúilleabháin. He was not a direct descendant of Dónal Cam's, but is believed to have had some connection by blood. He was often referred to as an 'O'Sullivan Beare' in his lifetime, and shown the kind of deference that would once have been accorded to a chieftain of the clan.

Murtaí inherited land holdings in Eyeries, Inches and Crumpane, though these were not his lands, as such; rather his role was that of a middleman who paid rent on them and in turn extracted rents from tenants of his own. While this would have provided some modest income and status, he looked elsewhere to make a more substantial living.

Murtaí is believed to have enlisted in the French army in 1739, most likely as an officer in Lord Clare's infantry regiment of the Irish Brigade. Little is known of his military experience, other than that he was probably wounded at the Battle of Lauffeld in Belgium in 1747, and was at some point promoted to the rank of Captain. He is more often remembered for his exploits as a recruiting officer for the French Army, an activity that earned him a fee of five guineas for each young man he enlisted.

Murtaí had a keep in the townland of Kilmichael on Dursey Island, a circular building known as the Corr Áit, whose remains may still be seen today. This was where he imprisoned at least some of the youths – presumably those who were enlisted by force - before transporting them to France on his sloop. Murtaí's favoured port of call was Nantes, and he would also have carried goods over and back.

Beara was traditionally a hotbed of smuggling activity, and Murtaí's father is known to have co-operated in the trade with the brothers Henry and John Puxley, the first of that family to settle at Dunboy, where they worked initially as agents of the Eyre family of Galway. Wool, butter and hides were sent out to France, and wine, brandy, tea and tobacco brought back. By avoiding customs and revenue charges, those involved could make substantial profits, but they ran the danger of arrest and imprisonment, and of losing small fortunes if their goods were seized.

At some point, the relationship between the O'Sullivans of Eyeriesbeg and the Puxley brothers broke down. The late Gerard Lyne, in his biography of Murtaí Óg, suggests that the most likely cause of the rift was Puxley's decision, in 1739, to report Murtaí to the authorities for his recruitment activities, which Puxley, as an English loyalist, would have seen as treasonous.

The rift became public when Henry and John Puxley, their nephews Henry and Walter Fitzsimons and a number of henchmen attacked the five sons of Murtagh mac Owen O'Sullivan of Rosmacowen on their way home from Mass at Christmas 1741. In this affray, Walter Fitzsimons shot Owen O'Sullivan dead, while all four of his brothers were wounded. No one was ever convicted for the crime. The O'Sullivans of Rosmacowen were allies of the O'Sullivans of Eyeriesbeg, and there was a further connection in that Murtaí later married Margaret O'Sullivan, a sister of the young man who was killed. It was inevitable, therefore, that he would henceforth regard the Puxleys as his enemies.

The rift was further exacerbated by the fact that, around the time Murtaí became a recruitment officer, Henry Puxley died and his brother John began seeking recognition as a respectable gentleman. He leased large tracts of land, including the former O'Sullivan Beare property at Dunboy and Murtaí's holding at Eyeries, and was appointed a salaried revenue officer, this last being on the basis that he would stamp out smuggling in Bantry Bay. If there had not been rivalry between the two before, there certainly was now. As an English Protestant, Puxley could carry arms and own land; as an Irish Catholic, and an officer of the French Army, Murtaí could legally do neither, which made him vulnerable to prosecution. Nonetheless, he continued to engage in smuggling and recruitment. There seems to have been some degree of hubris in this, his public taunting of Puxley, and indeed, of the English Protestant establishment; one of his more daring exploits as a recruitment officer was to persuade forty-nine soldiers of the English garrison in Cork to desert and enlist in the French Army.

Things came to a head when, according to tradition, Puxley or his men killed a young cousin of Murtaí's named Denis O'Sullivan, who had boasted of Murtaí's military prowess. Muireann Ní Shúilleabháin of Dursey travelled to Dunboy to denounce Puxley for the killing, and threaten him with the vengeance of Murtaí. Puxley responded by leading a party to her home on the island and setting fire to the thatch. That she survived the destruction of her home was a veritable miracle.

Murtaí Óg took personally the killing of his cousin and harassment of his foster mother, and challenged Puxley to a duel. Puxley declined, adding insult to injury by declaring: "It does not become an English gentleman to fight an Irish Papist." And so, on the morning of Sunday the 10th of March 1754, Murtaí Óg and his companions Domhnall Ó Conaill and Little John Sullivan, along with his nephew Henry Leary, lay in wait at Darby Harrington's forge at Finaha. When Puxley was passing on horseback on his way to church, most likely accompanied by his wife Mary, Murtaí stepped out to confront him. There are various accounts of the altercation that followed: some say the two men rowed, and shots were exchanged; others claim that Puxley had no chance to defend himself. One way or another, it is accepted that Murtaí Óg O'Sullivan shot John Puxley dead.

Murtaí was now a marked man. It did not help that he went almost immediately to the local Catholic church and boasted to the congregation of his deed: "My people, John Puxley will do you no more harm. All here whom he wronged are now avenged. I shot him this day." At the inquest on the 18th of March, Murtaí was identified as one of Puxley's killers, along with Darby Harrington, Henry Leary, Little John Sullivan and Domhnall Ó Conaill.

Harrington and Leary were the first to be charged in relation to the killing. Neither was judged to have had a hand in it, and both were promptly acquitted.

Murtaí remained in Beara for some weeks. A reward of £200 was offered for his capture, and a party of soldiers, under Colonel Boothby, arrived at Dunboy to pursue him in April. But Murtaí appears to have already left for France, bringing with him the forty-nine deserters from the garrison in Cork. Lyne concludes that this latter exploit was far more upsetting to the authorities than the murder of John Puxley.

It is hard to imagine how Murtaí, having engaged in so public and serious a crime, would dare to return to Beara thereafter, but return he did, to visit his wife and son at their home in Eyeriesbeg. The authorities were duly informed of his presence – according to local tradition, by Tim Scully, a Corkman married in the area whom Murtaí had put out of his home for beating his wife. A second expedition, this time commanded by Lieutenant Teavil Appleton, was dispatched by ship from Cork on the 2nd of May, arriving at Dunboy at midnight two days later. Appleton and his party, accompanied by the Fitzsimons brothers and a number of local guides, set out almost at once for Eyeriesbeg, marching over Miskish in darkness and torrential rain.

They arrived at Murtaí's home around 4am. It was probably the bad weather that compelled Murtaí to have posted so few of his men – he is believed to have had twenty with him - as sentries, but those he had posted did not see the raiders approaching until they were almost on the property, and even then, the household is said to have been alerted to their arrival by a barking dog.

Fire was exchanged between the two parties - those in the household, and those gathered outside - but at some point Murtaí's wife and son, along with the other women and children, were allowed to leave the property. Appleton then ordered the thatched roof set on fire, and Murtaí, knowing it could not be extinguished, instructed his men to make a run for it one by one. They had to exit the house by the front door, but the raiders' only real interest was in Murtaí and his two cohorts, Ó Conaill and Little John Sullivan, so most of the others were let go. Ó Conaill and Sullivan were among the last to emerge from the burning house, and they were promptly arrested. Murtaí himself came out last, armed with a carbine; fire was exchanged, and he was shot dead.

Murtaí's body was conveyed by horseback to Castletownbere. Local reaction to his demise appears to have been mixed. Many saw him as a patriot and hero, while others viewed him with contempt. According to local tradition, a woman whose son he had conscripted was given permission to view the corpse. The boy had been taken with such force from the bed they'd shared that he'd torn her breast and left it scarred, and now, given her chance for revenge, she beat Murtaí's face with her shoe.

Shortly after his death, Murtaí's sloop was destroyed, and his body is said to have been dragged to Cork behind the raiders' ship, the *Pelrose*. His head was cut off and spiked above the South Gate, and his body interred nearby, in either Cat Fort or the army barracks. This brought to an ignominious end a life full of daring and adventure. Murtaí's companion, Domhnall Ó Conaill, composed a *marbhna*, or elegy, while awaiting his own fate in prison at Gallows Green. This poem has been translated by any number of authors; these lines are from Gerard Lyne's version:

"Murtaí, dear Master,
How regal were you!
Cruel, cruel, you are lifeless –
Fair head severed too
From your beautiful body
And aloft as a show."

Ó Conaill and Little John Sullivan were duly executed, and their heads were spiked on either side of Murtaí Óg's.

4

JACQUES FONTAINE

The most stirring written account of life in Beara in the early 18th century is undoubtedly that of the Frenchman, and sometime fisheries entrepreneur, Jacques Fontaine.

Fontaine was a Huguenot who fled persecution in France in 1685. He spent some years in England before moving, with his wife Anne and their six children, to Cork in 1694. The family settled in the city centre, where Fontaine ran a successful textiles business and served in a voluntary capacity as minister to the Huguenot community.

Towards the end of the century, Fontaine's business faltered when the Parliament of Great Britain passed an act prohibiting the export of manufactured woollen goods from Ireland. He sought out an alternative source of income, consulting with Colonel Beecher, who had extensive fisheries at Baltimore, and Colonel Townsend, who likewise had fisheries at Castlehaven, before deciding to become a farmer and fisherman on the shores of Berehaven.

In 1699, Fontaine rented three farms in Rosmacowen, at rents of £100, £31.10s and £18. He settled a number of Huguenot families on his land as tenants, and formed a partnership with some merchants in London to catch and export fish, which were generally abundant in the waters around Berehaven. Fontaine had already acquired a vessel, the 40-ton ketch the *Robert*, and with his new partners he now acquired two more, the 50-ton vessels the *Goodwill* and the *Judith*. He also set up a salting-house near his home.

Fontaine began his first season, in May 1700, by setting his crews to fishing cod off Dursey Island. They had little luck, and he switched to salmon, again without success. In July, he set six boats and forty-five men to fishing for herring. His hopes were high: "One single draught in a large shoal of herring might pay our expenses for one, two or even three years." But they fared just as poorly, and he lost money on the season.

Fontaine and his partners sent the *Judith* and the *Robert* to trade in Spain. In his memoir, he claimed the captain of the *Robert* sold her in France on the sly, and remained there to enjoy his ill-gotten gains. It was then decided to send the *Goodwill* to Virginia for tobacco, and she was kitted out with a second deck, at a cost of £80. Fontaine had not fish enough to make up a cargo, so he added beef, butter, cheese and candles, to make a full value of £450. They intended selling these goods in Madeira, investing in wine which they would then sell in Barbados, where they would take on sugar, rum and molasses to sell in Virginia, buying as much tobacco as they could with the proceeds.

The captain of the *Goodwill* arrived in Madeira to find so many vessels there before him that he had no option but to sell his cargo cheap; he proceeded to Barbados with a cargo of wine, which he again had no choice but to offload at a poor price. After paying his crew, he was left with just £130 to purchase sugar, rum and molasses. He sailed for Virginia, where again there were so many vessels before him that his goods would have fetched a pitiful price, while a premium was demanded for tobacco. He took on a pilot, who offered to bring him upriver to a place called Patuxent, where he reckoned his goods would fetch a far better price. The pilot was proved right: no vessel had been that far upriver in six months, and the captain made so much on his half-cargo from Barbados that he could afford a full cargo of tobacco, cramming it in everywhere, even in his cabin and the sailors' beds.

When the *Goodwill* arrived back in Berehaven, Fontaine directed the captain to sell the tobacco in London. He was having a far better fishing season, and already had a cargo ready to go; all he asked was that the *Goodwill* return as speedily as possible. He kept a detailed record of the fish he processed that year; included were two hundred thousand cured herrings, two hundred hogsheads of pressed herrings, two hundred barrels of pickled herrings, twelve tierces of salmon, seven thousand eight hundred dried codfish and two thousand dried flukes. That same year, Fontaine was engaged in building a stone house, with towers and a slate roof, at his base in Rosmacowen; in the meantime, he and his family lived at one end of a storehouse filled to the rafters with fish.

Fontaine hoped to export his catch to the Italian port city of Leghorn (or Livorno as it is known today), and expected to earn as much as £1,500, but it transpired that his London partners, fearing the threat of war, had directed the *Goodwill* to retrieve their reserves of wine from Spain. As a result, it was well into the spring of 1702 before Fontaine could transport the fish, thereby missing the Lenten market in Leghorn completely and ensuring that his agents could only command a poor price for his produce. He claimed to have not received a single farthing from the venture, and split from his London partners soon after.

Apart from his farming and fisheries interests, Fontaine served as a Justice of the Peace in Berehaven, and arranged for the trials and convictions of any number of local smugglers and bandits. This made him hugely unpopular, and marked him out as an inevitable target for reprisal.

On the 1st of June 1704 a French privateer with ten guns, a crew of eighty and four locals acting as guides, laid siege to his new home. Fontaine and his family, and seven others, defended the household against the Frenchmen's cannons and musket shot, barricading the windows with mattresses and books and firing incessantly on their attackers. The younger children busied themselves loading the muskets for those who were older and robust enough to fire them.

Fontaine gives a gripping account of the encounter in his memoir, describing with glee how the cannonballs "made no more impression on our stone walls than if they were so many apples!" The battle raged for eight hours, but only one of his men, a Frenchman named Claude Bonnet, suffered an injury, and even that was merely a flesh wound in his arm. Meanwhile the French suffered the loss of three men and had several more seriously injured before they retreated to their boats. The privateer remained at anchor in the harbour, and Fontaine worried that the Frenchmen might attack again, but they obviously thought better of the enterprise and put to sail.

Fontaine's defence of his home made him famous throughout Europe, and the Government was so impressed by his valour that it awarded him a pension of five shillings a day for the rest of his life.

Fontaine was determined to remain in Berehaven. He fortified his household, building a turf bank eighteen feet in thickness facing the sea, and mounting six cannons upon it. When he appealed to the authorities for assistance, they promptly furnished him with five hundred cannon balls and four barrels of powder. Once, when Fontaine was away in London, his wife Anne observed a suspicious looking vessel approaching their home. She had all the cannons loaded, and fired one off as a warning. The vessel turned instead for Bere Island, where the pirates made off with some cattle.

Despite all the Fontaines' precautions, their home remained a target for attack. On Saturday the 8th of October 1708 another French privateer arrived in the harbour, flying under English colours by way of deception. At midnight, the ship deposited a raiding party of eighty men, under the command of two local Irish lieutenants, some distance down along the shore. They crept eastwards in silence, stooping low, so no one saw them until they were within sight of the house.

As soon as the alarm was raised, Fontaine, his family and four young cowherds prepared their weapons. The raiders were already upon them; they set fire to the malthouse to the east, the stacks of hay, straw and grain to the north and east, and the cowhouse, stable and fish press to the west of the house. In the confusion of smoke and noise,

Fontaine managed to cover the windows of his property with sheepskins and ox skins doused in water. The raiders responded by knocking slates off the roof; they made several attempts to set fire to it with burning straw, but the Fontaines extinguished the flames each time.

One of the enemy lieutenants was a former tenant of Fontaine's named Sullivan who had been proclaimed an outlaw and had fled to France. Fontaine claimed to have supported this man's wife and family in his absence, and he was particularly incensed that Sullivan was now using his knowledge of the locality and the particulars of the Fontaine household against him.

Fontaine later claimed that hundreds of his Irish neighbours had gathered to observe the battle from a vantage point nearby, hoping to see him defeated. As the conflict continued, he was eventually injured, not by enemy fire but by his own weapon, which he had overloaded with powder; it blew up and broke three of his ribs and his collarbone. His wife Anne, on establishing his wounds were not fatal, immediately assumed command of the defence.

The French succeeded in breaching the wall of the tower on the northeastern corner of the building. The household continued firing on them from behind a makeshift barricade, until the French at last called on them to surrender, and Fontaine, fearing for his family's safety, agreed to terms that would allow them all their lives and liberty.

The raiding party carried off all they could from the household, filling three boats of their own, and three more of Fontaine's, with plunder. They also took Fontaine hostage, to his great chagrin, as this violated the terms of his surrender. On board their ship, he remonstrated with the captain, but to no avail; the next morning, the vessel set sail for Dursey.

Fontaine's wife followed by land and, hailing the vessel at the Dursey Sound with her apron tied to the end of a stick, negotiated his return for a ransom of £100. When she succeeded in raising only £30 of this, the ship's captain agreed to exchange Fontaine for his son Peter, whom he carried off to Saint-Malo in Brittany.

Fontaine travelled to Bantry to have his wounds seen to by a surgeon, while Anne went on to Cork to raise the £70 needed to ransom Peter. The Bishop lent her twenty guineas, but the merchants of Cork persuaded her to give it back, as they believed Peter's release could be secured without any further payment. As soon as he was fit enough, Fontaine himself rode to Kinsale and presented his case to the Chief Magistrate. As a retaliatory measure, all the French officers kept prisoner there, and in Plymouth, were placed in chains, and the outcry in France was so great that the Governor of Brest commanded the captain of the privateer to bring Peter home, without any further ransom payment.

Fontaine and his family were awarded £800 compensation, levied on the county of Cork, for the destruction of their household and business enterprises at Rosmacowen. They moved to Dublin, settling in a large house at one corner of Stephen's Green. Here, Fontaine ran a private school, hiring masters to teach writing, drawing, dancing and fencing, and teaching Latin, Greek, Geography, Mathematics and Fortification himself.

Most of the Fontaine children emigrated to America, and established themselves in Virginia. One of the French Huguenot families Fontaine had settled in Rosmacowen also moved to America. Originally known as the de Crocketagnes, they changed their name to Crockett; one of their descendants was the great folk hero Davy Crockett, who died at the Alamo.

On their deaths – in 1720 and 1728 respectively – Anne and Jacques Fontaine were buried in the Huguenot Cemetery on Merrion Row. Nothing remains now of their home at Bank, Rosmacowen, but even in the late 20th century locals would point out 'Fontaine's hops' growing wild in the area, a reminder of one man's industry and ambition three hundred years after his passing.

5

THE BERE ISLAND LONGBOAT AND
THEOBALD WOLFE TONE

The oldest surviving vessel of the French navy is a longboat seized off
Bere Island in 1796, and now on display at the National Museum of
Ireland, Collins Barracks, Dublin. The vessel belonged to the *Résolue*,
one of the forty-four ships of l'Expédition d'Irlande, organised by the
First French Republic with the encouragement of Theobald Wolfe Tone
and others of the Society of Young Irelanders, which intended
conveying fifteen thousand soldiers to Bantry Bay to spark an uprising
against English rule in Ireland.

Wolfe Tone was an unlikely revolutionary. Born in Dublin on the 20th of
June 1763, he was the son of a coach maker, and studied law at Trinity
College. He graduated in February 1788, and qualified as a barrister a
few years later at King's Inns.

In September 1791, Tone, himself an Anglican, published a pamphlet
titled *An Argument on behalf of the Catholics of Ireland,* in which he
argued that Catholics, who represented three-quarters of the
population, should be given the right to vote. That same year he
founded the United Irishmen with Thomas Russell, Napper Tandy and
others, with a view to forming a political union between Catholics and
Protestants and demanding a fully independent parliament for Ireland.

The United Irishmen soon evolved into a radical political movement and the Government, fearing its growing power, began jailing its leaders. In 1795, Tone fled to America to avoid arrest. He then went to France, where he helped persuade the authorities to organise l'Expédition d'Irlande. The fleet, of thirty frigates and fourteen supply ships, under the command of Vice-Admiral Morand de Galles, and an army commanded by General Lazare Hoche, was due to leave Brest in September 1796, but was delayed until December, hardly an ideal time of year for such an enterprise. The fleet was split before it ever left the coast of France, and *La Fraternité*, with Morand and Hoche on board, was blown off course and forced to return to port.

Tone had been appointed an Adjutant-General and was himself on board the 80-gun *Indomptable*, which, on the 21st of December, arrived at the point off Mizen Head where the fleet was to rendezvous. It was only then that they opened their orders from Morand and Hoche and learned that they were to land in Bantry Bay and march on Cork before sweeping northwards through the country.

The fleet sailed west, to the mouth of Bantry Bay, and took on some local pilots off Dursey Island. A storm was blowing, and even with their assistance, only fifteen ships managed to enter Bantry Bay, with the rest divided between those that managed to cast anchor and those that were blown back out to sea. The *Indomptable* was among those that made it into the harbour, along with the *Immortalité*, carrying General Emmanuel de Grouchy, the second-in-command who was now in charge of the army.

According to local tradition, the arrival of the French was witnessed by the congregation leaving Mass at Cahermore. The late Bernie Den Mick O'Sullivan often recalled how his grandmother, Mary O'Sullivan of Killaugh, Cahermore, had told him that her own grandmother could remember clearly this momentous event from her childhood. As the crowd stepped outside, the fog that had shrouded the sea all morning began to lift, and they were suddenly confronted by the sight of this huge fleet of ships. Fearing they were about to be attacked, they ran back inside the church, where the priest led them in praying for safety.

Tone kept a diary of his time in Bantry Bay. On the 22nd of December, he recorded that his ship had cast anchor off Bere Island at "half-past six… being still four leagues from our landing place." They were, he wrote, so close to land that he could have thrown a biscuit ashore. The next day, he recorded that the night before "it blew a heavy gale from the eastward with snow. The wind is still high, and as usual right ahead; I dread a visit from the English, and altogether I am in great uneasiness."

On the 24th of December, Tone recorded that Grouchy had presided over a council of war, at which it had been agreed to press ahead and effect a landing. They had a force of six thousand five hundred men, "all tried soldiers who had seen fire." Tone bemoaned their lack of supplies, but remained grimly optimistic of their chances of success. "We have not one guinea; we have not a tent; we have not a horse to draw our four pieces of artillery. The General-in-Chief marches on foot; we have left all our baggage behind us. We have nothing but the arms in our hands, the clothes on our backs, and a good courage, but that is sufficient." Their progress was stymied not by lack of courage, of course, but by the "infernal easterly wind… though we have been underway three or four hours, and made, I believe, three hundred tacks, we do not seem to my eyes to have gained one hundred yards in a straight line. Damn it! Damn it!"

A day later, on the 25th of December, Tone wrote that the wind continued against them: "Our situation is now as critical as possible, for it is morally certain that this day or tomorrow on the morning the English fleet will be in the harbour's mouth, and then adieu to everything." That evening, at 6.30pm, the Admiral's frigate ran by, and one of its officers hailed the *Indomptable* with a semaphone, ordering its captain to cut its cable and put to sea at once. It was no longer possible to fight against the wind, and the best hope for the fleet was that it would return to Brest in safety. "The frigate," wrote Tone, "then pursued her course, leaving us all in the utmost astonishment."

On the 29th of December, he recorded gravely: "At four this morning the Commodore made the signal to steer for France; so there is an end of our expedition for the present, perhaps for ever."

The *Résolue*, commanded by Rear Admiral Neilly, lost its mast in a collision with another frigate, and Lieutenant Guillaume Proteau was sent out on the 38-foot longboat – or Admiral's barge - to seek another ship to tow the *Résolue* to safety. However, Proteau and his crew were driven ashore at Bere Island, making them the only men from the entire expedition to effect a landing, though they were promptly arrested by the authorities and had their vessel seized.

Proteau's longboat remained in the area for more than a century, before being taken to Bantry House in 1898. The vessel was presented to the National Museum in 1944, and was displayed at the National Maritime Museum of Ireland, Dun Laoghaire, from 1977 to 2003. It was then sent to Liverpool Museum to be restored, and may now be seen at Collins Barracks, Dublin.

Wolfe Tone hoped the French could be persuaded to attempt another invasion of Ireland, but by the time the United Irishmen organised an open rebellion in 1798, it was all he could do to persuade them to engage in a number of raids around the Irish coast. One of these was led by General Humbert, a veteran of the Expédition d'Irlande fiasco, who landed a force of one thousand one hundred soldiers at Killala, Co Mayo on the 23rd of August, and briefly declared Connaught a republic before being defeated by the English at the Battle of Ballinamuck. Around the same time, Napper Tandy landed with a smaller force at Rathlin, learned of Humbert's defeat, and fled to Norway.

Tone himself left the Baye de Camaret in late September on board the *Hoche*, commanded by Admiral Bombart, and accompanied by nine other vessels. This little fleet was scattered by the winds, and only four of the vessels - the *Hoche*, the *Loire*, the *Biche* and the *Résolue* - arrived off Lough Swilly on the 10th of October. They might have effected a landing the next morning but for the arrival of a British fleet, under John Borlase Warren. Bombart ordered his other vessels to make good their escape, while he faced down the English on the *Hoche*. Tone was entreatied to leave on the *Biche*; as an Irishman he would be shown no mercy by the English in the event of the *Hoche* being captured, but he refused, preferring instead to fight with the Frenchmen who had come to his country's aid.

Bombart and his crew fought for six hours – with Tone commanding one of the batteries – before being taken. The officers were marched to Letterkenny, where the Earl of Cavan had them to breakfast. Tone was in French uniform, but had the misfortune to be recognised by Sir George Hill, who remarked: "Mr Tone, I am happy to see you." Tone is said to have replied, "Sir George, I am happy to see you. How are Lady Hill and your family?" But the civilities ended there. Tone was arrested and put in handcuffs; he was taken first to Derry, and then to Dublin, where he was court martialled on the 10th of November.

Tone was sentenced to execution. He asked that he be shot as a French soldier, but instead he was condemned to be hanged. Tone avoided the indignity of the noose by cutting an artery in his neck with a penknife, though it took a further eight days for him to die. He was buried in Bodenstown, Co Kildare.

In 1994, divers Liam Salmon and Frank Hurley found an anchor buried in mud, facing northwest on the seabed near Ahabeg, just east of Castletownbere. The letters IND were inscribed on the shank, and local historians believe it must have come from Tone's vessel, the *Indomptable*. Beara Historical Society had the anchor refurbished by the late John Tim O'Sullivan and Denis O'Driscoll, and it now takes pride of place in Locmiquélic Gardens, across from Dinish Bridge at the eastern approach to Castletownbere. The gardens are named after the town in Brittany, France with which Castletownbere is twinned.

Theobald Wolfe Tone

The Bere Island Longboat

6

BEARA LIGHTHOUSES

The Roancarrig

In 1838, the Coastguard in Castletownbere requested that a lighthouse be built on Roancarrigmore, a few miles from shore between Rosmacowen and Bere Island, at the eastern end of Berehaven Harbour. The lighthouse, like so many around the Irish coast, was designed by the engineer George Halpin, and construction was completed – by a Mr Howard of Limerick – in 1847. The light was established on the 1st of August that same year, housed in a 60-foot high white tower with a black band.

Berehaven Lighthouse, as it was called initially, eventually became known as the Roancarrigmore Lighthouse, or more often locally as the Roancarrig.

For many years, the rock was home to a number of lighthouse keepers and their families, but towards the end of the 19th century it was ruled that the keepers' children should be educated in schools on the mainland. Thereafter, the families were housed in new dwellings east of Castletownbere, and the keepers went back and forth as their service was required.

The lighthouse keepers' dwellings were the scene of a minor drama during the War of Independence. At 12.15am on the 23rd of July 1920 they were raided by a party of thirty men, in disguise and armed with revolvers.

The shore keeper Frank Hill and his wife were in one of the houses when the men rushed in, shouting, "Hands up! Don't be alarmed!", and demanded explosives and firearms. Hill explained that there were none at the station, but the men insisted on searching the two houses and the store. They removed two telescopes and one Morse lantern, but left a roll of money untouched. The tracks of a motorcar could be seen by the eastern gate in the morning.

The Roancarrig lighthouse was manned until the 23rd of September 1975, when the light was converted from vapourised paraffin to electricity, and it was no longer required that it be tended.

In 2012, the Roancarrig became the first Irish lighthouse to be decommissioned, and since then, the light, installed on a 7 metre high tower of stainless steel, has run on solar power.

Roancarrigmore, comprising the island itself, the lighthouse, an adjacent two storey dwelling with six single beds, and a number of stores, was sold in recent times and is now in private hands.

The Roancarrig Lighthouse (Beara Historical Society)

Ardnakinna

A beacon was first established at Ardnakinna, at the western tip of Bere Island, in 1850, in a tower 50 feet 6 inches high to the balcony. It was tended by a local man, but he was let go in 1863, when the beacon was abandoned.

Thereafter, any number of appeals were made to re-establish the beacon, but it was not until 1965 that it was finally agreed to convert the tower to a lighthouse.

This was accomplished by installing a lantern from an obsolete light vessel, mounted on a concrete blocking. The tower was painted white to increase its visibility to ships entering the harbour.

The lighthouse was never manned, but continues to be maintained by staff at the Castletownbere Helicopter Base.

The Calf

The Royal Navy first proposed that a lighthouse be built on the Bull Rock, off Dursey Island at the western tip of the Beara peninsula, in 1846. However, the project was postponed for several years by Trinity House, the organisation that had responsibility for the lighthouses around the coasts of Britain and Ireland. By the time they looked into the matter with any degree of seriousness, they decided that the Calf Rock would make a more suitable location. This was disputed by local fishermen, who knew well how exposed it would be to the winter storms, but their warnings were dismissed, and Halpin was commissioned to prepare plans for the project. He proposed that the tower should be of cast iron, with floors of Valentia slate. The contract to build it was won, in 1861, by Henry Grissell of Regent's Canal Iron Works, London.

There was some confusion over who owned the Calf, and at one point a notice was posted on the rock itself, requesting the owner to come forward. As it happened, the titleholder turned out to be none other than Queen Victoria, who was persuaded to part with it for the sum of £26.5s.0d.

Grissell completed the lighthouse tower in August 1864. A kitchen and storehouse were built as well, these being hacked out of the rock and roofed with brick and cement. The following year, the lantern and optic were installed, bringing the height of the lighthouse to 121 feet, while the light itself, 136 feet above high water, was finally established on the 30th of June 1866. The Calf Rock light, along with that of the Fastnet further east along the coast, served as a guide to vessels arriving from America, and the two were regarded as being the most important along the south coast.

On their time off, the Calf Rock lighthouse keepers lived with their families at newly constructed dwellings on the mainland at Dursey Sound. Those on shore leave kept a close eye on the lighthouse, particularly in bad weather. One night in 1869, a section of the balcony rail was swept away in a storm. One of the men on shore saw what he took to be flags raised in distress by the lighthouse keepers. He secured a boat and raised a crew of six local men, and they rowed out to sea on what they believed to be a rescue mission. As they drew close to the rock, they saw the keepers signal that they were not in danger after all. The crew turned their boat to return to shore, but sadly, it capsized; all seven were drowned and their bodies were never recovered. According to local tradition, another boat was seen putting out from shore just an hour before theirs; this vessel was never identified, and it came to be regarded as an omen of their fate.

The year after this tragedy, it was decided to strengthen the base of the tower by adding a skirt of cast iron and filling it with rubble. This may well have proved counterproductive, for, early on the morning of the 27th of November 1881, a mighty storm snapped off practically the entire tower above the reinforced base and swept it into the sea. There were three workmen on the rock along with the three keepers, and all six took shelter in a tiny storehouse while the storm raged around them. Their names were: Thomas Fortune, chief keeper; John Young, assistant keeper; John Harrington, of Dursey, helper; John Byrne, of Kingstown, County Dublin, mason; and John Kelly and John Lowry, labourers. Kelly was, like Harrington, a Dursey Island man, and was married to the widow of one of those who perished off the Calf twelve years before.

Two British gunboats, the *Seahorse* and the *Amelia*, stood by for several days, hoping to effect their rescue, but the weather remained too treacherous to even attempt it. Their efforts were hampered by the fact that the 63-foot long gaff, normally used to convey the men to and from supply boats, had also been lost in the storm.

Some smaller boats, captained by a Dursey man named Michael O'Shea, got near enough to land supplies of mutton and bread and collect some letters from the keepers in an airtight satchel, but again, they judged it too dangerous to try taking the men off the rock. The keepers' predicament was reported on daily in newspapers, here and abroad, by reporters sent especially to Dursey Sound.

The Cork Examiner of the 5th of December reproduced a letter from the head keeper, Thomas Fortune, in which he described how he and Lowry had been the last to go to bed on the night of the storm. He had not been lying down for fifteen minutes when there were flashes of lightning and the sea struck the tower three or four times in succession. At 4am, he reported, the lantern was blown clean off. He ran and closed the lantern and balcony doors before rousing the others. He directed Kelly and Lowry to the safety of the west house, where Young had already taken shelter, while he, Harrington and Byrne secured everything they could in the tower and drilled holes in the woodwork to allow the seawater to pass through. They kept at it until 8am. Half an hour later, another great storm blew up, and three landings of the tower were blown off as cleanly as the lantern. The men made for the west house, before deciding they'd all be safer in the kitchen, another building on the eastern side of the rock. There they remained, in their wet clothes, and mostly without fire, for the next several days. Fortune later reported that the water was up to their knees for most of that time, and they could not lie down to sleep.

It finally fell to a party of Dursey Island men, captained by Michael O'Shea, to put out in three small boats and attempt a rescue on the morning of Thursday the 8th of December. O'Shea had the contract for supplying provisions to the keepers, and knew the waters around the rock better than anyone. With him were his son Michael, Daniel and Denis Healy, Tade Dudley, Darby O'Sullivan and Batt Lynch.

When the weather abated briefly, the keepers threw out a lifebuoy, with a rope attached, and it was taken on board by O'Shea and his crew. They attached a thicker rope, an inch and a half in diameter, to the buoy, and the keepers hauled it back onto the rock. They donned their lifejackets and then, one by one, they attached themselves to the rope and dashed down the rock into the sea. O'Shea and his crew dragged them into his boat. From there, they were transferred to the other Dursey vessels and conveyed from them to the safety of the *Seahorse*. Fortune was last to leave the rock, and was enveloped in "a cloud of sea" so dense the rescue party were surprised he came through it unscathed.

The Calf Rock

Capt Gravener of the *Seahorse* was so impressed by the rescuers' bravery that he presented O'Shea with £5 out of his own pocket, and gave another £5 to the crews of each of his boats. They were later honoured at a ceremony in London, where O'Shea was awarded a gold medal for his valour.

The ruin of the Calf Rock Lighthouse

The Bull

Almost as soon as the Calf Rock lighthouse was destroyed, a temporary light was established at the west end of Dursey Island, and plans were drawn up for a new lighthouse on the Bull Rock. This too belonged to Queen Victoria, who parted with it for the sum of £21.

Work on the Bull Rock lighthouse was if anything even more challenging than that on the Calf. For a start, more than three hundred steps had to be cut into the rock to allow access to the site of the tower. Nearly sixteen thousand cubic yards of rock had first to be excavated, and spars and derricks had then to be constructed, before work could commence on the lighthouse tower, the keepers' dwellings and stores. The optic, when it was finally installed, was the largest in the country. The light and fog signal were established on the 1st of January 1889. The fog signal was initially an explosive device, but this was replaced by a more sophisticated trumpet system in 1902; there were three trumpets, powered by an air compressor, and the general rule was that when the fog was so dense that the keepers could no longer see the Calf Rock three miles away, they started blowing the horn.

While the Bull Rock lighthouse and its dwellings were more secure than those on the Calf, the keepers braved storms and hurricanes, and were often marooned for weeks at a time. In 1937, the dwellings were damaged by a fall of rock, but no one was injured.

A series of modernisations of the Bull Rock lighthouse began in 1974, when the light was first powered by electricity. The fog signal was discontinued in 1989, and the light was finally automated and the keepers withdrawn from the Bull Rock just two years later, on the 31st of March 1991. From October 2000, the light has run on solar power.

The Bull Rock

The Bull Rock Lighthouse

The old dwellings on the Bull Rock

7

THE PUXLEYS AND THE ALLIHIES MINES

Henry and John Puxley are believed to have moved to Castletownbere around 1723, to work as agents of the Eyres of Galway, who owned large tracts of land on the Beara peninsula. They became involved in the smuggling trade, initially co-operating with the dominant local family, the O'Sullivans. On the death of Henry Puxley, his brother John became his heir, and acquired substantial land holdings in the area. He was appointed a revenue officer, and came into direct conflict with the O'Sullivans, supposedly because he objected to their involvement in recruiting young men to the French army. John Puxley was shot dead by Murtaí Óg O'Sullivan in March 1754.

John Puxley's son Henry (1744 – 1803) expanded the family's land holdings in Beara. He married Sarah Lavallin of Cork, and their son John Lavallin Puxley (1772 – 1856) inherited what was by now a substantial estate. He leased a property in Llethrllestry near Carmarthen in Wales, and it seems likely he would have settled there as an absentee landlord were it not for the discovery of copper on his lands in Beara, a development that gave rise to his fame – and sometime notoriety - as 'Copper John', for having pioneered modern copper mining in the area.

Puxley was alerted to the possibility of there being copper on his lands in Allihies by Colonel Robert Hall, who had first come to Bantry Bay in 1796 to assist in repelling the French army raised by Wolfe Tone. Among Hall's soldiers were a number of Cornishmen, former miners who advised him there were ancient mine workings in the area.

Most of the mineral rights in the areas neighbouring Puxley's holdings were owned by Robert Hedges-Eyre of Macroom Castle, from whom he leased them for a period of thirty-one years. Puxley then formed the Allihies Mining Company, becoming the principal partner with forty-six of its sixty-four shares. Thomas Parker held twelve of the remaining shares, and Edward Pogson six.

Parker became the first managing director of the company, hiring a Cornish captain named Edward Nettle to run the mines on a salary of £100 a year. Mining commenced at Dooneen in May 1812, and had minor success. The following year, mining commenced at what became known as the Mountain Mine, and this proved to be far more productive.

Copper John Puxley's illegitimate brother Edward Puxley owned two sloops, the *St Michael* and the *Jane*. These were engaged in transporting the ore from Ballydonegan beach to the cove by Puxley's home at Dunboy, whence it was transported by larger ships – such as the *Industry* – to be sold at Swansea. The first cargo of seventy-five tons was sent out in August 1813. Eight shipments were exported in 1814, and ten the year after. Sometimes the ore was shipped out directly from Ballydonegan, which proved to be very exposed in winter.

Captain Nettle left the Mines in December 1815 and was replaced by captains Richard Martin and John Reed, both of whom would remain there for over thirty years.

For a time, the ore from Berehaven was sold directly to a company called the Llanelli Copper Works, as Puxley felt it was not getting a fair price in Swansea. Transporting the ore to Wales proved to be a dangerous endeavour. On the 24th of January 1818, the *St Michael*, captained by Cornelius Harrington, sprang a leak off the Bar of Llanelli and ran aground on Whiteford Sands. The ship was saved, but £450 worth of ore was lost.

In August of that year, the arrangement to sell directly to Llanelli Copper Works fell through when the company complained of the inferior quality of the Berehaven ore. Shipments were resumed to Swansea once more. On the 3rd of December the same year the *John and Mary* of Kinsale, captained by Dan Dawson, sank en route to Swansea in the channel off Cardigan Bay. The crew survived, but salvage was impossible and the mining company made an insurance claim of £1,168.

In light of these accidents, and the difficulty of getting insurance for the older ships available to ferry the ore, Puxley decided it would be more practical for the mining company to build a boat of its own. This presented problems of registration, so he then elected to take on the cost himself. In March 1819, he contracted a Mr Roberts of Milford to build the new schooner. Puxley was in Tenby for the summer and took a personal interest in the boat's construction, liaising with the foreman, Captain Grey.

The mining company's transport ships were involved in further incidents throughout 1819. In April, the captain of the *Nancy* threw several tons of ore overboard and put into Youghal when the boat sprang a leak en route to Swansea. In September, the company's Swansea agent, Thomas Jenkins, complained of the "crazy" condition of two of their ships, the *Margaret* and the *Matty*. The company lost another vessel on the 8th of November when the *Friendship* of Kinsale sank, again en route to Swansea; again, the crew was saved, but the cargo of fifty-eight tons of ore was lost. On this occasion, Jenkins had failed to insure the ore, so there was no compensation for its loss.

That same month, the *Henrietta*, as Puxley called his first schooner – after his daughter – was registered in Swansea and embarked on its maiden voyage, carrying coal to Cork before making the return journey with ore from Berehaven. Being a new ship, she was cheaper to insure, and proved to be invaluable to the mining company, not least when she was used to import potatoes to feed the miners and their families when famine threatened in 1822.

In January of that year, the company acknowledged as lost a ship called the *Gannet*, captained by John Casey, that had taken on a load of ore at Ballydonegan a few weeks previously, having been forced by the weather to lay up at Ballycrovane for a month. The insurers paid in full for the lost ore. In October the same year, one of Edward Puxley's smaller ships, the *St Michael*, ran onto the rocks at Ballydonegan; ten tons of ore, out of a total of thirty, were lost.

More ships were commissioned. Edward Puxley had two new sloops built, the *Sally* in January 1823 and the *John* in August. Transporting ore from Ballydonegan continued to present difficulties, particularly in winter, so John Puxley had a road built over the mountains. Transport was slower by road, but was possible in most weather conditions. In early 1825, Puxley launched a second schooner, the *Allihies*. That same year, production rose to three thousand tons, and dividends paid £175 a share.

Most of the equipment required in the mines was transported by sea. When Puxley bought an engine from the Ross Island mine in Killarney in 1829, he had Captain Reed dismantle it and arranged to transport the pieces, including an eight-ton bob, from the quay at Milltown to Ballydonegan. A Swansea ship, the *Fox*, commanded by Captain Kempthorne, was engaged for this purpose. Kempthorne was paid £100 for the transportation job, and a further £30 to cover the considerable damage suffered by his vessel as the bob was being loaded.

Up to 1830, Edward Puxley brought the ore from Ballydonegan to Dunboy on his sloop the *Sally*, whence it was transported to Swansea on John Puxley's schooners the *Henrietta* and the *Allihies*; they usually made twelve voyages a year. In 1831, Puxley had a third schooner, the 80-ton *Miner*, built at Ipswich, intending that all three schooners would transport the ore directly from Ballydonegan thereafter. A year later, he had another schooner built at Ipswich; he sold the *Allihies* and transferred its name to this latest vessel. In 1835, he brought the size of his fleet to four with the commissioning of a 126-ton vessel, the *Waterwitch*.

One of Edward Puxley's sloops, the *Jane*, was wrecked at Lickbarrahane in June 1840, with the loss of two hundred half-barrels of gunpowder and other sundries intended for the mines. John Puxley blamed this incident on the captain and crew for leaving the vessel unattended, so presumably it came adrift and was irreparably damaged on the rocks.

RA Williams, in his book *The Berehaven Copper Mines*, speculates that Puxley may have lost the *Miner* in 1850 and another schooner, the *Brothers*, in 1854. These vessels seem to have been replaced by two others, the *Swanzey* and the *Albion*.

Copper John Puxley died at Tenby in Wales in 1856, leaving the mines at Allihies to his eldest grandson John Simon Lavallin Puxley. On his death three years later, at the age of twenty-nine, his brother Henry took possession of the property. The mines continued exporting ore to Swansea, and two more Puxley vessels, the *Allihies* and the *Swanzey*, were wrecked or lost in 1860 and 1865 respectively.

Henry Puxley embarked on an ambitious extension to the family mansion at Dunboy, but put a halt to the development in 1872, following the death in childbirth of his wife Katherine. Puxley had sold his interest in the Allihies mines for £100,000 a few years previously – to a new company, the Berehaven Mining Company - and he never again returned to Ireland. In 1873, the new company had a vessel wrecked in a storm at Ballydonegan; this augured badly for the company, which wound up its operations - after several years of losses – in 1884. The mines were worked for several periods in the 20th century, but never again as profitably as they had been under the Puxleys' stewardship.

One legacy of the boom years is the strand at Ballydonegan, whose sand is said to derive from the ore dressing operations at the mines.

8

DURSEY ISLAND

Penny Durell's *Discover Dursey* was published in 1996, and remains the definitive history of what is County Cork's most westerly inhabited island, and the only one in Ireland connected to the mainland by cable car. Dursey is four miles long, and comprises three townlands: Ballynacallagh, Kilmichael and Tilickafinna. Stone boundaries uncovered by turf cutting suggest that it was farmed thousands of years ago, while the earliest evidence of a church dates to the beginning of the fourteenth century.

Dursey is known in Irish as *Oileán Baoi*, through its association with Baoi, the Cailleach Bhéara. Its present name is believed to date back a thousand years to its association with the Vikings, and is derived from either 'Thjorsey' – meaning 'bull's island' – or Thor's Island, after the Nordic god. The Vikings are believed to have used the island as a holding station for captured slaves.

In the late sixteenth century, Diarmuid O'Sullivan, an uncle of Dónal Cam O'Sullivan Beare, and father to the historian Philip, built a stronghold on Oileán Beag, connected to Dursey by a drawbridge. Shortly before the fall of Dunboy, George Carew dispatched Captain John Bostock to take the castle on Oileán Beag. This he did with little effort, executing the defenders and dismantling the fort. Then his troops rounded up every man, woman and child they could find on the island. Some they put to the sword; the rest they bound together and flung to their deaths from the cliff-tops at Áit an Fheoir.

The signal tower

After Dónal Cam fled to Spain, ownership of Dursey passed to his cousin Owen O'Sullivan and his descendants, but later it passed out of the family entirely. The island was re-settled, and for the next few centuries its inhabitants survived by farming, fishing and helping themselves to whatever came in on the tide.

The Signal Tower on Dursey

In the early nineteenth century many of the islanders were employed in the construction of a signal tower on Cnoc Mór, at the western end of the island, to guard against possible invasion by Napoleon Bonaparte's forces. The signal tower was one of a number of defences built along the coast that included Martello towers and military batteries. The contractor, Benjamin Ball, would also oversee the construction of towers at Black Ball Head, Bere Island and Sheep's Head.

Work commenced in September 1804, when stone was quarried at the bottom of Cnoc Mór and carried uphill in wheelbarrows and baskets. Men were paid 2d a day for their labours, and women 1d, and this was reputedly the first time most could afford to buy shoes.

The tower rose two storeys high, with an entrance on the first floor that was only accessible by ladder. Work stalled within a few years, as the threat of a French invasion passed, and the project was never actually completed. A succession of officers lived in the building. Relations between them and the local community were initially strained, as when a party of islanders made off with the flagstaff, and were only compelled to return it when the garrison took a woman hostage. However, the tower soon became a place where locals gathered in the evenings to chat and play cards with the officers. With the defeat of Napoleon in 1814, the signal tower on Dursey, along with most of those along the shore, fell into disuse, and it was never occupied again.

Seine fishing

Seine fishing brought a period of prosperity to Dursey in the latter decades of the nineteenth century, when the mackerel grounds in New England collapsed and Berehaven stepped up to supply the American market.

Each of the three villages on Dursey had its own seine boat and a smaller companion vessel, known as the 'foll'er', or 'follower'. Typically, the seine boat would have a crew of ten and the foll'er a crew of six. They fished at night, and the 'huer', or captain, would issue commands from the stern of the seine boat. When he spotted fish, he would order his crew to throw out the net, and the two boats would draw it in around the catch, which was then hauled on board the foll'er.

The fish were counted in 'casts' of three, with forty-two casts making up the 'long hundred'. The catch was carried up in baskets from the landing place at Ballynacallagh, and the women, often assisted by their children, did most of the work in gutting, washing and salting the fish in barrels. After a few weeks, the fish were transferred to new barrels and re-salted, and were then transported to the mainland by boat to Castletownbere by horse and cart. From there, the fish were shipped to Scandinavia and on to New Bedford, Massachusetts. Much of the business was conducted by local agents such as Jerry Kelly at Lehanmore, and PJ O'Sullivan, Johnny Willie O'Sullivan and Henry Harrington in Allihies.

The mackerel season began in early September and ended in November, and often provided the islanders with their entire income for the year. Most households would also salt fish for their own consumption.

The market for cured mackerel fell away in the 1920s, revived in the war years of the early 1940s, and then collapsed completely.

An eviction

Up until the early twentieth century, the people on Dursey were tenant farmers. Just like those on the mainland, they were often in dispute with their landlords, and their agents, over rent. One such dispute made the headlines in 1905. On the morning of the 25th of April that year, the islanders observed the approach of an Admiralty vessel called the *Stormcock*, which had put out from Bantry the evening before, and gathered to meet it at the eastern end of the island. Four households on Dursey were in arrears on their rent, and the islanders seem to have had some intimation that there was an eviction party on board.

The *Stormcock* went first to the western end of the island, dislodging a party of thirty RIC men under District-Inspector Armstrong of Bantry at an inlet called Pluice before steaming on towards Ballynacallagh. On board were Mr Harrell RM, County Inspector Fawcett, and District-Inspectors Rowan and Hearden of Millstreet and Castletownbere, along with at least another hundred and thirty RIC. The islanders rained stones on the policemen as they disembarked, but soon came under attack themselves from Armstrong's forces, which came on them from behind. A fierce melee ensued. The island men fought with their fists, the police with batons and the butt ends of their rifles. One islander, James O'Leary, suffered an injury to his hand warding off a bayonet thrust at him by a policeman.

The RIC eventually subdued the crowd and proceeded to Ballynacallagh, where they entered the house of a family whose rent was four years overdue and started carrying their possessions outside. The family consisted of a husband and wife, their two young children, and his sister and elderly parents. The husband was known to have suffered health issues over the previous several years, but the landlord's agent, a man named Turner, refused to negotiate a compromise with him.

The parish priest, Rev Patrick Barton, and the nationalist MP James Gilhooly, arrived on the island soon after. Again, they tried to reason with Turner, but he rebuffed their efforts, and the eviction proceeded. However, eviction notices were not served on the other three families whose rent was overdue.

The agents, along with thirty policemen, set up camp at Ballynacallagh, intending to safeguard the caretakers who were to be installed in the home of the evicted family. The family were themselves accommodated in a zinc-roofed shelter erected in haste by their neighbours.

The eviction was reported on in the national press, and caused outrage, not least at the ridiculous expense that had gone into making an example of one hapless family. Fr Barton and Gilhooly organised a public meeting in Allihies, which attracted a huge crowd from throughout Beara and led directly to the founding of several local branches of the United Irish League to campaign for land reform. Meanwhile, a subscription was got up to support the evictees.

On the 3rd of May the case was discussed in Parliament, where the Liverpool MP TP O'Connor decried the expenditure of at least £700 in public funds on the recovery of rental arrears amounting to just £39. The matter was raised again the next day and on several occasions subsequently; on the 17th of July, James Gilhooly complained that there were still twelve policemen under camp on the island.

It was not until September that the matter was resolved, when the tenants paid their rent and costs on the understanding that the Estates Commissioners would advance them a long-term loan to purchase their property.

Shipwrecks

Discover Dursey includes a chapter entitled *Shipwrecks and Maritime Mishaps,* which accounts for many of the vessels that were damaged or lost around the island. Penny Durell searched far and wide for information on these. One valuable source was the Schools Folklore Collection, compiled by the Folklore Commission in the 1930s. This involved schoolchildren collecting local stories from their elders, relatives and neighbours who might never otherwise have left a record.

"Unfortunately, the children who wrote those stories wouldn't have dates for when the boats were wrecked," says Penny. "But their informants might remember that it happened on Christmas Day, for instance, or on a Sunday. Or they might have given information on the circumstances of their sinking, and sometimes I could then corroborate the stories and work out what year it was. I also researched the general Folklore Collections, when they went around and interviewed people. And then there were the accounts in newspapers such as the Cork Constitution and the Cork Examiner."

One story handed down locally concerns the night in 1822 there was a terrible storm, and two boats were wrecked in the Dursey Sound. One was a small boat belonging to a landlord's agent named Seán Óg O'Sullivan, who was drunk and ignored the efforts made by another boatman in his vicinity to get him to safety; he and his boat eventually disappeared in the churning waves off Béal Átha Bó. The second vessel was a schooner that took shelter below the old monastery. "The islanders were worried the boat would be destroyed, and signalled to the crew to pull in closer to land," says Penny. "But the mariners must have thought the islanders were trying to lure them to destruction. In fact the storm drove the ship across the sound and smashed it against the rocks at Ballinacarriga.

"All the crew were drowned except for one man who was pulled unconscious from the waves. On the shore, a nursing mother gave him milk to revive him. Three bodies were later recovered from the sea. Tadhg Pats showed me where their graves were; there was nothing to mark them, but his father would have told him the location. They wouldn't have known what faith the victims were, they would have just buried the bodies where they brought them ashore."

Years later, a man named Lowney from Ballaghboy was in a public-house in Wales, where he heard a man badmouthing the people of Dursey, who he claimed had lured his boat to its destruction. Lowney remonstrated with the speaker, whom he recognised: "Isn't it true that those people saved you from the sea? Didn't a mother's milk restore you to life?"

The place where the schooner is wrecked is still known as Carraig an Iarrainn, 'the rock of the iron'. "The remains of the ship could still be seen there at low tide as recently as the '60s," says Penny.

Apart from the records she uncovered in Ireland, Penny's main source of information was Lloyd's List in London. The List began life as a weekly shipping intelligence journal in 1734, and was then published daily until 2013, when it was adapted to a digital format. Penny accessed historical issues of the journal - which includes accounts of shipwrecks and accidents at sea - on microfilm at Guildhall Library in the City of London. "My husband David's parents lived down in Guildford," she explains, "so any time we went to visit, I'd pop up to Guildhall on the train - it only took half an hour to Waterloo station - and I'd methodically skim through the microfilm, looking out for any mention of Berehaven or West Cork. It was very useful; I'd get quite factual, reliable accounts.

"Most of the footnotes in my chapter on shipwrecks refer to Lloyd's List or Lloyd's Register. It's a quarter century since I wrote *Discover Dursey*, and I daresay the information I got from Lloyd's has since been made available online, so it'd be far easier to do that research now."

Some of the vessels that got into trouble were crossing the Atlantic. "The *Reward* was one of those. It was coming from Philadelphia to London when it encountered thick fog and ran onto the rocks near Dursey. That happened on the 12th of July 1847. The vessel was damaged but it carried on; it managed to get into Berehaven, but it had then to be repaired before it could cross to Sunderland."

More often than not, however, the boats were cargo vessels plying their trade along the coast. "There weren't huge numbers going across to America, but there were definitely ones coming from England. One I mention in the book is the *Effort*, a small trading vessel from Bideford in Devon that was on its way to Limerick with various goods when it came to grief on the southwest tip of Dursey. That was in 1831. And there's another that had come from Wales, a sloop called the *Valiant* from Cardigan that sank off Crow Head in 1838. I did a bit of research to work out which boat that was, and I found out quite a lot about it."

The *Valiant* was a 73-ton sloop, owned and captained by Daniel Davies, which had made three return journeys between Cardigan or Liverpool and Castlemaine, Dingle and Bantry between January and June 1838. Lloyd's List of the 26th of November that same year contains a telegram from Berehaven confirming its destruction. "The *Effort* and the *Valiant* were both small vessels," says Penny, "with three or four people on board."

Collecting wreck was an important part of the coastal economy until recent times. "Materials that came in on the tide, wood and so on, would often have been quite valuable. If the wood was on deck, and you had rough weather, it might get washed off into the sea. In fact, there are several accounts of people finding goods and then the coastguard coming along and saying, that belongs to the Crown. And then those who'd found it would sneak up and make off with it anyway, in the same way that they stole wood out of the beams in the signal tower."

Penny's book includes an account of a Spanish vessel that was wrecked at Cuas a' Ghearraigh on the south side of the Reen peninsula some time in the first half of the 19th century. All the crew were drowned. The boat was carrying a cargo of hemp, some of which the Dursey islanders retrieved with can hooks; it was later used to make ropes and nets. They also recovered the body of the captain and buried it nearby, having found nine gold coins, each with a value of seven guineas, in his pockets. One Ballinacarriga man later bought a red cow with the single coin that was his share of the spoils.

Some shipwrecks are commemorated in local place-names, such as Foill an Ime – the Cliff of the Butter – on the north side of Dursey. "This is where a small boat with a cargo of butter struck a cliff in the fog. The islanders must have thought, this is a bonanza. I know nothing about what happened to those on board, or whether they survived or not, but of course the people must have benefitted from it; they would all have got free butter."

A number of local families claim descent from men who survived their boats being wrecked on the coast around Dursey. The first Harrington Causkey to settle in the area, for instance, was one of the crew of a coaster that lost its way in thick fog and came ashore near Crow Head in the early 18th century; his son or grandson moved across the sound to Dursey to live in 'the house of the white rock' from which Tilickafinna takes its name. Similarly, the Merwicks and one branch of the O'Dwyer family are descended from two Arklow men who swam ashore near Garnish when their fishing vessel was destroyed in a storm.

9

THE USS SULLIVANS

Few in Ireland were aware of the sacrifice of the five Sullivan brothers of Waterloo, Iowa, or of their connection to Beara, until the American gunship the *USS Sullivans* visited Castletownbere in 2003. The brothers – George, Frank, Eugene, Matt and Al – were the grandsons of a couple named Tom and Mary Bridget O'Sullivan who left Adrigole for America in 1849, at the height of the Great Famine.

The Sullivan boys had their first taste of adventure on the water when, as children, they found an old boat, plugged its holes with mud and took it onto the river. The boat began sinking, and the four eldest swam to safety, leaving Al, the youngest, to fend for himself. Luckily, some adults went to save him. Their grandmother was furious at the older boys for abandoning their brother, and punished them severely. The rule thereafter was, they were always to stick together.

George and Frank, the eldest brothers, each did four years service in the Navy, on the *USS Hovey*, before returning to Waterloo. But then, after the Japanese attacked Pearl Harbour in December 1941, all five resolved to sign up as Marines. Al, the youngest, had married at seventeen, and fathered a child a year later, but even he could not be dissuaded. Given his family commitments, the recruitment office was reluctant to accept him, but the brothers insisted that all five of them be taken, or none at all. They also made it a condition that they would serve together on one ship. In February 1942 they were assigned to the *USS Juneau*.

The *Juneau* operated in the Atlantic for a spell, and then in the South Pacific. The US had invaded Guadalcanal, and the Marines were defending the islands at the southern end of the Solomon chain against attack by the Japanese. On Friday the 13th of November, the *Juneau* was struck by a Japanese torpedo and destroyed. Four of the Sullivans – Frank, Eugene, Matt and Al - are believed to have died in the initial explosion, while George, the eldest, was blown clear into the sea and managed to get onto a life raft.

Sadly, there was great confusion over whose responsibility it was to check for survivors. The captains of the *Juneau*'s sister ships concluded there were none, and sailed away into safer waters. Similarly, the crew of a B-17 air force plane in the area, who might have spotted the survivors, filed a standard report, not realising the onus was on them to initiate a rescue mission.

The men who had survived – as many as one hundred and fifteen - were left to the mercy of the elements. Some later reported that George Sullivan was stricken with grief, screaming his brothers' names as he swam around among the dead and wounded, wiping the oil and blood from their faces in hope of finding Frank, Eugene, Matt or Al. He was injured himself, and like the rest, he suffered greatly over the next three days. The men had neither food nor water; by day, they were at the mercy of the sun, and when it sank, they shivered in the cold. Worse again, the bodies and blood in the water all around them began attracting sharks.

By the fourth night, George was delirious. He told his companions he was going for a bath, took his clothes off and swam away from the raft. Allen Heyn, who survived the ordeal, recalled later how "the white of his body must have flashed and shown up more, because a shark came and grabbed him and that was the end."

Only thirteen men were rescued.

The US Navy did not announce the loss of the *Juneau* or its crew for several weeks, but Tom and Alleta Sullivan knew there was something amiss when they stopped receiving letters from the boys. Then they began hearing rumours, from neighbours whose sons were also in the service, that the *Juneau* had been torpedoed.

At last, on the morning of the 11th of January 1943, just as Tom was preparing to go to work, three naval officers arrived at the Sullivan home in a black sedan. It fell to the senior officer, Lieutenant Commander Truman Jones, to inform them that all five of the Sullivan brothers were missing in action, presumed dead.

Tom and Alleta accepted the news with grace, and later campaigned for the war effort. A few days after learning of their sons' fate, they received a personal letter of condolence from President Theodore Roosevelt, and subsequently, at St Patrick's Cathedral in New York, they were presented with a silver medal and rosary beads from Pope Pius XII.

As a direct consequence of the Sullivan brothers' deaths, the US War Department adopted its Sole Survivor Policy, which protects people from the draft or combat duty if they have lost a family member in military service.

The US Navy named a ship in honour of the brothers, the first time an American naval vessel was named after more than one person. The *Sullivans DD-537* was launched in April 1943 by Aletta Sullivan, and served in World War II and the Korean War. The vessel was decommissioned in 1965 and donated to the Buffalo and Erie County Naval and Military Park in Buffalo, New York.

A second vessel was then named after the brothers: the *Sullivans DDG-68* was launched by Al Sullivan's granddaughter, Kelly Ann Sullivan Loughren, on the 12th of August 1995. This vessel bore the motto: We Stick Together.

In 2008, the Grout Museum in the brothers' hometown of Waterloo, Iowa opened a new wing, dedicated to the memory of the Sullivan boys. The Sullivan Brothers Iowa Veterans Museum honours the service of all Iowa veterans from the Civil War to the present, and includes more than one thousand five hundred interviews collected through the Voices of Iowa Oral History Project, as well as thirty-five interactive exhibits and an electronic Wall of Honour.

Waterloo has also named a building - at West 4th and Commercial St - the Five Sullivan Brothers Convention Centre. It features a display on the Sullivan brothers and a 'We Stick Together' commemorative mosaic.

The Sullivan brothers' story inspired the Hollywood movie of 1944, *The Fighting Sullivans*, directed by Lloyd Bacon and starring Edward Ryan, John Campbell, James Cardwell, John Alvin and George Offerman. The movie took some license with real events, suggesting that all five brothers were killed at the same time, but its depiction of their fierce family loyalty won audiences' hearts. *The Fighting Sullivans* was nominated for an Academy Award for Best Story, losing to the Bing Crosby musical, *Going My Way*.

The Sullivans were also the subject of a number of books, including *The Fighting Sullivans: How Hollywood and the Military Make Heroes* by Bruce Kuklick, and *We Band of Brothers: The Sullivans & World War II*, written by John R Setterfield and published by Mid-Prairie Books in 1995, which is said to have helped inspire the Steven Spielberg movie, *Saving Private Ryan*.

Al's son James had two children, John Sullivan and Kelly Sullivan-Loughren, who were present when the *USS Sullivan*, accompanied by vessels of the Irish and French navies, sailed into Berehaven and docked west of Adrigole on the 30th of August 2003. John and Kelly laid a wreath a mile offshore to commemorate the Sullivan brothers, and attended the unveiling of a plaque at the old family homestead, commemorating Tom and Mary Bridget O'Sullivan, who had left it all those years before, and the brothers - George, Frank, Eugene, Matt and Al – whose sacrifice won all five posthumous Purple Hearts and the admiration of America.

Waterloo, Iowa
January 1943

Bureau of Naval Personnel

Dear Sirs:

I am writing you in regards to a rumor going
around that my five sons were killed in action in
November. A mother from here came and told me she
got a letter from her son and he heard my five sons
were killed.

It is all over town now, and I am so worried.
My five sons joined the Navy together a year ago, Jan.
3, 1942. They are on the Cruiser, U.S.S. JUNEAU. The
last I heard from them was Nov. 8th. That is, it was
dated Nov. 8th, U.S. Navy.

Their names are, George T., Francis Henry, Joseph
E., Madison A., and Albert L. If it is so, please let
me know the truth. I am to christen the U.S.S. TAWASA,
Feb. 12th, at Portland, Oregon. If anything has happened
to my five sons, I will still christen the ship as it was
their wish that I do so. I hated to bother you, but it
has worried me so that I wanted to know if it was true.
So please tell me. It was hard to give five sons all
at once to the Navy, but I am proud of my boys that they
can serve and help protect their country. George and
Francis served four years on the U.S.S. HOVEY, and I had
the pleasure to go aboard their ship in 1937.

I am so happy the Navy has bestowed the honor on
me to christen the U.S.S. TAWASA. My husband and daughter are going to Portland with me. I remain,

Sincerely,

/s/ Mrs. Aleta Sullivan
98 Adams Street
Waterloo, Iowa

*A letter from Aletta Sullivan enquiring after the fate of her five sons, dated January
1943*

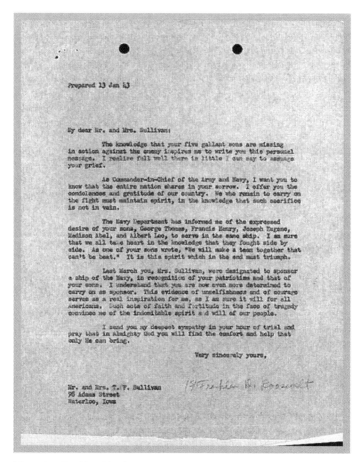

A letter from President Theodore Roosevelt sympathising with Tom and Aletta Sullivan on the deaths of their five sons, dated the 23rd of January 1943

PART 2: PEOPLE OF THE SEA

1

TED O'SULLIVAN
BERE ISLAND

Bere Island native and retired teacher Ted O'Sullivan is the author of *Bere Island: A Short History,* and divides his time between the island and Cork city, where he lectures at UCC. He traces the arrival of the British military on Bere Island to shortly after the aborted French invasion of 1796.

"The British Navy set up camp within a year of Wolfe Tone coming into the harbour," he says. "The first thing they did was build the pier. Some archaeologists who have done work on the island claim the pier was built in 1800, but local folklore says they started cutting the stone for it in 1797, and they had it well built by 1800. The signal towers were all built in the 1800s, in the Napoleonic era. Then Napoleon was defeated, at Waterloo, and all those towers became obsolete."

Although there was a small garrison on Bere Island all through the 19th century, Ted believes it was not necessarily well-managed, or a priority with the authorities. "You had correspondence and reports that indicate the garrisons often didn't show up at all; it certainly wasn't very military-like. They had a beautiful building at the east end of the island, an officers' mess that was like a landlord's house, but as often as not there were very few in residence."

Ted O'Sullivan

That began to change in the late 19th century, when the value of
Berehaven harbour began to be better appreciated. In those days, the
Navy depended almost entirely on steam power. "As a result, the ships
needed very elaborate servicing. The boilers had to be scraped to get
rid of all the tar; it wouldn't have been very efficient, and they would
have had to be replaced on a regular basis as they simply wore out.
The dreadnoughts, like the *HMS Furious*, were steam-driven.
Everything was in those days. Even the gun turrets were steam-driven.
I saw a documentary a few years ago about the Battle of Jutland, and
they were showing how they fired the guns; they had a little wheel that
they would open. There was a steam-powered turbine, and that
stopped it moving. You needed steam power just to elevate the gun.
Nothing worked without it. But it took forty-eight hours from the time
they put in the first firelighters till they got full steam. And in the
meantime, they were sitting ducks."

The British invested heavily in Bere Island between 1898 and 1903.
"The historian Robert Fisk estimates they spent £4 million that time,

which would be like spending billions today. They put three huge gun batteries at the east end, and three batteries at the west end. They had lookout towers, a communications system and a barracks. And there was a big garrison there then.

"There was huge work in building the batteries. In the 1901 census, every house had a lodger, and the lodger would be a carpenter or a plumber or a tradesman or a builder's labourer or whatever. So there was big money in it."

The development also resulted in a large number of local people being evicted. "On the eviction notice, it said they would be compensated. But actually it was the landlords got compensation, not the tenants. A lot of them were let back in then, but it was under new agreements; they were called tenants at will. I found one document in the British Archives in Kew, that said they were actually camouflage. If you sailed into Bantry Bay, and you saw farmers in a field cutting hay, you'd never expect a gun to fire out between the haycocks. So it suited the British to have these people back in their farmhouses, working their farms. It suited them to have cattle in the fields. That was all camouflage for the guns; they were invisible from the sea. Once airplanes were invented, it was different, of course, because then you could see them from the air."

British Atlantic fleet in Berehaven, 1914/15 (Beara Historical Society)

During the First World War, some of the weapons on Bere Island were re-purposed elsewhere. "The two big nine-inch guns were taken out that time. One from the lower battery was taken to England to fire against the zeppelins. The local story was that the other gun, from the Rerrin Battery, which had never been fired, was put on the *HMS Indefatigable*, which was a dreadnought in the Battle of Jutland. That gun wound up at the bottom of the sea."

From 1917, Bere Island found itself playing host to the American Navy as well as the British for a few years, when the US established bases at Whiddy Island and Berehaven to safeguard shipping from attack by German U-boats and destroyers. Whiddy was a base for seaplanes, while Berehaven sheltered US battleships such as the *Florida*, the *Utah*, the *Oklahoma* and the *Nevada* - each with a crew of one thousand sailors - along with up to eleven submarines. At one point, a baseball diamond was marked out at the British Admiralty grounds at Rerrin so the ships' crews could compete against each other. The *Utah*, the *Oklahoma* and the *Nevada* were later destroyed in the Japanese attack on Pearl Harbour, Hawaii.

USS Utah with balloon in Berehaven, 1918 (Beara Historical Society)

The Troubles

Bere Island was the scene of one of the most infamous raids of the War of Independence, when, on the 5th of June 1918, the local Volunteers removed fifty-two boxes, each containing 56lb of gun cotton, from the Navy store and spirited them across the harbour in a rowboat, somehow avoiding detection by the British Navy ships at anchor and the searchlights flashing all around the shore. The Bere Island IRA later burned down a wooden pavilion at the British military's sports ground, and the site was converted to an internment camp, where prominent figures such as Alfred O'Rahilly, Seán Collins (brother of Michael Collins) and Canon O'Kennedy of St Flannan's College, Ennis were kept prisoner.

Cumann na mBan was particularly active on the island. "Some of the women used go to the dances at the British Army camp, but they'd only dance with a man if he gave them a bullet. So they'd go home with a bunch of bullets in their pockets. They were involved in communication with the prisoners and general intelligence gathering. After the Truce many of the prisoners couldn't be repatriated immediately and Cumann na mBan organised for the prisoners to visit farms on the island and help out with the harvest before they were returned home."

The Treaty of December 1921 was opposed by most of the IRA men in Beara, and the island became a place of refuge for a number of those on the run. "When the Free State Army came raiding, the IRA men crossed what was known as the Red Line, and they couldn't be followed, because that was officially under British rule, under the Union Jack. They were actually hiding under the skirts of the British Army.

"The Free State Army had a garrison in the Workhouse in Castletownbere. They were watching every ferry coming out of Bere Ireland; they knew well the boys were in there. Timmy the Tailor told me that one time there were six people sitting at the table in his house for breakfast with his mother and father, and they got out on the coal boat to England. That was the boat that brought in coal for the electricity generating station on the island, and the heating in the barracks. So they escaped to Leeds. And in 1924, when my grandfather died, a lot of fellows got out by mingling with the mourners on the *Princess Beara*."

Even after the Civil War, the Bere Island chapter of Cumann na mBan remained active, spying on the British garrison until its evacuation in 1938. "Throughout those years, you had to have a permit to cross the Red Line. But there was one woman got a job in the school, and she'd question every child who came in. 'Who are you now? Who's your Daddy, and what's he doing? And where did he come from? And what rank is he?' There were two post offices, one British and the other Irish, and she'd go into the Irish post office on her way home and brief the postmistress, who was second-in-command of Cumann na mBan. They knew more about what was going on in the fort than the British did. They knew everything."

Fishing

Bere Island has had a long association with fishing, although, much like on the mainland, there have been lean times as well as periods of prosperity. According to local tradition, the pilchard industry attracted Cornish 'cutters' to the island in the mid-18th century. "That was when all the unusual surnames came into Bere Island. They'd come in for a season and go away again. But an odd fellow took a shine to a local woman and didn't go any further."

By 1824, the British Army could report that at least two-thirds of the island's population of two thousand was solely dependent on fishing, and there were one thousand employed in the industry, with sixteen hookers and ninety yawls operating out of Lawrence Cove.

In the early decades of the 20th century, seining for mackerel was the most popular fishing activity on the island. There were as many as thirty seine boats in 1913, working out of Greenane, Lawrence Cove, Trá Ciarán and other points around the island, "and each would have worked with a second boat, the follower. There would have been sixteen men between the two boats. They were going strong up until

1923/24, but then the American market closed for mackerel, and that was the end of it really. It continued on a smaller scale for a little while, and there was a bit of a revival during the Second World War, but by 1945 the seine boats were all gone again."

Ted's family moved to Cork in his childhood. He remembers that on one occasion when he returned to the island as a teenager, some Chinese boats had come in "and they were buying everything. They were particularly fond of mullet, and fellows my age got a few bob supplying them."

World War II

Berehaven was a Treaty Port, and the British authorities maintained a garrison on Bere Island until 1938, when they handed over jurisdiction to the Irish state. The military presence was a boon for businesses in Castletownbere, but also for local suppliers on the island. "My father used say, 'come up here, I'll show you the most productive acre in western Europe.' This one acre produced more vegetables than any other market garden in Ireland. They used to grow cabbage there nearly eleven months of the year. My father said the British Army had an insatiable appetite for cabbage, they couldn't get enough of it. Jim Crowley has that garden now. He did a reclamation job on it, and I went in to have a look. There's a ridge of rock there, and there's pure black earth. The people who had it were Murphys, and you could see that it was obviously very well looked after."

The Irish Army took over the military stations on Bere Island shortly before World War II broke out in Europe. "During the war, they closed the western entrance to the harbour, for security reasons, and you could only enter the harbour through the eastern entrance. Any boat that came in the western entrance was fired on. On one occasion, the skipper of a fishing-boat running before a storm sought permission to come in the western entrance. I don't know how he did it, but he was granted permission. By way of thanks, he sent a bucket of fish to the commanding officer in Rerrin, who would have been Slater, I suppose.

And Slater, in front of the locals in Rerrin, sent back the fish, saying, 'don't do it again; the next time we'll shoot you.'"

The submarine

In the 1960s, a German who had been a submarine captain in World War I arrived in Castletownbere on holiday. The local historians Connie Murphy and Gerdie Harrington brought him out to Bere Island at his request. "In 1916, he had brought the submarine into Berehaven and they ran up on the Colt Rock, when the tide was going out. They were right under the gun batteries at Ardnakinna and Derrycreeveen. It was during the night of a full moon, and when the tide went out they were left high and dry on the rocks. They all had their life jackets ready to go, but they were worried that if they jumped out they'd be fired on. Next thing, the tide turned and the boat started to lift, and they slipped off the rock and went out again.

"That time the captain came back, in 1962 or '63, he wanted to see the gun battery. So Connie and Gerdie brought him in to show him the Reenduff battery and the Derrycreeveen battery, and it was only then he realised how lucky they were that they hadn't been blown out of it."

2

JEROME HARRINGTON

BLACKBALL

Jerome Harrington of Blackball, Cahermore is eighty-seven years old, and has been fishing since he was thirteen. "I started in 1946," he says. "That was my last year in school. I started with a boat from Crookhaven that came into the harbour below, a half-decker called the *Shamrock*. There were three in the boat besides myself. I was ten weeks in her, and I was only home the once. I got seven pounds for the ten weeks; a lot of money that time."

Jerome remembers that fish were plentiful, but the fishing-gear was primitive. "It wasn't like what you have now. The equipment today is no comparison. There were pots that time, and there was only one entrance into them. You'd put your hand in the top, but the conger could be there before you. The only way you could move the conger was to put your hand beneath its tail and point it out. That was a tricky job.

"There were no lights in the boat, and it was all night work; the lobsters would go in the nighttime better. You'd get two lobsters inside in the pot, so if you had even ten pots you might get twenty lobsters. We had thirty-six pots. They were the old pots; they used make them themselves. The money we got for the fish was nothing at all, but everything was cheap. The boats were cheap, the gear was cheap. In the '50s you could buy a trawler – a 60-footer - for €3,500. You wouldn't get a punt for that now. The money wasn't there, but at the same time, they were happier times."

Jerome Harrington

The lobsters mostly went to France. "That was the big market all the time. A Frenchman used to come around in a cutter. Peggy Leg, they called him, because he had only the one leg. He'd come into the harbour here buying fish."

Jerome remembers that were no small boats in the Loch when he started fishing. "There was no local boat, only the boats from Crookhaven. My grandfather fished here in the '30s, and a few more beside him, but then the family went away, to the States. The crowd from the south came up here then, from Crookhaven and Goleen and Hare Island. They'd give two hours rowing coming up, and they'd tie up in the Loch for the night, or if it was fine they'd stay outside. It was rough going. We slept in the boat ourselves, when we were potting; we had two bags of hay to lay on and we slept soundly."

The weather

Fishermen had always to contend with the weather, and Jerome remembers tales of the foul summer of 1914 still being spoken of in his childhood, decades later. "My grandfather had a 26-foot wooden boat. There was no engine, but he had a couple of sons able to handle the oars. There was plenty of stuff coming in that time on the tide. Bags of flour, and boxes of meat. They lived off what they'd get on the shore. They were used to handling boats in rough weather, but the weather was so bad that year that there was only three days in the month of July they got out in the harbour. That'll tell you. They got no hay or turf that year either. Another year then, they say the calves died from the heat in the month of May, but what year that was I don't know.

"That was all before my time; my grandfather died of an asthma attack at the age of 75."

Jerome's parents went to work in America, and he was himself born in New York. "Then we moved home. That was eighty-three years ago, when I was three, and I never went back since. I don't remember anything of it. We came home in Black '37; that was a savage year. We had eight feet of snow. My father had to go out the window upstairs, he couldn't get out the door. Cattle died in the sheds in some places, but not here; we were luckier.

"In the '40s, going to school, we used have wooden clogs, and we'd skate across the rivers to Cahermore. The month of February you'd get a black easterly wind. We're getting a different pattern of weather now, the whole thing is changed, but I think it's just cycles."

The worst storm Jerome remembers was in '44. "The sea ran up in the middle of the night and took the fence by the corner there, and drove it right into the other field down below. I saw the boats below in the harbour left up in the fields. Down by Dudley's house below, it knocked the reek. We never heard it; there was no wind, we never felt a puff of it. It must have been there was something built up outside, like an explosion. A tsunami, maybe. They talk about global warming and all this, but I just wonder."

Jerome remembers that only one of the neighbouring houses had a thatched roof, and that too was lifted in a storm. "That was Shea's old house up the hill. Himself and the wife were inside in bed one time; we got a northwest gale, and they lost the thatch to the squall. It was a full moon-lit night. He looked up and saw all the stars, and he said to his wife, 'wake up, my girl, we're the biggest hotel in Ireland!'"

Living conditions

In Jerome's childhood, life was simpler in many ways. "There was no car outside the house. It was a big thing to have a bicycle, even. But people had all the news. A pipe of tobacco and a cup of tea, and they'd be happy. And if they got a glass of whiskey, it was all the better. The money wasn't there. They'd walk to Castletown with the cattle, and if they couldn't sell them they'd walk them back home. We weren't bad, but the Dursey crowd had it worse. And the Bere Island crowd too, coming into town in the open boats with no shelter, depending on the old Seagull engine, and walking across the hill with their bageens of shopping in bad weather.

"A woman getting married that time… they had big families. They were baking non-stop, washing, darning. They hadn't much time to think. The man had it some biteen better, but 'twas hard going. The gramophone was the only thing in the house. No wireless, no television, no electrics. You had the lantern for milking the cow, with the candle inside in it. The bicycle lamp came in then; they were a great improvement."

People were largely self-sufficient. "We'd have two barrels of salted fish; connor and pollock. Three or four times a week we'd eat fish, and we were lucky to have it. You'd have your own meat then; you'd kill a cow and a pig. The bacon that time was grand stuff. The quality of it; you could smell the next door neighbour's bacon cooking. You grew your own vegetables, and the artificial manure that time was guano; you used nothing more than that.

"They had their own hens then. And they made soup that time, with the chicken and the vegetables, that'd heat you down to your toes. That soup, by Jesus! That was the cure for the cold."

People hunted as well. "You had the rabbit; they'd hunt them with ferrets. You'd get a half-crown for a rabbit. But the myxomatosis came out then, and that finished it. It put everyone off when they'd see the rabbit dying. But they were a grand feed. There's plenty of them around again, and no one touching them. We went after the birds too, dazzling them inside in the bushes. Thrushes. Blackbirds. We ate them both. The youth today wouldn't eat them, would they?"

People went visiting in the evenings, but the best occasions were often a station or a wake. "And if it was a wake, it could be twelve o'clock before they'd leave, after the Rosary. Some of them wouldn't go at all, they'd stay the night. In some parts of the country, they'd have a bottle of men's urine in the house. They'd shake it on your clothes to keep the dead away from you when you were leaving. Sure you'd have to burn the suit! I didn't see it, but I heard yards about it."

The War Years

Jerome remembers how World War II impinged on life in Beara. "We'd have black curtains on the windows, and we'd draw them tight so the planes couldn't see the light from the paraffin oil lamp. People believed in the fairies that time, and between the fairies and the planes overhead, we had to watch out for ourselves!"

Ireland was neutral, but Irish vessels were sometimes targeted. Early in the war, in October 1940, a cargo ship from Limerick named the *Kerry Head* was sunk by a German plane off Sheep's Head, with the loss of all its crew. "I was at school the same day. You'd see the smoke from the top of the hill, and people saw part of the structure of the boat being carried west by the tide past Dursey Head. They reckon the plane went down too; the trawlers picked up its wing. There was a lot of dirty work done that time."

British vessels fishing off the Irish coast were vulnerable to attack. "I remember one Sunday in '44, a plane came right down over the hill here - a German plane - and machine-gunned an English trawler off of Blackball. The skipper on the trawler got a bullet in his belly. He was taken to hospital but it didn't kill him."

The war years were a great time for collecting wreck along the shore. "There was plenty of stuff coming in. Firewood, and stuff like that. The beachcombing… 'twas like a kind of disease. I used to go out in the middle of the night, and I'd head away to Cahermore strand across the fields. A southeast wind would bring the wreck in. In '44, the last year of the war, I remember there were fifty-three men taking wreck on the Cahermore strand. Food, biscuits, chocolates. Tablets of every description. Tobacco. They were all sealed up in containers.

"Sonny Dudley had a punt, we went after wreck in that. The two Sheas, John and Tim, and myself and Sonny. You could pick what you wanted from the strand out. The four of us would split up what we got. A bale of rubber was worth £10 or £12, depending on the weight. The rubber would come in a solid block, and they bought it in town, in Peter Murphy's. There was a lot of money made on them. A bicycle that time… you'd get a good Raleigh for a pound, but a pound was hard got if you were working."

Jerome remembers an occasion when they got their hooks around a box of sweet tobacco, "in four-pound cardboard containers. They were all smokers round here, so we gave it out to the neighbours. Then the guards got word of it. That time the guards were on bicycles. Riordan was a guard west in the Mines, and he came into us here on his bicycle. My father told him he never smoked, and he had no tobacco. Riordan went into Dennehy's west, and got nothing there either. Micheál - a granduncle to PJ Dudley - was in the pub in Allihies, and Riordan the guard came in; he was mad for whiskey. Micheál was sitting inside and he watching Riordan in his peaked cap. 'Tobacco poacher!' he said. 'It's out in the street you should be, not drinking whiskey in here with your uniform on you!' He gave him the works, and Riordan drank his whiskey fast and got out!"

The sand boat

In the late '40s, the government gave out vouchers for sand that could be used as fertiliser. A sand boat operated out of the pier at Blackball, supplying the local farmers. "They used to go out the harbour with two ash oars. They'd anchor then on the south side of the harbour, and they'd drop the dredge. They'd pull the dredge behind them then, and they'd fill the boat. She was a small boateen, she wouldn't take much of a ton anyway. They worked every tide. There'd be horses and carts down by the pier. You'd get your voucher, so the sand cost very little.

"But those men were like steel. They didn't know their own strength, and they getting no grub. They did a power of work, pulling those oars. Sure there's no one could pull the oars now."

Cargo ships

After the War, Jerome went working on the coasters in England. "I was in Lancaster, and in Newcastle for the coal. I was all over. They were drinking on the ship that time. The captain of the boat had a bottle of whiskey beside him at the wheel. It was something frightening.

"I was on a cargo ship then, one of the sugar ships, called the *Crystal Diamond*, going to the West Indies. You had three lookouts; you had a man on the wing of the bridge, a man on the monkey island, and a man on the focus ahead. Three on watch the whole time. You were told how to send in reports, and you reported every light and port you passed. You'd report everything."

On the trawlers

In the '50s and '60s, there were only four trawlers fishing out of Castletownbere. "They were Biggs's boats, from Bantry. I worked for Biggs, and they did what they liked. We got no returns back; we just got the brown envelope with some couple of pounds inside it. We went fishing out of Howth, and we got talking to other crews in the pub, and they were getting double our money. So we said to the skippers, what's going on, like? We were being wronged badly. But we got united that time, we tied up the boats above in Bantry, and the strike was on. And Biggs sold the boats. Denis and Billy and Dónal O'Driscoll bought the *Marguerite*. The *Johnny Mary* then was bought by Micky Donoghue from Bantry. The *Staravaise* went to a man named Adams from Skibbereen. And the *Johanna Mary* went to Dublin.

"They all worked up from that. Billy O'Driscoll was a good fisherman, and he was the first to start up in Castletown, buying a boat of his own. His brother Kieran was a skipper at 16, if he was that at all. One time Billy took an interest in going ashore. He got into cows, and built a big shed inside in Skerkin. I stayed in their house a few times. Billy was inside for the best part of a year, quite happy he seemed, and he had a small boat doing a bit of potting. But he took a fit one Sunday evening and came back to Castletown. He took over from Kieran again, and went back fishing."

Jerome fished with Dónal O'Driscoll. "I gave three years with him, at the herring. Most of the fish went to Holland. They paid the best prices going. They'd take them fresh the most time, but they'd take them salted too. Dunmore was a busy place that time, 'twas like a city. We'd only fish the five days, and Sunday was a day of rest. But one morning in '61, Billy O'Driscoll was on the pier and there were two priests out walking. All the northern Irish boats were out fishing, and one of the priests said to Billy, how come ye're not out? And Billy said, because it's a Sunday. Well, said the priest, if you had Mass, there's nothing wrong with going out there and making an honest pound, if there's money to be made. And that opened the gap. That finished Sunday! Our day of refreshment!

"It was nice to have the weekend off that time, you'd go down the pier and talk to people. I go in to the pier in town now and again, but not too often anymore. Anyone you'd meet now off a boat would have his phone in his hand. There's no talk. Go into a doctor's surgery now, down in Bantry or anywhere, and it's the same. Not one word spoken. They just look at their phones. It's no good for the mind."

Jerome reckons the most profitable years he had fishing were at the herring. "The best week I had, I made £90. That was in '62, and the average week's wage that time would have been a fiver. But if you work that out again, the man on shore might fare better. You'd be so many weeks tied up with bad weather and so on. We hadn't the same boats to go out that time as they have now. The boat would be at the pier all the winter. We'd put the fish to market on the lorry, but the lorry might miss the market, and we'd have to pay for it anyway."

Jerome spent eight years crewing with Frank Downey, Joe Joe O'Sullivan and Mick Orpen. "Frank was a steady man. He was on a share and a quarter. He had the full intention of getting a boat of his own all the time. He didn't drink or smoke, and what he made he saved. Joe Joe was a good man too; he smoked but he didn't drink. But after eight years saving, they still couldn't get the boat on their own. It was €3,500, from Chambers of Kilkeal. Frank asked if I could give them a hand, but I couldn't that time. So they went to Finbar Murphy in Bere Island to back them, to get her clear. It was hard to put £1,000 together that time.

"You'd get a punt there now, for €12,000."

Piseogs

There were many piseogs associated with fishing. "You'd never stick the point of a knife into the mast or the deck, or anything, for that matter. And you wouldn't move anything out of the boat on a Monday morning, in case it would take the luck. Back in the '50s, we took this boat called the *Carbery Lass* to Baltimore for an overhaul on the slip. There was another boat there with boxes of mackerel on the deck, so I went down across the pier and asked could I have one for my breakfast. Ask the skipper there, they said. So I did, but he reckoned they were all sold. I was kind of surprised he wouldn't give me one. But I got talking to one of the crew after. The skipper wouldn't give me the mackerel, he said, in case I'd take his luck."

Marriage

Jerome was thirty-three when he married, "and that time we were making £30-35 a week for the four days. We were at the whitefish, working the Kish Bank in Dublin Bay. That was a dangerous place at night with all the ships going up and down there. One night I was on watch. I was a chain smoker that time, and I lit my pipe on the stove back of the wheelhouse, and in the time I was gone, the boat went right around. Instead of going northwest, it was going northeast on the compass. There was a big ship going down the bay on the other side at the same time. I was a lucky man that we didn't hit her.

"After I met Ann, I packed the fishing up then, on the big boats anyway. That was fifty-two years ago. I was on the Council then, but I'd go fishing in the summertime, in my own boat."

Lobsters

Jerome spent many years potting for lobsters and crayfish. "The biggest lobster I ever caught was eleven pounds. But Seán Cotter caught one that was thirteen pounds. We were fishing north in Ballinskelligs. I had a half-decker that time, a 33-foot boat. That was in '58. My brother Patrick and Christy Murphy and myself were fishing out around Two Head Island, out the mouth of Derrynane. We went into Lucey's in Derrynane, thinking he'd buy our lobsters. But he said, 'where'd ye buy the pots?' And when we said, 'Sheehan's in Castletown,' he wouldn't take our crays. We had to steam right back into Castletown, and land our fish inside to Sheehan's. That was the thing; they gave you the pots for nothing, but they had a claim then on your fish."

Jerome today

Jerome's health was poor for a long time. "I was asthmatic for twenty-five years. I was in Bantry Hospital one time for six weeks, and they put me off the Council. It wasn't safe to have me on the road, my breathing was so bad. I tried everything to cure it. The one place I had relief was out in the boat. Once I was out in the sea air, I was grand; the salt was great for the asthma. In the end, I got this notion; I got stumps of red weed down in the strand and brought it home and boiled it. I threw whiskey into it. Honey and cloves. It turned pure brown, and I drank it warm. And from that day to this, I had no attack of asthma. Never.

"I get checked up now once a year. I take one tablet for blood pressure, and that's it. In my time, a man of seventy was counted very old. That was pension age. When they got the pension, they'd say, I have my death cert got. But they're living longer today. They're going to more doctors, getting tablets for this and that, keeping them going."

Jerome still fishes as often as he can, but the fish are nowhere near as plentiful as they were in his youth, a situation he attributes to the boats being too big and too powerful. "If they cut the power down, and let no boat go over 600 horse-power, there'd still be plenty of fish. I said that years ago. The fish have no chance. The herring are nearly cleared out now. And the mackerel, you don't know what's going to happen there either.

"The last few years I haven't seen a sunfish. They were very popular one time. They're very big fish, you just see the fin sticking up. I had one nearly caught, but he got away from me. The sunfish, you'd cook them; the oil is very good for the system."

Even the days he's not fishing, Jerome goes down to check on his boat. "There was a woman there by the pier last summer. I had the old bicycle. It's one of the old Raleighs, there's no gears on it. The woman asked me how old it was. She's eighty anyway, I said, and I'm a few years older. You're not, she said. I am, I'm eighty-six. And she took a picture of myself and the bicycle.

"But that's it. I put in a lifetime fishing, seventy years anyway. And I cycle down to the harbour regular still; if you give up at all, you're finished."

3

BILLY BLACK

CASTLETOWNBERE

Billy Black of Castletownbere was the third generation in his family to work painting lighthouses around the coast, including those on the Roancarrig in Berehaven and the Bull Rock, off Dursey Island. His grandfather James was a Scotsman who fought in the Great War before moving to Dublin with his three brothers and two stepbrothers, all of whom were painters. Billy's father William was born in Dublin, and met his mother while working with the lighthouse service in Beara. Initially, the couple lived in Dublin, before moving back to Castletownbere with their young family in 1948.

One of Billy's earliest memories of the town is of a Spanish boat coming into the pier with the remains of five seamen, the crew of another vessel who'd perished at sea. "We all went down to see that," he says. "I remember there were blankets thrown over the bodies, and the fishermen were having their meal at the same time, sitting on deck."

*L – R: Billy's grandfather James Black, and father William Black Sr, at
the Hook Lighthouse, Co Waterford, c. 1935 © Billy Black*

On another occasion, the crew of a Spanish vessel tried to get Billy and
two of his schoolmates - the Morrissey brothers – drunk. "I was
coming up to thirteen at the time. We were drinking wine from the
bag, and I was starting to get groggy, so I came home. I fell in the door,
and my sister Noreen said, 'what in the name of God is wrong with
you? You're drunk!' 'I'm not,' I said. 'Get up to bed,' she said, 'before
Father comes in.' Because he'd have bloody murdered me, you know.

"But with that, he came in. We had a garage up near McIlhennys, and
he said to me, 'go up and get a tin of green paint.' He wanted it for the
next day. 'All right, Daddy,' I said. The night was wet, but up I went
and eventually I found the tin. The lid wasn't fully closed down, and I
smeared myself with paint; it was all over me, but I didn't notice, with
me being drunk and the night being so wet. Dick and Noel O'Driscoll
were coming down the road with me, and they noticed, and they said,
'are you okay? You'd want to hold the tin right, you know.'"

*L – R: Jim Joe and Geoffrey Morrissey on the old pier at
Castletownbere, 1951 © Gerdie Harrington*

When Billy got in the door, his father took one look and said, 'Holy Jesus, what happened you?' "And with that, I collapsed; I went down in a heap on the floor. I was put to bed, and Noreen cleaned the paint off me with paraffin oil. I came downstairs the next morning and my father was just going out to work. I thought he'd give me a hiding. 'Do you think you'll continue drinking?' he said. 'No, Daddy.' 'Well then, let that be a lesson to you.' Out the door he went, and there was no more about it."

The local boats

Only a handful of locals were fishing when Billy first lived in Castletownbere. "Timmy Lynch and Jimmy O'Neill, the Rock, they had a small boat that was wrecked out the back of the Protestant churchyard. John Michael O'Neill was fishing as well, and Willie Murphy, Droum; he was supplying fish to Castletown when nobody else was. He'd come in on the Friday; he'd have the boxes of fish there in the Square.

"The O'Sheas – Gerry, Teddy and Pierce – started here as well; they started small. Gerry had the boat, but he moved to Howth and fished out of there for many years. Then he went across to Fleetwood; he was making better money there because he was getting the prime fish."

Billy remembers the fuss when the Lynches had a new boat built. "That was the *Ros Bhéarra*. She came into the pier and we all thought she was the *Queen Mary*."

In the 1950s, Biggs of Bantry sold off their boats, and they all came up to Castletownbere. "What were their names? The *Staravaise*, the *Raingoose*, the *Deirdre*, the *Johanna Mary*, the *Casamara*, and the *Marguerite*.

"The king of fishing that time was Billy O'Driscoll. Billy came up with the *Casamara*, and the next boat he had was the *Raingoose*. That was fairly new, a lovely varnished boat. Dónal then, his brother, had the *Staravaise*; she had a kind of a straight bow, you could see the keel at the back."

Denis, another of the O'Driscoll brothers, was fishing with two Bantry men in Glengarriff on a boat called the *Hidden Treasure* when they were asked to come to the assistance of the *William Buzz*, a Swansea trawler that had gone aground at Cametrignane. "The *Hidden Treasure* came up to unload the coal, to lighten the boat. Eventually they got it off the rocks, and Denis came up to my mother's for tea; my mother had the restaurant where the chipper is now. My sister Pat took a fancy to him, they started dating and they married later. The funny thing was, he told me to come down to the pier one night for some fish. He said to me, 'have ye relations in Cork?' When Denis was in the army, he'd stayed on Patrick's Hill with a family called the Murphys. It turned out they were our first cousins."

It transpired also that Billy and Denis had met in Dublin many years before. "When I was seven, our first communion class from Milltown School were brought out to Ballsbridge as a treat, to see the military tattoo, a demonstration of army equipment. I asked Denis, 'did you ever hear of the tattoo?' 'I did,' he said. And I said, 'when we were youngsters we thought it was great.' Denis couldn't believe I'd been at it. 'Describe it,' he said. I told him we'd walked in, and there were two soldiers on sentry duty, walking back and forth. And Denis said, 'I was one of them, I was on duty the five days it was on.'"

Joining Irish Lights

William Black had retired from Irish Lights when the family moved to Castletownbere, but eventually he went back, and he got Billy in with him. "I was twenty when I joined, in 1956. The Roancarrig was my first stop. I was on there for fourteen weeks, and then we were shifted up to Inishtrahull, off Malin Head. We were there for the building of the lighthouse. And then I went to the Skelligs."

It was on Skellig Michael that Billy had his first accident. "I was line fishing off the rocks, with a weight and goat's hair as bait. I'd step on the line as I threw it out, but one time it snapped in under my kneecap, and the hook – a pollock hook it was – got stuck right in. The lightkeeper that was with me, Matt Coughlan, was from Schull and his father was a doctor. And he was Assistant Keeper (AK), next in rank to the Principal Keeper (PK). Matt cut the line and helped to carry me up to the dwelling. We had a long way to go, and when we got there, my leg had started to swell. So what happens out there is, the PK has the emergency kit, and he goes on the phone and gets instructions. He'd amputate the leg if necessary. So the PK wanted to operate, to get the hook out. He opened the box, but I said, 'you're not going near my leg,' and I went to work on it myself. I sliced it on one side, and I forced the barb through and pulled it out."

Billy remembers being present the first time a helicopter made a night landing at a lighthouse for a medical emergency. "I was back working on Inishtrahull. Danny O'Sullivan was one of the lightkeepers there, and his son Eugene came out cooking. There was a big job on, dismantling the lantern. There were two lighthouses there, so they had to demolish one and build up the other, and put the fog signal on it. But next thing, the young fellow, Eugene, had appendicitis. It was night, and they had to get him ashore. It's a pretty big island, about three miles long, and there's a football field. We put eight lights out on that, and the helicopter came down and picked Eugene up to take him away for treatment. Before that - before there were helicopters - the PK would have carried out the appendix operation himself."

The Bull Rock

Billy's family had a long association with the Bull Rock. He remembers his grandfather describing how tough conditions were in his day. Often, the meat they'd bring out would go off in a few days. "But it wouldn't be thrown out. They'd boil it up, and then they'd let the pot rest for the night. Next morning there'd be a layer of fat on it, and all the bugs would be floating in the fat. So they'd take the fat off, and the bugs, and they'd peel potatoes and onions and make up a good stew. It's hard to credit now, but they'd sooner do that than part with the meat."

Billy's father and grandfather worked there together in the war years. "They were out in 1943. And in the evening, after all the bombing raids, this German plane used to pass by. Not that high, just over the water. The German used to wave out through the window, and they'd all wave back, but one day he was shot out of the sky."

It was inevitable that Billy would work on the Bull himself, and he did so regularly. On one occasion, in '58, he witnessed Dónal O'Driscoll steer his trawler, the *Staravaise*, through the tunnel in the rock. The following year, Billy and his father witnessed his brother Jimmy narrowly escape disaster when the boat he was fishing on, the *Lochloy*, struck a submerged rock to the south. "We were working away, and Hegarty the PK said, 'come out, there's a boat sinking.' So we came out and the keepers were on the radio and they were talking back and forth. And they were saying, 'who was steering?' There were three Jimmys on the boat; Jimmy Jack and Jimmy Harrington from Bere Island, and my brother Jimmy. My father of course nearly lost it; he thought it was our Jimmy was steering, though it turned out he wasn't. We were watching away when Gerard O'Shea came along and took the three off the boat. The boat sank but she went on a shelf beyond the Cow, and for three days we'd look out and we'd see her mast sticking up, and the third day she went down."

Painting the lighthouse

The Blacks would paint the dwellings and the stores on the Bull, but the most dangerous job was painting the lighthouse itself. "We had a cradle, with a double pulley lock, and we'd come down from the top. There'd be two of us in it, the two painters, and two more on the ropes above, so the cradle wouldn't tip over. That'd be a summer job; you'd wait till the weather was good. Two of us would do it in two days; you had a day for the white, then another for the black band. The white was an enamel paint, and the band was vegetable black, with a matt finish. We didn't mind the height; anything over forty feet, we'd get paid extra anyway.

"We got noise money too, tuppence an hour when the foghorn was sounding. There were three trumpets on the Bull, all faced in different directions. Long ago, on a foggy night, they were that loud they could be heard in Bantry. Our dwellings were right under the trumpets, and you'd be just going to sleep when they'd start up. You might get two days of that, constant, night and day. You wouldn't sleep at all. They had this monitor that registered how long the foghorn was sounding, on a sheet, and the lads used come out and give it a little encouragement, so we'd get more noise money."

The painters worked a fifty-four hour week, with Sundays off and a week's leave for every six weeks served. "If you had a storm and you had so many days overdue, in the month of March or something, the cutter went out to pick you up. There were three boats served the Bull Rock; the *Velonia*. the *Nabro*, and the *Ierne*. They'd be in and out with provisions.

"The longest I spent out was sixteen weeks; that was on the Blaskets. If you got stuck, there were emergency supplies. You had plenty of cans of bully beef and sardines, and the dog biscuits, in a big container. They were rock hard, but if you dipped them in hot water, they swelled out, like slices of bread. They were actually quite nice to eat."

The men would often bake in the evenings. "We'd have condensed milk, and we'd make our own yeast bread. Out on the Bull, there was a stove with two burners, and an oven on top of it. We used to make yeast bread. One time, I made my first attempt at scones. They were lovely and brown on top, and I buttered them and everything and put them on the table. Six of them. My father came in and said, 'oh great.' So he picked up one, and he tapped it on the table, and it was as hard as a rock. 'Throw them out,' he said. And I did. My father was standing outside after with Dillon the PK, and the seagulls were pecking at the scones, and Dillon says, 'Jesus, look at that; the seagulls can't manage them either!'"

Out on the Bull, the men would supplement their diet by catching fish off the rocks, or potting for crayfish and lobsters. "I'll tell you one thing that happened me. We used to go cliff climbing for eggs. We used to have a big long rope and every two feet of it would have a knot. We'd tie it to the stanchion above and climb down. Jimmy Maguire was with me; he was the helper for a mechanic out there, Paudie O'Shea. I was climbing down for the razorbill and puffins' eggs, and Jimmy was above, paying out the rope. I got onto a ledge, and I thought I had more rope, but there was none. There was nothing for it but to jump.

"The drop was twenty-five feet, but anyway, I went for it; I dived into the sea. I was going for the ladder, but the swell started to take me out. I was all cut, but I held my head. What I did was, I went down three feet under, and I frog-stroked out of it; I got around to the north side and I was out of the current completely. Then I had a fair old swim around to the other side, but I got out of the water. By that time, Jimmy thought I was lost, and he'd gone up to tell the others. Jim Hegarty the PK and my father came down, thinking I was gone, but then they saw my head appear. I got a right earful from my father, and Hegarty then, by right he should have reported me, but I begged him not to; I'd have been fired if he did. Hegarty said, 'okay, I don't think you'll be doing that again.' And I said, 'no, I don't think so.' So he let it go."

Hobbies

The lightkeepers and workmen all had their own ways of occupying themselves in the evenings. "There was one keeper named Dillon who made souvenirs, and he was making so much out of that he retired and moved back to Dublin and employed six more in the business. My father used to do the ship in the bottle; the Dimple Haig bottles with the three sides were his favourite. What I did out there was, I'd collect eggs, and I'd blow them. The gannets' eggs were great to make an omelette. You'd feed two men with one gannet's egg. It's very rich; you don't need any salt.

"I used to collect old chests of drawers. The old ones were pure mahogany. They'd be dovetailed and all that. I used to cut them up and make a case. I had plenty of putty and glass, and my diamond cutter, to cut the glass for the front. Then I'd put eggs in the case. I'd start with the gannet's egg in the centre, and then the razorbill beside it, down to the stormy petrel. The stormy petrels used land at night, and they'd go in under the Mizen hut. They had a very colourful little egg. How we discovered them was, they got in under the floor and at nighttime they'd start twerping. You'd hear them. We lifted a plank and there were hundreds of them in there. You'd put the light on and they wouldn't move.

"But making the cases of eggs… that's what I did for a pastime."

Leaving the Bull

Anyone leaving the Bull Rock had to be lifted by winch from the brass ladder onto the boat, and risked being dunked in the tide by the keepers above. "With the rise of the tide, there could be an eight or nine foot swell up and down. You'd throw your mattress into the boat, and then you had to wait for the swell to come up and you'd jump. But the lads, if they didn't like you, they'd say, 'don't wear your good suit going ashore.'

"Anyway, I came down one time in my overalls, and my father said, 'what are you doing in those?' 'Oh,' I said, 'I was told not to wear my good suit.' And he said, 'nonsense!' The two boys were on the winch, and anyway I was quick enough. I stood on the stick; I didn't sit on it. And then, when the tide was coming up, I brought up my legs and scrambled up along the rope. The water just skimmed off my ass. But when my father was going out, they dunked him in the sea halfway down to his waist. In his good suit!"

The Roancarrig

Billy worked on the Roancarrig often. He and his father were there one time, chipping off all the coats of paint that had accumulated on the buildings, burning the paint off the doors and woodwork, and pumicing the surfaces to smooth them off. It was slow, repetitive work, and it tested their patience. "My father had to write a report every day, and because it was the same old, same old, he'd just put 'ditto.' Next thing, he got a letter from head office asking, 'what's all this *ditto* about?' My father was mad. He said to me, 'go down and get every bag of paint we've burned off.' There were six and a half coal-bags full of it, and we put them in the magazine.

"About three weeks later, the commissioners came down on an inspection. There were five of them, and here were the two of us standing in our white overalls. Anyway, my father said, 'I have something to say; I got a very nasty letter down from head office.' 'What was that?' they said. He showed them the letter while I threw out the bags from the magazine. 'And what's all this?' they said. 'That's all the paint we burned off the walls and the doors,' said my father, 'and that's what all the *ditto* was about!'"

Back Row L – R: Billy Henehan, John Noel Crowley and Billy Polly. Kneeling, Billy Black at the Roancarrig Lighthouse, 1956 © Billy Black

The Fastnet

Billy worked as a glazier as well as painting, and he could be dispatched anywhere around the coast at short notice, even on his week off. He would often install new lantern lights, or dismantle the old ones. Again, this was a family tradition; his grandfather had dismantled the old lantern light on Skellig Michael.

On one occasion, Billy and his father were given the job of installing a new lightning conductor on the Fastnet. Again, they had to work from a cradle, "but towards the end, instead of using the cradle, we used the bosun's chair. It was nice and light."

One of the keepers on the Fastnet was a character named Pa Crowley, who was notoriously impervious to the cold. "Pa used to go around in his shirt in the wintertime, with the sleeves rolled up. They couldn't understand it, how he could go around like that, winter and summer the same. When the commissioners would come on the rock in May, they'd be in uniform, the 'lilywhites', with a special white cap. The lads used to be giving out to Pa, as they'd have to dress up for the inspection. One of the commissioners said to him one time, 'I hear you're a very healthy man.' 'I am,' said Pa. 'And do you know why? I have a cast-iron pot, and what I do is, when I'm ashore, I collect wild spinach. Not cultivated spinach, the wild stuff, and I boil the sugar out of it. Then I let it rest before I bottle it. And I take two big soupspoons of that every day.'

"I didn't believe it till I saw it myself. It came out of the bottle like ink, a pure black liquid. But Pa reckoned that's what made him so healthy."

Leaving Irish Lights

After he'd served his time, Billy was offered a permanent position with Irish Lights, like his father and grandfather before him, but he declined, choosing instead to work independently as a painter, while developing a keen interest in photography. "My father nearly lost it when I turned down the job," he says. "But that was before the helicopters came in, and I'd have been stuck out there too long. After that, the painting was put out to contract; there were no more permanent jobs."

4

KIERAN O'DRISCOLL
CASTLETOWNBERE

Kieran O'Driscoll is one of the most prominent trawlermen in Castletownbere. He became the youngest skipper on the whole Irish coast when he commissioned his first vessel, the *St Gervase,* in 1968. He has since owned and skippered the trawlers the *Spes Nova,* the *Loinnir,* the *Siobhána,* the *Draíocht na Mara* and the *Solunday,* and continues to pot lobsters at a time of life when most would be happy to retire.

Kieran's family have been associated with the fishing industry in Castletownbere since the early 1950s, when his brothers Billy, Denis and Dónal bought their first boat, the *Marguerite,* from Biggs of Bantry. Biggs is today more often associated with the wholesale and oil delivery businesses, but the company dominated the fishing industry in Berehaven for many years until, in 1951, their skippers and crews went on strike for better conditions and pay.

"Biggs packed it in that time, and the skippers bought the boats," Kieran remembers. "Billy continued fishing the *Raingoose* for a Dublin fish dealer for ten years, and then he bought her. She was a 70-footer, a massive boat at the time. It was actually a submarine commander who had her built. There was a little saucer he kept as a souvenir at the back of the cabin; it was all cracked from when the submarine was torpedoed. She was a lovely boat; Billy fished her for seven or eight years.

Kieran O'Driscoll, 2019

"I was only fourteen and a half when I started fishing, in January '53. I was on with Billy. My first outing was to Dungarvan, and then we came back and fished out of Kenmare. We were targeting the haddock and whiting mostly. We used to send a lorry of our own away to Dublin every night."

That autumn, Billy brought the *Raingoose* into Castletownbere. "Johnny Sheehan had the old ice plant that time. They used to do block ice. Great big blocks of it. We used to get five or six tons of that, and we'd have to crush it ourselves. It meant that we could stay out a couple of days longer. We'd go fishing north of the Bull Rock, and we'd come into Garnish, working at night. Before the ice, we'd have to come in every day. In Castletown, there was an old wooden pier, and the old sleepers would float away in the southeast gales. You might be walking down and you'd put your foot between them. There wasn't much of a local industry at that time. Timmy Lynch would do a bit of herring in the wintertime, but that was all, and Billy Murphy did a bit of scalloping, but he used to work from the slip further up."

Kieran was only sixteen when he first skippered the boat. "Billy bought a big motorbike, and decided to do a tour of Ireland with his girlfriend, Sheila. There were very good lads on the boat, but none of them would take her over, and Billy said to me one day, 'you'll have to take her, there's no one else wants to do it.' I was actually the cook up till then. So Billy brought me up to the wheelhouse for a week, and that's how I learned the ropes. But I liked it, you know. All the crew were established. There'd be a crew of six that time; they were good men, they were nice to me, actually. It wasn't easy to go back to the deck then, after that."

Skippers' Graduation, 1967 Back Row L – R: Captain Dave Warner, Frank Downey, Michael Joe O'Driscoll, Kieran O'Driscoll, PJ Dudley, Unknown, Joe Joe O'Sullivan, Dónal O'Driscoll and Michael J Murphy TD Front Row L – R: Denis Drake (BIM), Denis O'Driscoll, Brendan O'Kelly (Chairman BIM), Canon Moriarty, Jim O'Connor (BIM) and Bill Deasy

Castletownbere Skippers, 1967 Back Row L – R: Frank
Downey, Michael Joe O'Driscoll, Kieran O'Driscoll, PJ Dudley,
Joe Joe O'Sullivan and Dónal O'Driscoll Front Row L – R:
Denis O'Driscoll, Brendan O'Kelly (Chairman BIM) and Bill
Deasy

*Skippers' Wives, 1967 Back Row L – R: Mary Drake, Nancy Teehan,
Phyllis O'Driscoll, Kitty O'Driscoll, Joan O'Connor and Margaret
Downey Front Row L – R: Agnes Carlton, Margaret Dudley, Maisie
O'Driscoll, Patricia O'Driscoll and Mary (Joe Joe) O'Sullivan*

Kieran O'Driscoll and PJ Dudley, 1968

The *St Gervase*

Kieran had his first boat, the *St Gervase*, built in Brittany in '68. "There was a special thing with the French that time... they made a loan available, at a cheap rate." He attributes the name he chose for the boat to a case of divine intervention. "I was on the *Patricia* with my brother Denis before that. We were in Crosshaven, having a job done. The Sherkin ferryman, who I knew very well, came down the pier and said, 'I'm taking a boat back to Baltimore tomorrow, would you go with me?' It would only take eight or nine hours, but he wasn't sure of the coast. So I said I'd go. They put everything we needed on board – as we thought - and we took off. But the engine started to splutter outside of Roche's Point. This man knew the engine inside out ... she was a petrol/paraffin engine... so he stopped to clear the filter, and when he went to start her again, it wouldn't start, and we realised we had no petrol. They had taken the gallons of petrol on shore in Crosshaven.

"We were drifting away for three or four days after that. We were down to our very last flare when a Belgian trawler picked us up, and they towed us into Kinsale."

Kieran's sister was home from Kenya at the time; she was a nun and her name was St Gervase. She told him that, when everyone else had presumed they'd drowned, she'd had this vision that they were still alive and would be found. "So I told her that day that when I got my first boat I would name it after her – and I did."

Denis O'Driscoll, Kieran O'Driscoll and BIM official at the arrival of the St Gervase *in Castletownbere, 1968*

Frank Downey had a new boat - the *Purple Heather* - built in France around the same time. Frank's previous boat was the *Seaflower*, which he sold to the Bere Island skipper Michael Crowley. The *Seaflower* sank off Carrigavaunaheen, near Ardgoom, on the 22nd of December 1968, with the loss of all five of its crew: Michael Crowley, Bernie Lynch, John Michael Sheehan, Noel Sheehan and Niall Crilly. "I remember we were back from Dunmore East the night the *Seaflower* got into trouble," says Kieran. "Frank rang me, and about four o'clock we got out away north to Kilmackilloge. We were walking along the route the boat had taken. Whatever way Frank spotted this thing sticking out of the water, he knew it was the *Seaflower*. Frank was real tough, but he started crying... he knew the men were gone."

Kieran and Frank both had bad luck with the French boats, when a fungus got into the woodwork on the decks just a few years after they'd been built. "We should have gone back to the builders. I remember this fellow at the time; he was with BIM. He came down and said, 'we're going to fight this. Don't go back to France.' But the Killybegs fellows went back, and they got the woodwork redone - for free - and they were fine after that. And the *St Gervase* would have been too, if I'd gone back. But we went by your man from BIM, and we never got a penny."

Developing the harbour

Fishing has changed hugely in Kieran's time at sea. "The first big change for me was sonar. That took getting used to, when we put it in first. When we were towing for herring, you might come on a spot, and then you might see another three or four hundred yards up ahead again. You'd cast the nets quarter of a mile either side of the shoal, instead of straight down. The sonar helped us get it right, you know."

In the early '70s, the harbour in Castletownbere underwent huge changes too. Kieran credits this development to a number of factors, including the support of Canon Moriarty, the local priest, and Erskine Childers, who served as Tánaiste, under Jack Lynch, from '69 to '73. "Childers used to stay with Sir James Baird at Waterfall House. We got to know him very well, and he was a great help. We got the money for dredging first, and then developing the harbour. That was in 1971. It was amazing how easy it seemed to happen once it got started. We got a Dutch dredger in, and she dredged the whole place in a matter of months. Then they got the piling finished in no time. They did Bantry as well, a little later. There was some energy that time."

The EU

In '73, Ireland joined what was then the European Economic Community and is now the European Union. The effect on the Irish fishing industry was largely negative, as Ireland conceded the right of other European nations, with better boats and processing facilities, to fish in its waters.

Kieran believes the government had little understanding of how the fishing industry operates. "That time now, in the '70s, when Garret FitzGerald was Minister for Foreign Affairs, the government knew what we needed, but they'd go across to Brussels and get next to nothing. There's negotiators have gone out there since and they've got less. The French didn't get any great deal when they entered the EU, but they're such good negotiators that they got things down the line. The farmers had a big lobby that time, and I'd say to get subsidies and that for the farming, the government here had to give up a lot of the fishing."

Kieran helped establish the Irish Fishermen's Organisation as a voice for the industry, and became its first Chairman, in '72. "We'd be up to Dublin, trying to get a 50-mile limit. I was involved for a few years; there was a heap of travelling involved, but we put things half-right anyway."

Kieran O'Driscoll addressing the National Fisheries Conference,
1972

He concedes that "there was good came out of the EU, but I don't
know did we take full advantage of it either. There were good grants,
and they set up the IFPO [the Irish Fish Producers Organisation] in '75
to better the market. Fish were being withdrawn, but you'd get paid
for it. Any fish that didn't clear at auction, you'd put dye on it and
dump it back into the sea. It mightn't have been that good an idea, but
it'd bring up your income anyway. It was after that really that fishing
was able to stand on its own feet."

The tuna

Kieran was one of the first in Castletownbere to fish for tuna. "That
started in '91, I suppose. We had to go away south to get the warm
waters. We went within two hundred miles of the Azores, and we'd be
four days steaming back, but it was a great fishery, you know."

The Draiocht na Mara

He remembers how close his vessel came to being caught in a ferocious storm one night northeast of the Azores. "It was our first year at the tuna, myself and Neilie Minihane. It was a lovely calm night, but I couldn't sleep. I was up in the wheelhouse, and there was this big ship passing, so I said I'd call them. And they said, 'you wouldn't want to be here this time tomorrow. There's winds of one hundred and fifty miles an hour streaming down... you'd want to go at least forty miles north of here to keep outside it.'

"There was no satellite forecasting that time, we usually depended on the BBC. We started hauling anyway. Neilie was a bit further north than we were. Sometime in the night, the dome on top of the wheelhouse was blown off. We turned the boat down before the wind. I was sure we weren't going to get out, but thankfully we did. We were just on the edge of the storm, I'd say. It lasted about two hours."

Crew

Kieran remembers how getting good men to crew the boat was not always an easy task. "It's important to get the right fellows. The trouble was, you were working very unsociable hours. That time now, in '71, the buyers wanted us to fish on Sunday nights for Monday morning, which was a big change. But we went along with them anyway. We started fishing on the Sunday, so that meant there was no weekend. We were going off Sunday morning, and you never knew if you were going to be one day away, or two or three, so you had to have a good night's sleep the night before. So that was Saturday night out for us."

That task is no easier today, he reckons. "Anyone who's doing well is spending a month at sea. It's tough going. The only way you can do that is to have a foreign crew. And that's not giving the employment to the Irish fellows anymore."

It has also become increasingly difficult to locate the fish. "Prawns are getting scarce now, they're pretty well fished out on the south coast. It comes in cycles, but it's hard to say where it's going anymore. In the herring at Dunmore East… one year it'd be slack, but it'd be better the next year. But the herring are not coming back now. The spawning beds there, south of Dunmore East, they're the best in Ireland. But there's Dutch beamers steaming back and forth through them, and it's definitely doing harm. The Department doesn't seem to be able to do anything about it, but that should have been closed down during the spawning time. I don't know what's going to happen it, really."

Potting for lobsters

In the early 2000s Kieran started a wellboat services company with his son Finbarr, who operates their vessel the *Solundoy* - a 300m^3 live fish carrier equipped to transport, grade, count and treat live salmon, trout and smolts – off Iceland. Kieran's younger son, Noel, is captain on Holland America Line cruise ships, but it is surely a sign of the times that none of the extended family fishes for a living any more.

Kieran himself keeps a small boat as a hobby and is still potting lobsters, just as he did as a young fellow on Sherkin. "I was still going to school when I started, I was twelve or thirteen, and we had a little boat – eighteen or twenty foot – and I fished ten pots on her. I got the pots in Bantry; I got an engine too, and the deal was I could pay for them when I got fish. But I wasn't getting many at the start. I had a big old tank, for holding them. I thought I could fill it, but I was putting nothing into it; I was putting the pots in the wrong place.

"But this old man, he was sitting in the same place every day, and one evening, he said, 'I'm going out with you tomorrow.' And I thought, 'where is this fellow going?' But anyway, he went out with me. He said, 'go over here now,' and he brought me to where there were these slits in the rock, going along. Every slit in the rock, he put a pot outside it. I'll never forget it; the following morning there were six lobsters in the first pot. After that, I always got fish. These things stay in your mind. He was a real old timer and he knew his stuff."

Kieran keeps his current boat at Ballycrovane. He has taught his daughter Mairéad and grandson Robert how to haul the pots, and the lobsters feature on the menu of Mairéad and her sister Eileen's seafood restaurant in Castletownbere. "I have ten pots," says Kieran, "and I go out every three days. One day I got twenty-seven fish; it was unreal." He chuckles. "But I put the pots out there again, and I only got five or six."

5

BARNEY MCGUINNESS
CASTLETOWNBERE

Barney McGuinness is the eldest of ten children and grew up in the east end of Castletownbere. He started fishing, aged fourteen, in 1957. "The boat was the *St Bernadette*. I remember it was lovely the first day out; it was a novelty, I suppose, at the beginning. The rest of the crew were all fully grown men. Big lads. You had Michael Crowley from Bere Island. Jimmy Murphy from Sherkin. Greg Conneally from Galway. Victor Lloyd was an Englishman, but he was off with a broken leg at that time. And then we had our skipper, Gerry O'Shea himself.

"Things weren't bad at all; there was no roaring or shouting, you just got on with it. We didn't go out far; we'd be fishing in the Dursey, north the Kenmare River and up that way. We wouldn't be far from land. No one went far off the land in those days anyway. Most of the boats, the seiners, they were in Bantry Bay, or north of the Bull, places like that. That was as far as they went. We used to go in there to Firkeal at night. Gerry used work nights, you know. He was the first one to start working the twenty-four hours. That was a big change. Although I was only a greenhorn, I learned to steer and all that. What he'd do, if he was going for a mug of tea, he'd put you in the wheelhouse. You'd know what to do; if the boat went too fast, you just pulled back the throttle. You'd be learning away from there the whole time."

Barney, Roy and Josie McGuinness

The *St Bernadette* mostly trawled on its own. "Three-hour tows we used do. The only time you'd go pairing was when you'd go to Dunmore. They'd be fishing for the herrings in Dunmore, and they'd go pairing then. And sometimes we'd trawl for the herrings ourselves. An ordinary time, you'd have maybe four on deck. You had to, for all the work that was in it. We used to have to haul the net; as soon as the doors came up, the hand work started straight away. You had to haul the net up, and shoot away again. Now all they do is throw the cod-end over the stern and it comes off the reel. There were days back then you could get fifty or sixty boxes of fish. You'd get haddock and a nice bit of prime at the Dursey. If you got nine or ten boxes, you had a great day. It was all timber boxes then, and we landed below, on the old wooden pier."

The one fish they always threw back was monk, a species that is highly prized today but was never eaten locally back then. "We were afraid of the monk, so we dumped them. We were afraid to even touch them, to be honest. The size of the mouth would frighten anyone. If we kept the monk, I suppose we'd have sold them, because some people would have known what they were, but they didn't realise we were catching them anyway."

At the time, there were no more than half a dozen boats in Castletownbere.

"The O'Driscolls had boats here, and Mick Orpen had a boat, but Frank Downey didn't yet. Then you had the lads from the south… the Deasys from Union Hall used land here all the time. You had a couple of Schull boats coming in too.

"There were a couple of 60-footers, and the rest of the boats would be 50 to 60ft. The boats were Irish built mostly. The *St Bernadette* was built in Meevagh. The *Ros Bhéara* was built below in Baltimore. There were a lot of boats built in Baltimore that time. Those that had the money went to Scotland and got the Scottish boats. There were some lovely Scottish boats brought in here. And things were really going ahead, in those days. It was the only employment here really."

For a long time, ice was brought down from Cork to preserve the fish, and then finally an ice plant was built next to Harrington's. "I used help Joe Sheehan in there, to take the ice out. It was terrible. They were hundredweight blocks, that you lifted by hand. And you had to crush the block; there was a crusher inside. It was fine ice; it used last, but my God, it was hard work."

All the fish was sent to Dublin, courtesy of two prominent dealers. "Nolan was mostly at it… but Molloy came at it then, and the O'Driscolls used send all their fish to Molloy. When we were up in Killybegs, it was all Nolan. We all found out that Nolan was about the best of them. Molloy had his own few charmers all right, but we always went to Nolan."

Barney fished on the *St Bernadette* for two years – from the age of fourteen to sixteen - until the skipper decided to try fishing out of

Howth. "I didn't go that time. I stayed in Castletown, and worked in the creamery. I was three years there, and then I went to Howth all right."

Castletownbere in the '60s

For a long time, fleets of British trawlers landed in Castletownbere, and then, in the early 1960s, for whatever reason, they stopped coming. "It was a shame. In the bad weather, or if they needed repairs, it was in here they came. Then all of a sudden they didn't come in anymore. But the Spanish and the French used come, especially at the tuna times. The pier on both sides, you couldn't move with them; it used be black with them that time.

"The Spanish, God love them… we thought we were poor… but to see the little bits of clothes they would have on them, like a piece of a rageen. Sure they lived on fish and potatoes. They were timber boats, would you believe that? Steam trawlers were all wooden. God almighty, they were great men. There were loads of them lost out there. Sure there's Spanish wrecks out there still, all along the bay. The skippers would be under pressure too. The weather they would go out in in those boats, you wouldn't put a dog out in it. The Frenchmen came over too, in those little 50-footers. When they were at the tuna, and had all the big poles up on them… you wouldn't believe it, that they came across from France. Jesus Christ, they were small boats."

At that time, there was only one hotel in Castletownbere, the Berehaven, and one restaurant, Titch's. "But there were loads of shops. Where Supervalu is now, that was known as Murphy's. Next shop up would be Joe Martin's. You had Dónal Harrington's the hardware shop. You had a grand little shop next to Martin's… Paddy Bawns's. Then McCarthy's was the next one… that was the pub and shop. You had Maud Harrington then, she used to do all the schoolbooks, the pens and pencils and all that. And then you had Charlie Moriarty's, that's Spar today. Then you had Breen's; that was a pub at the back, but Mrs Breen had all the women's magazines out front."

Young people mostly socialised at the dancehalls; Ardgroom and the Lake House in Tuosist were particular favourites. "The craic was ninety in the Lake House; we'd go there on a Friday night. That was a night out, any Friday night, for a long time. Then that went by the wayside. It was a shame. It's funny how the wheel turns; the place is for sale today."

Killybegs

After leaving the creamery in Castletownbere, Barney fished in Howth for a time, and then he moved to Killybegs. "That was something else. The pubs in Killybegs were open till two or three in the morning, legally. We were working down in Killala Bay. I was on a boat called the *Girl Eileen*. And I was with James McCloud on the *Mirana*, while the lads were on holidays, I was six or eight weeks with James. A Scotsman. He's a big shareholder in Gundry's now. Himself and Albert Swann started Gundry's, a long time later, of course."

Killybegs had a much bigger fleet than Castletownbere. "And the boats were way bigger. There were up to thirty of them; the most were 56-footers, but Albert Swann would have had a 60-footer. The *Radiance* would have been the biggest boat up there. There was a man we used to call Johnny Forty. He had a big old Dutch ship, with a big high wheelhouse. She'd have been a good 70ft-odd, that one. He was nicknamed Johnny Forty because any time they'd ask, 'how did you do that time?', he'd say, 'forty boxes!'.

"But they were all getting bigger boats before long. All the McKennas had boats there, and most of them lived around Killybegs. Then you had the blow-ins, of course. The Moores came up from Dingle, and they all married Killybegs women. That's the way the world goes. I was with Mossie Moore on the *Girl Eileen*."

Barney admits he made "great money" in Killybegs. "Fishing was better, but the lifestyle was different there too. There was some serious drinking done. Only the fellows who were living there had beds, we were sleeping on the boats the whole time. How in the name of Christ we didn't get lost, half of us, I'll never know. It's often I think about it, truthfully. There was definitely somebody up there looking after me, because by God we used take chances, there was no doubt about it. Some of the pubs used open at midnight. It was crazy… it was honestly crazy. You'd be in at the weekend, and you'd never work after midday on Saturday. You had only to walk up the pier and you were at the Harbour Bar… that was for starters. And then we'd go to the Atlantic and we'd work our way around the town.

"They had one of the finest dance halls up there, the Forester's Ballroom. Oh God Almighty, a fine hall. And the best of bands. I've seen them all. I can go back and say I've seen the likes of Kathy Durkan and Philomena Begley; they were only starting out then, they were only young girls up on the stage. Margo came down there. She was only about six weeks on the road when she came to the Forester's. Saturday night was Forester's, and Sunday night was St Mary's out in Drumkennealy. That was only four miles out the road. So you had two dancehalls there, with the finest of bands."

Glasgow and Hull

Barney stayed three years in Killybegs. He married, and with his wife he moved to Scotland. "I got work there with the Glasgow County Council. There was a massive difference in the money between the fishing and the Council, but the hours were easier, and it was good money anyway. Things weren't dear in those days. Even though I was staying in lodgings, they were cheap for the week as well. You always had a few pounds in your pocket. You look at today; they're up there in Cork, and they're getting good money, but the rent is crazy. The rent would take what you'd make.

"I did six or seven weeks with the Council until I got some money together, and then the two of us moved south to Hull. My sister Toni was working there already."

The boats in Hull were owned by companies, rather than individuals or families, as they would have been in Ireland. "The owners were bastards because they were all getting massive money from the government. There was about twenty-two of a crew on each of them. There had to be; you were working twenty-four hour days – twenty-one days in a row - to keep them going. None of the Hull boats worked the North Sea at all; Grimsby had the smaller boats for that. The Hull boats went working off Newfoundland, or Greenland, or up around Iceland. Or up the White Sea. Cod and haddock, we were after. You had nearly a week steaming up there, and another coming home. That's what made the trips so long. You worked in unmerciful bad weather; if you didn't, it prolonged the trip. You always kept fishing because the skipper was under fierce pressure; he'd get the sack before one of the crew did. That was the pressure you had up there to be a skipper. If you didn't deliver, you were out."

The fishing off Iceland was particularly rewarding. "A thousand kits was a good week's fishing. One kit would be ten stone, about a box and a half. So you're talking about one thousand five hundred boxes of fish. Prices were good. If you made £10,000, that was good money. We used to get £22 a week in those days, and £7 to the thousand. Every £1,000 the ship made, you got seven. And by God, I'm telling you, did we live like lords. The old beer over was only one and thru'pence or something. We used work it out, that if you went out with a fiver, you'd still have the price of fish and chips going home. You got less than forty-eight hours on shore after a trip, but when you had done six trips, you got a fortnight's holiday pay. It was three weeks a trip, so you worked for eighteen weeks and you got your holiday pay then."

Even when Barney had earned two weeks off, he'd often be pressed into fishing anyway. "They'd all be shouting at you, 'would you go out?' In the winter, that was the best time because you could call the shots with them then. They'd give you third hand's pay. There was a bosun and third hand on the deck, you see. And they'd give you a third hand's pay because all the fellows that'd be out all year wouldn't go out for Christmas. The married men wouldn't go, so it was murder trying to get anyone. They'd give you an extra few bob to go, or a bottle of whiskey and a case of beer. And it worked, I tell you."

Up around Iceland, the boats fished far from shore. "We could be eighty to one hundred miles out, and you wouldn't see the land at all.

It was only water all around. And the bad weather would take you over. We got swamped a few times. Mother of God, to see it coming down on top of you. Man, the weight behind that stuff. It was no joke.

"And we used ice up, you know. You'd be on deck, and you had axes, knocking the ice off the mast and the railings and everything. The boat would be top heavy, and you had to do that, to keep the boat afloat. You should see the lumps that'd come off. That year I was telling you about, the *St Grenard* got lost running off bad weather, and there were three others went down that same week. They all iced up and they turned over. Only one man was saved."

One time, off Iceland, Barney witnessed a volcanic eruption in the sea. "That was twenty or thirty miles out. There it was, the old rock would come up, and it boiling away still, you know. That was a spectacle."

In the '60s and '70s, Britain came increasingly into dispute with Iceland over fishing in its waters, and the 'Cod Wars' concluded with Iceland expanding its limits to two hundred nautical miles. The effect on the British fishing industry was catastrophic, with thousands being put out of work. "That was the end of it really. And Margaret Thatcher pulled the money anyway. Oh God, it was a shame to see the ships that went into the dry dock to get cut up. The Irish slipped up bad that time; they should have bought them. There were ships going for scrap price. The best of ships, and nobody buying them. I couldn't understand for the life of me how they didn't buy them. Marses had four lovely ships. Good honest to God sea ships. They were all steel in them days. Hamlyn's, the gang I was with, they had a couple. The *St Ives*… she was nearly a brand new ship altogether. She'd have been only seven or eight years old, I'd say. She was one of the nicest boats above there, and yet they left her go to the scrapyard."

Back to Castletownbere

Barney came full circle in the end, returning to his home port of Castletownbere in the 1990s, to work on the *San Pablo* with Mick 'Slim'

O'Sullivan and the *Martha David* with Paddy O'Connor before retiring from the sea.

Asked whether he ever found anything unusual in the nets in all his years fishing, Barney shakes his head. "We never picked up anything special," he chuckles. "We never got that mermaid we were after. She didn't turn up, no."

6

TIMMY LYNCH
CASTLETOWNBERE

Timmy Lynch lives at the east end of Castletownbere. He fished out of Howth most of his adult life, having begun working with his father in Berehaven when he was fourteen. He is now retired.

"My father was fishing long before I started," says Timmy. "There were British trawlers coming in to Castletownbere after the War, big steamboats, 100- to 120-footers. My father went away with one of them, the *Bahama.* He was with a fellow by the name of Alex Smith. They fished out of Milford Haven, but they'd come up here to Berehaven. There was a pile of fish off the west coast that time. They were doing really well."

When he'd saved some money, Timmy's father moved home and got his own small boat, the *Grove.* "She was about forty feet, and he fished her with my uncle Donie, and I don't know did Timmy Crowley fish with them as well. Gerry O'Shea started with my father too; Gerry was only fourteen that time, when he left school. They were all young. My grandmother sold the fish. They'd sell them locally, and inside in Kenmare and Bantry as well, and I think they used even go to Killarney. My father drove the van.

John Martin and Timmy Lynch in Howth, 1972

Timmy Lynch and Norman Caslin in Howth, 1971

"But most of the fish went to Dublin that time, and then it was going to Clayton Love in Cork. The amount of fish that was out there was unreal; it was no bother catching it, the price was the problem."

In those days, "no one in Castletownbere could afford a big boat. You couldn't really make money from fishing full-time, so my father used to work at the quarry there, where Centra is now. I don't know what he was getting, maybe £4 a week; it wasn't much anyway."

Scalloping

Timmy's father often went scalloping, in Berehaven and Portmagee, Co Kerry.

"He worked with Laurence Heffernan here in town; they'd fish out the back of Dinish, off Frenchman's Point. They'd sell the scallops to Willie Murphy, and they were sent on to England. Prices were shocking. In the '50s and '60s, they'd get a pound a bag for the scallops. There were forty casts in the bag, and three scallops in the cast, so that was what you got; £1 for one hundred and twenty scallops."

Things did not always go smoothly when they were scalloping in Portmagee. "They were hunted out of there one time. They were up in court, and the judge said, 'Frenchmen and Corkmen, I never want to see ye in Portmagee again!' They didn't like the type of fishing they were doing, the dredging; they were cleaning the beds, I'd say. My uncle Donie went aboard with the local lads, to show them how it was done, but when they got the thing right, they turned against him then, you know."

The price for scallops was no better when Timmy started fishing them himself. "We might get one hundred or two hundred scallops in a day, but there'd be two or three of us; one each side of the dredge, and one at the back. In five days fishing, we might make £5 between the three of us. To put that in perspective; I knew a fellow joined the ESB in 1959, and he was getting £4 90d a week. The creamery were the biggest employers in Castletown that time, they had eighteen men working, lorry drivers and so on, and they were paying the same wages as the

ESB, or maybe a bit less, maybe £4 50d a week. But we'd be lucky to make that between three of us."

Childhood

Timmy's life revolved around fishing from his early childhood. "Even as kids, we'd pick winkles on the strand. That was a hard job. My brother John used do it with me. Eugene Dunne in Adrigole was buying the winkles; I think he was sending them to France.

"But we were mad for fishing. We used to catch whiting, as a pastime, out over there near Bere Island. Every harbour was full of fish that time. And the mackerel? They'd nearly come ashore. We didn't do too much whitefishing, only pollock with lines. The boats might trawl a bit all right, at night-time. They might get a box of plaice or something, but the price for that was poor as well."

He remembers going aboard an English boat with his cousins Teddy and Seán O'Shea one night when he was twelve, "and she was full from rail to rail with whitefish. Hundreds of boxes. And the fish were still alive, so they weren't after hauling too far away from the harbour's mouth. There'd be two boats, with the one net between them. They used call them two-to-one shots; one haul in the day, and they'd fill the trawler up. They used to take them in to gut them then, out the back of Dinish."

When Timmy started fishing with his father, in the '50s, "we'd fish herring by night, out in the harbour. Michael McCarthy was the agent for the French that time. They used to come in here for bait, for the long lines. We often gave them herring, at a pound a box. My father used to work in the quarry by day, and we'd fish at night. We might get ten boxes, sometimes twenty. We'd build them up, and Michael would let us know when they were coming in. If we were fishing three or four nights a week, we might get £40 or £50. There'd be Jimmy the Rock and my father, and my brother John and myself. They were making more money at the herring that time than my father made in the quarry and Jimmy made in the creamery.

"The long-liners come in here still, but it's a different system now. They go through the machine: if it misses, it misses; if it catches, it catches. They were fine fish that time; they're small now. They're fished out, I'd say."

The English, the Spanish and the French

Timmy says of the English boats that "there were a lot of them coming in; they'd fish away through the winter, but they'd only tie up overnight and go away again. It was a three-mile limit that time. Dr Power was the man who'd look after the men who got injured at sea. His surgery was where the Berehaven Pharmacy is now. If they were badly injured they'd be sent away to Cork; I don't think there was even an ambulance that time.

"The English were getting way more money than we were. They'd be out there fourteen days; that was their trip the time my father was on them. They'd have a couple thousand boxes. They were making the money, but our boats weren't. It's the same today; all our boats are tied up, but the Spanish, are they tied up? Not at all. Our guys can't fish any herring now, the herring are too small, but the Dutch are still fishing. Strange, isn't it?"

He remembers that the Spanish boats "had counter sterns on them, and they'd steam all night. They were pair fishing; they weren't single like they are now. There'd be two of them with the one net; they'd shoot and let it go all day. They'd haul the net then, and put the fish in one boat. And the next day, the other boat would take his turn. They'd go up off the north coast, off Donegal, and they'd tow back in. One big haul they were after. These lads were icing the fish, but the mackerel and herring they'd be salting."

They'd spend longer in town than the English. "The Spanish were okay, they'd spend money, but the French... when they'd come in, they were very hostile, you know. They'd be chasing girls around and everything. And they'd clean the cockles along the beaches. They shouldn't be allowed do that; you wouldn't be allowed do that in France."

In the '50s, the French would fish for tuna with poles. "It was the '80s when they started fishing them with nets. Before that, there'd be a big fleet of French trawlers; they'd come into Kinsale, with the big poles on them. They weren't big boats like they have now. The boat we bought, the *John Martin*, she was the *Scoobadoo* before we had her, and when we bought her there were poles on her still, but sure we didn't want them."

Howth and Dunmore East

Timmy was only seventeen when he moved to Dublin. "I left here on the 27th of December 1960. I fished out of Howth for the next forty years, so I was forty-seven years in Dublin altogether. There's only a few boats left there now, but one time there were sixty or seventy trawlers in Howth. They were all small boats, 50- or 60-footers. Gerry O'Shea had two boats, and Seán had one. And Teddy had the *John Carol*. We got our own trawler then, John and I, in 1969. We called her the *John Martin*, after John's two sons. They have a bigger trawler now, the *Ablana*. They work all down the east coast."

In the '60s, they often fished out of Dunmore East. "That was when the big boats came in then. They were coming from all over. Kerry. Donegal. There was up to eighty or one hundred boats in Dunmore that time. There was some herring out there; sure it was a goldmine. If you had a good herring season, you were laughing. You were home and dry."

The Northern Irish boats came down too, but Timmy does not remember them with fondness. "The less said the better. They were the same then as they are now. You can see the carry-on out of them. They wanted it their way. It was our waters, and our fish, but they'd undercut you with the buyers. If they were selling one hundred cran, they'd give the buyer twenty for himself. The brown envelope. And we'd be stopped from fishing. Quotas full, they said. But the Northern Irish just kept going."

The EU

Timmy agrees that Ireland got a raw deal when we joined the EU. "You ask me what went wrong? The government didn't understand the fishing, I suppose, and we didn't negotiate enough. We were all inside a six or seven mile limit that time. Now it's one hundred miles."

Better equipment has helped the fishermen, but often it has been at the expense of the stocks. "Things are serious now. The catching power is unreal. It's not boxes any more, or crans; it's tons. The easiest thing to do is blame the Spaniards, but we did a lot of damage ourselves. I was asked a question at a function one time, in Dublin. Michael Woods was the Minister, and he said, 'how would you bring the fishing back when it's going down?' I didn't have to think. I just said, 'increase the mesh.' Those were my very words. And he said to me, 'we couldn't do that; the scientists wouldn't allow it.' The scientists were coming out of college, they had degrees and everything. I had no degree, though I was fishing since I was that height. He turned around to me and said, 'you didn't even have to think about it.' But what was there to think about? And this was way back in the '70s.

"This craic that I see now is trawling up and down the bays. I'm totally against it. It's being banned now, but it's too late. The cow's gone out, the horse is on the road; close the gate now if you want to, it doesn't matter. There's no whitefish. No herring. No mackerel. All they're catching is sprat, and you tell me they're not herring? What's they're calling sprat is young herring, they have to be small some time. I reckon they're killing tons and tons of small ladeens. It's the most serious thing I've ever seen, is those big trawlers going up and down the bays. And they blame the Spaniards."

Timmy remembers when Mornington, a fish plant in Drogheda, was conducting a survey in the Irish Sea. "I was only a crewman on one of the trawlers at the time, and we had the scientists with us. We were out fishing sprat for the fishmeal, and I reckon three quarters of the stuff we were catching was small plaice, dabs, codling, haddock and whiting; they were only that size. And I said to the scientist, 'God, there's an awful lot of small fish in that.' He turned around to me and said, 'there's a good share of sprat there too.' He was writing in the book, and he was putting it all down as sprat. He didn't care; he was going to get his wages next Thursday. And stands by there's nothing there today."

7

MARGARET DOWNEY-HARRINGTON
TRALAHAN

Margaret Downey-Harrington of Tralahan is a director of Fast Fish. She owns the trawler the *Sea Spray*, and was a founding member of the women's organisation, Mná na Mara.

Early days

Margaret has had a lifelong association with the fishing industry, her father, William Murphy of South Droum, having fished for a living since before she was born. "His boat had been a lifeboat," says Margaret. "She came in on the tide from God knows where, and Timmy Lynch of Garranes picked her up and sold her to my father. She was a twin-ended boat; clinker built, wooden, about twenty feet long. I was born in 1940, and that was the boat we had then, so he must have got her in the '30s. I think it was £5 he bought her for. My father left school at the age of fourteen, but he was an avid reader. There were not a lot of books around, and there was no library that time either, but he'd read up on things, and figure them out. These boats weren't really fit for purpose, but he put a lorry engine into her, and it worked. Now, there was no gearbox, but they managed away with it.

Margaret Downey-Harrington with the Lifetime Achievement
Award presented by BIM in 2019 in recognition of her work with
Mná na Mara

"How far they could go would depend on what they were fishing. My father used fish the herring and the mackerel below in the harbour. The seine fishing was gone at this stage; he would get the sling rolled up in a bundle, and he'd figure it out from there. He'd go down to Harrington's and buy the lead you'd put on the roof of the house, and he'd cut it into strips and wind it around the footrope to weigh down the net.

"When my father was fishing out here in the harbour, there was no such thing as flasks. What they'd have is bread and butter, and the bottle of tea in a sock. You'd have the bit of land, and the cow, so you made your own butter. You'd have the vegetables and the spuds and what have you. We were very well off, really. There was a furze bush down in Parknoe, which is the field in front of the house. And if the lads were out at sea, and they were needed, there was a white tablecloth put over that bush. It could be seen even if they were away down beyond the Walter Scott. It didn't happen too often. But I remember the day my grandmother died, that was one of the days they had to be hauled in. That was how the SOS was sent."

The herring and mackerel sold locally. "If they got six or seven boxes, they considered it a good night's fishing. And if they made a pound a box, it'd be as much as they'd get for it. Danny Bob McCarthy of Star Seafoods in Kenmare… he passed away in February, but that was his business. I remember Danny coming to my father and buying boxes of herring and mackerel, putting them in the back of the car and selling them house to house. And that's how Star Seafoods started off. That was where the market was."

William fished lobsters in the summertime. "He'd go from here up to the Dursey and over across the bay to Kilcrohane, all along the shore. It was a long distance when you think about it, for the gear they had. In my father's time, the lobsters and crayfish were collected. There was a Frenchman built a pond down in Goleen, and he used to send a lorry. It might be every week or every second week, and he'd come to all the fishermen around here, pick up all the lobsters and the crayfish and bring them back to the pond in Goleen. That guy was in contact with the factory over in France, and they had two boats. They had tanks in the boats, and the lobsters and crawfish were transported live from Goleen over to France."

William had a second vessel, a rowboat, for the scalloping. "We sent the scallops to Billingsgate Market in London. They went off in a bag, in the shell. My mother made out the set of forms to go with each consignment, every two weeks or so. Or she'd get me to fill them in. I was seven or eight years old, and I'd say I was the only child that age who knew what a certificate of origin was."

The pier William built in the '40s is still there today. "There's a pool in the rock by the side of it, where he drilled a hole to let the water in and out. He could put the scallops in there, and the pool would fill up as the tide came in. It was a natural holding place for the scallops, and they were dead safe in there. The tide would only go down so far because he had plugged the rock with sandbags. But then when they wanted to shift the scallops, he'd pull out the plugs and the pond would dry out naturally, and way you'd go, you'd pick up your scallops and put them into the bags.

"I used have to go into the shops for the bags. Murphy's, Dónal Harrington's and Warner's. They all sold feed that time; chicken mash, meal, and corn for the animals. People wouldn't buy the whole bag, as it'd be too expensive, but they'd buy a stone of it. So the shops would have bags left, and my job was to go in and collect them on my way home from school in the evening. They were jute bags, and when I brought them home we'd flake the divil out of them. There was a pillar out in the yard, and we'd flake them off that. That was how we got the residue out of them. You couldn't wash them because the jute would go hard if it got wet."

When they'd filled the bags up with scallops, they'd bind the tops and pack them off to Billingsgate. "They went by bus to Bantry, by train to Cork, by train again to Rosslare, across on the boat, then on the train from Fishguard to Billingsgate Market. And that set of forms that I would have filled in on the kitchen table at home, we'd give it to Timmy who drove the bus. It was the one set of forms and it'd arrive with the scallops in London. It never got lost, and there was never a consignment went astray. They'd go on a Tuesday, and we'd get a telegram on the Friday to say how much they made. What was under the line was the price, and what was over was the number of fish. So it might say 'two at two shillings.' But it was like incognito, because no one reading that would have a clue what it meant unless they were buying or selling fish."

The English trawlers

In Margaret's childhood, English trawlers arrived regularly into Berehaven. "The fishermen would go out to them and pilot them in. It was a thing that everybody did. Everyone had their own trawler, and no one stepped on your toes. If the trawler my father piloted was seen coming in, another man wouldn't go out to it. They fully respected all of this. The trawler then would give us fish, and they'd have such a selection.

"The first chart I ever saw was one that a trawler skipper gave to my father. A chart of Bantry Bay. This used to come out in the evening, after dinner. The table would be cleared, and it was fascinating; you could see where everything was. Before that, they had it all in their heads. They gave my father a drawing of a net as well, and based on that he made a trawl that he used to fish out here for plaice and white sole and lemon sole and what have you. And it worked. My father was a man before his time."

The EEC

In the early '60s, there was already talk of Ireland joining the European Economic Community. "The Dept of the Marine came down that time and started collecting data. The fishermen used to fill in a weekly log, a return. My father was to collect it from the boats on a weekly basis. So he'd have all these forms. The fishermen would say they had so many boxes of A, B, C and D. That then was put into a book, on a monthly basis, and that was what was returned to the Dept. And that was what was used as a yardstick when it came to the negotiating table when we joined the EEC. But they didn't negotiate properly."

Marriage to Frank Downey

In 1961, Margaret married Frank Downey of Bere Island, who would become known as one of the most progressive fishermen in Castletownbere. "In those days, we had the Bantry boats, the fifty-foot trawlers. They were fished by the O'Driscoll brothers from Sherkin, fishermen from Schull, and lads from here: my husband Frank, Joe Joe O'Sullivan, Mick Orpen, and my brother Mick Murphy. They fished on those boats when it was down to Bantry they were going to land. But then, it got that they were consuming too much fuel going back and forth to the fishing grounds, and they couldn't go out so far, because the capacity for the fuel wasn't great. So they got the okay from Fastnet Fisheries to come in here to land. And that definitely worked, as it was a saving on fuel."

Like others in Castletownbere, Frank eventually bought a secondhand trawler in Scotland. "There was nothing wrong with those boats; the only thing they suffered from was age. But it gradually came to where our fishermen, our lads, were able to get new boats built to their own specifications and requirements, and get them fit for purpose. This was a huge step forward. BIM had come in to support the industry; they had a boatyard in Baltimore, a boatyard in Dingle, a boatyard in Killybegs, and a boatyard in Skerries. This was wonderful, because they were building fifty-footers, and the boats were a great success."

Kieran O'Driscoll (first on left) and Frank Downey (second from left) signing for their new trawlers the St Gervase *and the* Purple Heather *in 1968*

Frank was one of those who took advantage of a loan from Credit Lyonnaise to have a new boat – the *Purple Heather* – purpose-built in France. Sadly, what should have been a huge step forward turned out a disaster. "The *Purple Heather* was a beautiful boat, and one of the biggest in Castletownbere at that time, but she went rotten. There were seven of them built in the same yard, and they all met the same fate. They'd lined the boats with African pine, which is fine, but used in wet conditions a fungus grows behind it. It'd smother the timber so it couldn't breathe, and it would be like pepper. As well as that, then, when they took down all the lining inside to investigate this thing, there was rot there as well. And then we got a copy of a telex message in our hands, to say the boat was inoperable and not destined for the use for which she was designed.

"The yard went into liquidation, though they went back building again. We took a case - I have files that high – but that dragged on for nine years, until eventually they settled out of court for the amount that was due. I mean, they could have paid for loss of income and all the rest of it down along the line, but it was settled for that. We had nothing that time. We had the loan from Credit Lyonnaise that we couldn't pay back without the boat. We had four small children, and we thanked God every night on our knees that the roof over our heads was our own. When we got married, we bought an old house and did it up. So the house was our own. We had no mortgage, so no one could put us out of it."

The only saving grace about the *Purple Heather* was that it came equipped with a seventeen-foot punt that was made of fibre glass rather than wood, and thus did not decay. "Frank said, 'I started off in a small boat, so I can do it again.' He bought an outboard engine, and went back fishing scallops in the punt. That was the connection with my father; we knew how to fish the scallops and what to do with them. I wrote to the address that we used to deliver to in London, the suppliers that my father worked with in the '40s and '50s. They weren't the same people, the business had been sold on, but they held the same name, and they answered my letter.

"We shelled the scallops that time. Frank would bring them in, and we'd work together, shelling them at night. We worked up a speed of seventy dozen an hour between the two of us. At that stage, we had an ice plant in Castletownbere, thanks to BIM, so we were able to get ice. We put the scallops into bags and iced them down, in polystyrene boxes. I was going around that time, gathering cardboard to wrap the polystyrene boxes in, because the strapping could break the polystyrene. My brother would take them on a Wednesday morning up to Cork airport, fly them to London and into the market. And next day we knew where we were."

At that time, with the *Purple Heather* tied up, the Downeys began travelling around the country to meetings of the Irish Fishermen's Organisation. "We learned that they were catching salmon at different places around the coast, and Frank said, 'I'm sure there's salmon out here that we could fish.' From having the *Purple Heather*, we knew suppliers of fishing gear, and we got some materials; the nets and whatever. That was in '72; at that time, you just went in and applied for a licence, so we got that too.

"People laughed at Frank when they saw him mounting the nets on the pier. They said, 'you're mad, there's no rivers here, so how could there be salmon?' But Frank said, 'I'm going to try.' He had six or seven nets mounted, but no one to go with him. This was in the seventeen-foot punt with the Honda outboard engine. Frank had never fished salmon before, and I hadn't either; we were two greenhorns, but I said I'd go with him. Lord rest my mother, she stepped in to mind the kids after school and be there when they got home, and I went off with Frank. It was night fishing, and we had nine salmon the first night. We came home, and I had to do the shopping and get the kids' lunches ready for school the next day, and cook the dinner and all the rest of it. We got a few hours sleep, and I went with him again, and we had nineteen salmon the next night. And then we had thirty-six the night after. So he had no problem getting a crewman after that."

When other fishermen saw how successful the Downeys were being, they thought to try their luck with the salmon as well. "Marine Stores was born out of that, for the simple reason that they came in to Frank and said, 'where can we get gear?' And Frank would say, 'ring this number and tell them I gave it to you.' This was going on for a while, but the next thing your man, Glanville in Dunmore East, came up and said he'd give us a discount if we sold the nets for him. We lived in the old house in Bank Place that time. There had been a shop at the front, but we'd made a dining room out of it. But we took the table and chairs out of that again and put them up in the attic. And we put the gear in there, and sold it from the house.

"Everybody had a go at the salmon, and they did reasonably well at it. But Frank then, he mounted a piece of a trawl with the three-inch mesh and he went out fishing mackerel. We got mackerel nets in from Finland, and the salmon nets had to go up in the attic then while we sold the mackerel nets. I remember being in bed one night, and whatever way I looked up at the ceiling, there were cracks in it. So I thought, we'd better get them out of here. So we bought the store down in the Square, and it worked a treat."

Mná na Mara

In November 2019, BIM presented Margaret with a Lifetime Achievement Award for her work with Mná na Mara, the organisation she helped found over fifty years ago as a support group for women whose menfolk were fishing. "Life was different that time. In the '70s, boats would go to Dunmore fishing the herring from the second week in November, into December, and they'd come back for Christmas. They they'd be gone again till the second or third week in January. So they were away a long time. We were all at that time young mothers, with young families. If you had one car, that was as much as you had. Once the boat would go, it'd stay in Dunmore. The men might come home for a weekend every three weeks or so, and then the car would be gone again. It wasn't that big a thing, but my mother and father at that stage were getting on in years, and they lived in Droum. It was only twenty minutes walk, but you'd want to be available.

"Mná na Mara used to meet once a week. We were all in the same boat; we were rearing children, but there were our parents to be looked after as well. There was no crèche, so we supported each other. If I wanted to go shopping or something like that, or to bring one of the kids to the doctor, I could ring one of the women and say, could you mind the other kids while I'm gone, for an hour or two?"

These days, everyone is easily contactable by satellite or mobile phone, but at that time, communications were a lot more primitive. "The only communication you had with the boats was on the radio. You bought a radio with a single sideband on it, which meant you could pick up the shipping frequency. All the lads had a time. They might say, 'I'll call you at four o'clock,' so you listened in at that time. They all had a signature tune. They'd whistle. For instance, if they were fishing north of the Dursey, the reception mightn't be that clear, but they'd whistle, and you'd know the tune, you'd know that they'd be all right. We mightn't hear what they said, the reception might be breaking up, but the whistle would penetrate. Frank's tune was *Bonny Dundee*.

"Years later, my son Aiden went fishing. Frank was sick that time, and Aiden was fishing the boat. He said he'd call me at three o'clock, and I said, 'fine, I'll be listening in.' So he called at three o'clock, and what did he whistle, only *Bonny Dundee*? And when he came home, I said, 'do you know you whistled Dad's tune?' He said, 'what tune?' I said, '*Bonny Dundee*.' And he said, 'I don't know *Bonny Dundee*.' 'Well,' I said, 'you whistled it today!'"

When the boats went east for the herring season, it was more difficult again to keep in touch. "We all knew each other here, of course. Take Pat O'Driscoll now. If I met Pat downtown, she'd say, 'did you hear from the lads?' All we wanted to know was, were they okay? So that formed a bond. But then, when the lads went to Dunmore, you'd be very anxious to know if they got there all right. So we made contact with the women there, to know could we ring them to ask if the boats got in okay. And they would do the same when the boats came up here. That was how Mná na Mara started."

Margaret remembers one occasion when Frank was fishing in Dunmore. He had ordered a part for the radio on the boat, but the shop rang to ask if he could clarify the specifications. Margaret told them she'd arrange for Frank to ring them back. "PJ O'Leary, God rest his soul, was the cook on the *Northern Dawn*. Whenever the boat came in, he would have to go ashore to do the shopping. And he'd always ring his wife Kathleen while he was in. So this particular day, I talked to Kathleen, and she said PJ would probably ring before the day was out. So I gave her the number, and said, 'would you ever tell him to get Frank to ring your man because he needs to talk to him about the part?'

"So PJ came up for the messages. It was a dirty day. The phone was up near the convent, and the village was beyond that again. He rang Kathleen and they had the chat, and then she said, 'by the way, will you ask Frank to ring this number?' PJ had no pencil on him to write it down, but he said, 'hang on a minute,' and he went out and got a piece of stick. 'What's the number again?' Kathleen called it out, and he went out and wrote the first few numbers in the mud southside of the phone box. Then he went back in and said, 'what's the next part of it?' And back out again to write the rest of it. So then he went down and got the messages in the shops, and he went back down to the boat. Frank was landing herrings below, and PJ said, 'Frank, go up to the phone box. There's a number written in the mud outside it, you're to ring that to get your part for the radio!'"

The *Sea Spray*

In 1977, the Downeys had a new trawler, the *Sea Spray*, built in Campbeltown, Scotland. "The *Sea Spray* was originally a whitefish boat, but Frank saw the possibility of putting in RSW tanks. John Tim did the conversion in here by the pier, and it worked a treat. So we changed over from whitefish, in boxes, to tanks that held mackerel and herring. The EU brought in regulations then, so you could choose to stay in the whitefish category, or you could go after pelagic fish; the herring and the mackerel. We chose the pelagic because we'd already put in the tanks. We're still in that category today, and it's not possible to change."

The Downeys then acquired a second trawler, the *Sea Sparkle,* which they devoted to whitefishing. Later, both vessels were sold on, and replaced with a much bigger trawler, also called the *Sea Spray,* in 2004.

Frank's passing

Frank was still a young man - in his late 40s - when he was diagnosed with motor neurone disease. "We had paid off the *Purple Heather* and the *Sea Spray,*" says Margaret. "So that was one thing; financially, we were in the clear. But Frank was always so capable and so in command of what he was doing, and now he was still fully aware of everything, his mind was still sharp, but his mobility was diminishing day by day."

As Frank's health failed, Margaret took over the management of both the fishing vessels and the Marine Stores, and she has run the business since his passing, aged fifty-six, in 1989. "I couldn't let that go down the Swanee, what Frank had worked for all his life. I kind of knew what to do. There were hiccups, of course, but I was able to calm troubled waters." She faced a serious challenge when the *Sea Sparkle* broke down a year later. "It was touch and go if we would be covered by the insurance. But the surveyor came down and took off the crankshaft, and he found a crack in it, so we managed to get the engine replaced."

The future

Margaret is very conscious of the effects of pollution and overfishing on the maritime environment. "A lot has been done on these issues," she says, "and there's still a lot more to be done." She remembers how her father's generation never had to worry about overfishing or damaging the stocks. "There were no rules and regulations that time, but they had a gentleman's agreement among themselves; nothing under a certain size was ever brought home. They'd be very careful of the ground they worked, but at the same time, freshening it up did wonders. It was the same when Frank put in the tanks on the *Sea Spray.*

There wasn't a quota system that time; you just went out and fished. A farmer has to cultivate the ground and keep it worthy of the crop. You have to do the same out there."

She has serious concerns for the future of the industry locally. "On the one hand, the fishermen have never seen so many mackerel on the ground as they have seen this year. Huge fish. And that's wonderful. But I fear for the future, that we'd lose control over what we have here, that it will be swept from under our noses if it's not protected and nurtured. Fishing is a beautiful occupation, but it has got very heavily regulated, and I think of the lads going out there sometimes, and what they have to put up with. It's rather daunting. They're caught every way they turn.

"Fishing itself is a tradition, and a lot of it is handed down from one generation to the next. If it isn't nurtured, it will be lost. And I may not see it, but I don't think I'm wrong; I can see a government further down the line – and it's not that far off - spending a fortune in trying to train fishermen in how to catch fish."

8

DERRY O'DONOVAN
CASTLETOWNBERE

Derry O'Donovan works as an agent for Spanish fishing vessels in Castletownbere, and is the Spanish Consul for Co Cork. In the 1970s, he formed a company, Cornelio O'Donovan Ltd, to operate his agency. This company has since expanded to represent Russian, Dutch, French, German and Japanese vessels, and operates four tug boats in Berehaven harbour.

Training for the priesthood

Derry was born in Millstreet, Co Cork, the son of a garda who later retired to Drimoleague. He moved to London at twelve to train as an Augustinian priest, living in a succession of monasteries in England and Spain, where he became fluent in Spanish. "At the time you had all these missionaries around, looking for lads to go away," he says. "I was one of a family of nine, and in those holy times, every family had a priest or two, or a couple of nuns. I was in various places when I was training, because this crowd had colleges all over the place. I was in Fuenterrabia/Irun for a time. France was that close, with the river between us. Then I was down in Navarra; I was there about five years. And then I came back to England."

Derry O'Donovan on the pier in Castletownbere, 1975

Eventually, Derry realised the priesthood was not for him. "When you're a young fellow you go through these phases; I did ten years and then I jumped ship, for want of a better word. I came back out, redundant. I had a brother trained the same as me. He was only twelve when he joined as well; he's often said he's very grateful that I took him away, because he'd probably be around Drimoleague now being a farmer or something. He left too, but he didn't come back to Ireland; he went to London. We had a sister in London, and he went up to her. He has restaurant businesses there now.

"Some of my buddies in the monastery stayed on. There were a couple of us from Co Cork. There was another fellow who left around the same time I did, but he went back to some other place and finished his training after. And now he's a priest. I've often said to myself, if I'd become a priest, I could have finished up out in Taiwan, though it was called Formosa then. If you had English, that was where they sent you."

Bantry

It was 1967 when Derry left the monastery. On his father's advice, he approached the superintendent in Bantry about joining An Garda Siochána. "The superintendent said, 'you're a good man, but have you any word of Irish?' 'I haven't,' I said. I'd learned Oxford English, Latin and Spanish, but that was no good, he said, unless I had a bit of Irish. So he gave me a ball of books and he said, 'go away and study them and come back in six months time.' 'But what'll I do in the meantime?' I said. 'I want something now, not in six months.' I didn't fancy having to learn Irish after going through the Latin and the Spanish. 'Look,' he said, 'there's an agent over there across the Square, Michael Carroll, he'd be delighted to have you.' So I went over and explained my position and Michael said, 'can you drive a car?' I said I could, that the monks had taught me. 'Can you speak Spanish?' he said. 'No bother.' 'Right, you can start straight away, boy.'

"So that was like my novitiate, looking after the Spanish boats in Bantry. I spent three years there, training."

Michael later wrote a book called *The Second Spanish Armada*, an account of how the Spanish fishing fleet made Bantry their base in the '50s. "If you check the end of that book, that's where I came in. Michael says they had a young fellow working with them, and he took off to Castletownbere and he took all the business with him. And that was me. Michael started writing that book when the Spanish started coming to Bantry after the War. Before that, going back even further, during the Civil War a lot of them used to come to Bere Island. The Murphys were agents for the Spanish in Lawrence's Cove. Mrs O'Shea, in Marinero's, was an agent too, and she used to work with Dr Power. And in Bantry, Murphy and O'Connor were agents as well as my own man. And then you had another agency in Renard Point as well. They were all the places there were agents for the Spanish."

In Bantry, the agents' interest shifted to Gulf Oil when it arrived in Whiddy Island in 1967. "The dollar was stronger than the peseta that time, and of course everybody went for the oil, with the result that the Spanish and all these foreign boats were a bit neglected. So the door was left open for any smart jackass like me to wade in. I was getting bored anyway; I was getting a good hand on what I was doing, I had no problems, and I thought I could do it for myself. All the Spanish wanted when they got off the boats was to meet someone who spoke the language. I used to do a lot of driving in those days, taking them to the airport. That was my job, and it was a piece of cake to me.

"So then, after three years, I jumped ship again and headed west to this beloved town."

Moving to Castletownbere

Derry made the move to Castletownbere in 1970. "I'd been coming down since '68/'69, as some of the Spanish used to come in here that time. They'd ship their fish from boat to boat. Not onto lorries; that didn't exist then. It was a quiet town, but the herring was becoming a big thing. A crewman might make £100 in a week, which was a lot of money that time."

Paddy Bawn Murphy and John Houlihan with Spanish trawlers at the old pier in Castletownbere, in the late 1950s or early '60s

The pier at Castletownbere, April 1969

Derry's work as an agent, particularly in those early days, was nothing if not diverse. One day, he could be supplying a boat with groceries; another, he could be bringing an injured fisherman to hospital. Very often, he was arranging repairs for vessels damaged at sea. "Back then, the boats were very poor quality; they were not like the modern boats you see now, they'd have a lot of breakdowns. I used to spend all my time going out to John Tim O'Sullivan in Cnocura. He had a workshop, where we'd go to get the welding done. I supplied all those kinds of services to the boats, because when the Spanish came in here, they had nobody to talk to them. Going back fifty years, people had a bit of Irish but not many spoke Spanish."

Derry estimates that he was dealing with "somewhere between four and five hundred Spanish boats. That's from here up to Rockall and down to the coast of France. In those days, nobody could see the boats. Now they see forty of them sheltering in Bantry Bay, and they think we're being robbed or something."

The boats Derry was dealing with back then were "20- to 30-metres, but they were the old sidewinders. They were what was called open boats, and a lot of them were steamboats. But all those boats are gone now. If there were five hundred of them there then, how many are there now? About one hundred. Of that five hundred in '69, you might see each of them once a year. But now there's one hundred, but you see every one of them seven times a month. So work that out; it looks as if there's more Spanish boats fishing now, but there's actually way less. And on top of that, in the old days, they were actually Spanish boats. But what are they now? Spanish boats fishing under French flags and German flags and Irish flags and English flags. So if you actually count how many Spanish boats there are at the moment, fishing under the Spanish flag, I doubt there's even fifty. But the total figure for the Spanish now would be roughly around one hundred boats."

Trawlers in the harbour at Castletownbere, 1976

When the Spanish came into Castletownbere, "it might be that they'd run out of food, and they'd take on what provisions they needed for so many days. Or they'd come in when the weather was bad, or to land a man who was injured, or they might be out of water or ice. There'd always be an order coming in for one hundred loaves of bread or something like that, there was always that happening. And that was a system that used work from 1939, let's say, to 1990.

"In the old days, if there was a puff of wind, they'd have to stop working. But now their catching capacity is way better, and they're shelter boats, where before, they were open boats. Fellows were often washed over the side. They'd have very bad accidents; I remember fishermen losing their hands and their legs. They'd try to work in bad weather, and you know what the weather is like."

Transport

After Eiranova opened on Dinish Island in the '90s, the whole idea of
how fish could be transported began to change. Instead of the boats
returning to Spain with their catch, they offloaded in Castletownbere,
and the fish was taken to Spain in refrigerated lorries. "In the '70s and
'80s, the average trip for a Spanish boat took about three weeks; from
the time they'd leave home, it took them probably three days to come
up, they fished for twelve days, and then they went back home. The
boats now can do three trips in the same time. The result is that 99% of
the boats are coming in to land either here or in Dingle or Killybegs.
No matter what way you look at it, Castletownbere is geographically
the nearest for the Spanish.

"In the old days, all the boats went back to Spain. Every one of them.
When Eiranova opened, they started the trend for putting the fish on
lorries. They had five Irish boats at the time – the *Dinish*, the *Dursey*
and so on – and they started that. The rest of them woke up then.
Eiranova were new to this territory, they never historically had boats
here. There was a crowd going into Bantry for years, they had about
one hundred and twenty boats out there, one company alone, and it
never dawned on them to use lorries. But then again, the facilities
didn't exist. The system they used then, they'd have three boats; two
would fish, and the third would go home. Then he'd come back, and
the next fellow would go home. That was the way they used work it in
the old days, but that system disappeared then, and the pair trawling
disappeared in the '80s."

Crews

The Spanish crewmen don't make a great deal of money, Derry says.
"They're not on a share, they're on some kind of percentage. At the
moment now, the Spanish have a problem getting crew. You have the
same thing here. Local men are not going out in the boats anymore.
The Spanish are the same; crewing is a big problem for them. On the
longliners now, it's all Indonesians. The owners are making money, but
the crews aren't really. In the old days, they were poor enough in

Spain, and if a lad went fishing, if he made €1,000 a month, back on the land they might only make €500. But ashore now, they're making just as much, so the incentive to go fishing isn't really there. The same has happened here; lads aren't going to go fishing now when they can make a living working in computers or something like that."

The Spanish boats are often at sea for three months at a time. "The way they were before, they'd be out for twenty days, and they'd be lucky if they got twenty-four hours ashore. If they landed on a Monday, they'd go back out on a Tuesday. If they landed on a Friday, they might be lucky and get the weekend out of it. Now, for every trip they do, they get one or two days off, so they get about twenty days when they go home after doing the three months. Before, they had no family time, so they're happier now. Most of the boats that would be out after Christmas, they'd leave home in January and they wouldn't see Spain again until the end of March, and then they'd probably get twenty days off. So they might get three or four batches of twenty-day breaks in the year.

"Some of the Spaniards would say it's a fine thing to be in the freezer boats in the Falklands; they do less time, and make more money. And even if they go that far, they wouldn't be gone from home so long. In the big freezers, off Norway or Newfoundland, they'd do better than that. But that's why they're not getting crews; there's very few of them Spanish any more. All the gill netters and the long liners, the crew would all be Indonesian bar the captain and the engineer, they'd still be Spanish. The captains have to be Spanish, or European anyway. But the crews might all be from Indonesia or Morocco, or Ghana and Senegal. All the fellows I knew in the beginning, they're all dead, so there's a new breed of people. I often asked after a fellow, and the word came back that he was dead for years."

The EU

Spain did not join the EU until 1986, but the impact on its fishing industry was huge, with many long-established companies getting out of the industry altogether. "Of the old companies I dealt with starting off," says Derry, "I would say that, straight across the board, 100% of them are gone. The companies that are there now would mostly have two or three boats. The big companies that used to go to Bantry – companies like Massó – they're basically gone. What happened was you had the older generation, the old men were working into their eighties, but then they handed over to the sons, and the sons didn't have the same interest."

Another factor was the generous grants offered to boat owners to scale back on tonnage. "Spain was a country where they always got very good money scrapping the boats. When they joined the EU, the maximum number of boats they could bring in was three hundred. Within a few years, that was gone down to two hundred, and I would swear that figure is now down to fifty. But of that three hundred, you must remember, some of them were scrapped, and others got out of it. They have a funny system in Spain, but it's a good system, actually. If I was an owner when Spain joined the EU, and let's say I had three boats and three licences, but with the first boat, I was only allowed so many of this species, and with the next, I was only allowed so much of another, and so on… well, what did they do? They scrapped two of the boats and kept one fishing, but the one fellow fishing was allowed use the catch for the other two as well. So he could catch as much fish with one boat.

"So they paid them to decommission their licenses, but they still allowed them to transfer their catch, a thing you cannot do in Ireland. The number of Spanish boats was reduced, but that one boat was way more catch efficient than its predecessors going back thirty or forty years. Believe it or not, there might have been forty Spanish boats up in Bantry Bay in December, but when you looked out at sea, there wasn't that many more of them out there."

Until Spain joined in '86, EU rules forbade them from fishing inside a two hundred mile limit off the coast of Ireland, and vessels that did so faced arrest. "When they were allowed in then, they could have three hundred boats between the coasts of Ireland, France, Scotland and Rockall, and that was it. But the numbers went down very quickly, because it was the first time, if you like, that they saw the writing on the wall. Up to then, before the EU, it was no man's land out there. The Russians and the Dutch and everyone were out there on the sea. But a lot of the old fellows bailed out of it then, a lot of the old men who'd been at it for years.

"At the moment now, there's no big company. Most of the people we deal with, there's one owner who might have one or two boats. And the figure is going down the whole time. They sold a lot of boats. Mercadona, the Spanish supermarket chain, they used land into the Co-op in Castletownbere. They had some boats out here, but they've taken them all away to Africa and places like that. They're all boats that are gone from here, though obviously they transferred their licences to somebody else."

The fishing stocks

In Ireland, there is always controversy over fishing stocks, and how much the Spanish boats are taking. "Looking at it now, most of the Spanish boats come in every six or seven days, so there's fish somewhere. Going back twenty years ago, it could take them fourteen days to fill a lorry, now they're doing it in seven or eight. The boats in the old days usen't freeze the fish at all. Now all these boats have freezing facilities. So they can work longer. I often see them now; for the first ten days they might catch and freeze the fish, and then they can put the frozen fish in different parts of the lorry when they're loading it.

"The stocks have held up away deep sea, but inshore I don't think they have. Having said that, you must remember that the French had a big fleet out there as well, and they're completely gone. The crowd that sold all those boats – they were called 'the musical boats', the *Melodie*, the *Concerto* and so on – they were one company alone that had twenty boats. There were three or four companies that time. Lorient and Concarnou, those ports had about one hundred and fifty boats, and they've got nothing now. The crowd that is based in Lorient now, I think they have twenty boats, but they're scattered all over Europe. But when do you ever see a French boat in Castletownbere?

They're gone. I know very little about them, but they had small boats one time, then they had bigger boats, and then they went away to other waters."

The Spanish and Castletownbere

The Spanish still send most of their fish back to market in Vigo, but Derry insists their spending in Castletownbere on supplies and stores is "unbelievable. Every boat takes a minimum of twenty-five thousand litres of diesel a week. Between the diesel and the food, it's something else, and the poor old agent like myself has to make a few bob as well. A lot of work goes into it, you know. I mean, you walk down the pier there, and someone would say, 'all you have to do is back up a truck and sign a few papers.' But it isn't that easy. You have to organise a lorry for when the boat gets in. Then you have to organise twenty-five thousand litres of diesel, and you get it from whoever is cheapest.

"When I started, I was the original of the species. But you have different companies acting as agents now, like Eiranova, and Monamar, which is my subsidiary. And then we do the tugs and all that as well. Monamar there, the last five or six weeks before Christmas, they were dealing with twenty-five boats a week. That's a horrendous amount of work, organising truckloads of diesel and the lorries to take the fish away. There was one fellow came in there a month ago, and he had five lorries of fish. They didn't know how to get help to unload it, so they had to go to the Co-op to get help. That was a turnaround, seeing the Co-op handling the fish for the Spanish."

Compared to other ports, there is ample work in Castletownbere for a number of agents. "We have a lot of advantages. Number one, we're right in the heart of it. Eiranova look after so many, Monamar look after so many, and Diarmuid my son is looking after the tugs and all that in the harbour. So the Spanish know they get a service. The only thing they're stuck for is space to tie up along the pier. We're getting another two hundred metres of pier, so hopefully that will improve things and bring in more business. You have to get more space, or control the space you have. I'm often at loggerheads with the harbour master, trying to make space, to shift a few boats. But he has the last call on that."

Derry estimates there are about one thousand three hundred Spanish landings a year, and each boat would have an average crew of ten. "The Spanish boats leave home with seventy or eighty thousand litres of diesel. Sometimes they take on diesel for the weight; the boats go all over the place when the tanks are empty. They'd take on twenty-five thousand litres when they come in here. There's an international system for pricing diesel, and it changes every day. One day Fast Fish might be cheaper than the other fellow; it goes around in circles like that. We go to whoever will give it the handiest. It's still a lot of money; it might work out at fifty cents a litre. You get a lorry then, to take away the fish; that's going to cost you another three or four thousand euros. I wouldn't want to see the total figures added up, but it'd be quite a lot of money, you know. In Castletownbere, the Spanish boats pay €400 per landing in harbour dues as well. €400 is not out of the way, but long ago it used to be way cheaper."

Developing the harbour

Derry remembers that when he first came to Castletownbere, the old wooden pier was just being replaced. "Where the lifeboat is now, you'll see the old pier there. I've got a postcard of it; you can see the water back of Sadler's, it used to go up to John Murphy's corner. When I came to town in '69, they were just finishing the pier. Dinish they started in Canon Moriarty's time, around '75. But that was a different ballgame; Dinish has gone ahead in leaps and bounds. First they built the pier inside in front of Eiranova, then they went east in front of the synchro-lift, and now they've gone out the other way.

"The only thing I'll say is, it developed quite quickly from the '70s, but Dinish was stopped there for a long time. Basically the fishermen didn't want a bigger pier because it would only bring in more foreign boats. It was 2010 before the pier was extended. There was no major dredging done before they knocked out the piece in front of Eiranova. And then they did the dredging, and then that green perch, that was always an awful stumbling block; if you came in there by that, you needed two hours on the tide to get into the port, and you'd be watching the tide for going out again. Now they've made a fine job of it, they've put the pier outside the thing. But it was very dead from the '80s up till 2010; the fishermen didn't want any extension, so there was nothing done for years. We would never have got this extension, but for the Department knowing that it was bringing in more boats. The figures are way up, in terms of the numbers of ships coming; in 2019, there were over six hundred and fifty ships, in spite of Eiranova's numbers being down, as they went to Dingle and places like that. And you have the sand crowd in as well, drawing coral sand from Iceland; that's a big development in the harbour, there were nineteen ships this year."

Communications

One of the biggest changes Derry has seen in his fifty years in Castletownbere is in communications. "When I came here first, there were only a hundred phones in the whole town. It was like we were still in the dark ages. We had a receiver, a ham radio; it was completely illegal. The Spanish would send you a message, 'we'll be in tomorrow with such a fellow,' but you wouldn't have a means to answer them at all. I lived next door to O'Donoghue's Bar, and I'd have the radio on the whole time, all over the house. I had an awful habit of leaving the radio on, and people didn't know if I was the KGB or what. It was very controlled that time; even if you used a transmitter, you'd nearly be locked up. The first job I had with Michael Carroll was listening to the radio. They'd have a special time; if the Spanish were coming in tomorrow, they'd call you at twelve noon or six o'clock. Then they got the system that they could call you through Valentia. That started in '71/'72. Even that's gone now; now they call you through satellite phones, or VHF. I remember being outside west with John Tim, and we'd see a Spanish boat coming in, and we'd have no way of contacting them or anything. No way at all. We'd be watching the Spanish coming in, and we wouldn't know if they were heading to Bantry or Castletownbere.

"How long is the mobile phone in? Twenty-five years? Before mobile phones, we got four payphones put in on Dinish Island. There used to be one, then we got four. Then after a while we got the Telex. You'd type out your message on a long tape and put it into the machine. Then there was the fax. I remember Gay Byrne had it on the Late Late Show. He had two faxes; he put the paper into one and it came out the other. It was like a miracle. I still have the faxes going below. I went over to Plymouth one time; there was an agent over there, and he said, 'I have a mobile phone.' The face of it was like the size of a battery, and he used carry it around with him everywhere. Then I got a big white one myself, with an aerial up on the roof. If you missed the call that time, they might never ring you back, and that's not all that long ago; the '80s maybe. And now the emails are coming in on WhatsApp."

9

VINCENT O'SULLIVAN, DÓNAL DEASY AND ANDREW O'SHEA

GLENGARRIFF

Vincent O'Sullivan, Dónal Deasy and Andrew O'Shea are all prominent members of the business community in Glengarriff. Vincent has been a boatman for seventy-six years, and operates Harbour Queen Ferries, while Dónal is the proprietor of Casey's Hotel and Andrew owns the Spinning Wheel gift shop.

Glengarriff has the advantage of being on the main road from Bantry to Kenmare, and has traditionally been the village in Beara that has profited most from tourism. Primary among its attractions are the Italian Gardens on Garnish Island, which is easily accessible by boat.

The British Navy

A number of Glengarriff businesses benefited from the presence of the British Navy in Berehaven. "The Eccles Hotel was originally known as the Glengarriff Inn," Dónal explains. "But John Eccles renamed it around 1790 when he developed it as a hotel for officers of the British Navy. It was the first purpose-built hotel in the country."

The village continued to have an association with the British military well into the 20th century. From 1918 – 20, the Eccles was used as a rest home for men who had been injured in World War I, and it was then occupied by the Essex Regiment during the War of Independence.

Dónal points out a small island in Glengarriff harbour that the British Navy used for semaphore drills. "They'd calibrate their guns in Bantry Bay that time. Their marksmen would use the different points along the shore that they had put up specifically for that purpose. People see these little pillars today, off the shoreline, and don't realise that's what they were built for."

Beyond Garnish Island is Whiddy, where the US established a naval air station during World War I, maintaining a number of seaplanes to watch over their ships in Berehaven. "There was a runway on the island that time, and the first American to lose his life in World War I was killed when he crashed his plane there."

The pier

The pier in Glengarriff, where the boatmen put out for Garnish Island, was built by the Bantry Bay Steamship Company. "It was known always as the Steamship Pier," says Andrew. "It was private property and there were two iron gates on it. And then, when the steamship company wound up, they handed the pier over to the Council. But even then, the Council used it themselves for years. The boatmen weren't allowed use it until 1970, when they got the *Harbour Queen*. Before that, they used a place called the Sand Quay. It was called that because they used to dredge the sand and land it there; the sand was used as fertiliser. The Sand Quay is still there. They used Tralahan strand as well, which is further over."

Dónal remembers that, historically, there was very little fishing in Glengarriff harbour. "There was a bit of scalloping all right, but there was never a herring fleet or anything like that."

The Lady Elsie *arriving at Glengarriff Pier (Beara Historical Society)*

The railway

Around the start of the twentieth century, plans were drawn up to build a railway line from Kenmare to Castletownbere, and on to Glengarriff and Bantry. This would have opened up the towns and villages around Bantry Bay, and especially Berehaven harbour, to a huge increase in shipping. For various reasons, the plans were never brought to fruition, but the project is still remembered in Glengarriff.

"They were going to use Garnish Island as a leg for a bridge across the harbour," says Dónal. "It was supposed to be bigger than the Forth Bridge in Scotland. But it would have been a disaster for Glengarriff, when you think of what's on Garnish now."

Garnish Island

Garnish Island, also known as Ilnacullen, was purchased by the Scottish businessman and Liberal MP John Annan Bryce and his wife Violet from the British War Office in 1910. They engaged the prominent architect Harold Peto to design a mansion and extensive gardens on the island. The mansion never materialised, but the Bryces did build a comfortable cottage, where they played host to a number of famous guests such as the writers George Bernard Shaw and George Russell (AE), while the gardens thrived in the mild micro-climate of Glengarriff harbour.

"The work Bryce did on developing the gardens went on for four years," says Vincent. "There were about one hundred men employed, and it cost at least £80,000 in the money of the day. It would have gone on longer, but the Great War brought a halt to it. The gardens opened to the public in 1925, and there were boats going in and out the whole time after that. But there were boatmen in Glengarriff long before the Bryces; my own father was a boatman in the 1890s.

"You had every nationality coming to Glengarriff, but a lot of them were English. At its peak, there were more than twenty boatmen working here. The boats they had initially were small; they could only carry twelve. The season started at Easter, there was a quiet period between that and Whit, and then it picked up for the summer. Now we have three ferries ourselves, there's two more in the Blue Pool, and Kevin Jer O'Sullivan has one at Ellen's Rock. The boats are bigger now, of course. The small boats weren't suitable for coach tours at all, when you'd have forty or fifty on each coach. We're geared up better for it now. One summer, there were at least eighty thousand went out to the island."

Garnish Island was gifted to the nation by the Bryces' son Richard in 1953, and is now maintained by the Office of Public Works.

Cruise liners

Vincent remembers cruise liners, which he thinks were German, arriving in Glengarriff before War World II. "The first time one came in after the War was on the 29th of July 1951. That was the *Coronia*; she was an English ship, I think she was registered in Liverpool. Other liners came in after that. They'd anchor about a mile and a half outside Garnish Island, and they had their own boats for coming in and out. I think the *Coronia* was thirty-two thousand tons.

"In the '60s and '70s, you had liners coming in every summer. There were probably four or five liners a year, with a few hundred passengers on each. In the early days, when they came on shore, they might spent a little time around Glengarriff, but after that, they mostly went to Killarney and Blarney, and sometimes to Gougane Barra. They'd just do a day trip and be gone again."

A cruise liner at Glengarriff

Dónal remembers visiting the cinema on board the *Coronia* in his childhood. "The crew were the ones who spent money in Glengarriff," he says, "and they spent serious amounts while they were here. They used to give us change to go out and buy cartons of Peter Stuyvesant cigarettes, and we'd be smoking them ourselves, at eight or nine years of age. Doc Ryan at one stage would have a table outside, full of Irish coffees. One fellow hired a horse; he was already drunk and he rode it in the door of Doc Ryan's. And of course the horse went berserk and caused havoc."

The passengers on the liners tended to be very wealthy people. "In the late '50s and '60s, you'd have four or five ships in over the summer," says Andrew. "The *Coronia* was a Cunard liner, top of the range. The *Andes* was a royal mail ship. And then you had two ships from the Swedish American line, and a few more Norwegian liners.

"In those days, you didn't go on holidays unless you had money, and you didn't go on a cruise liner unless you had an awful lot of money. The passengers had the shore excursions organised for them, and it was all done through American Express Travel on Grafton St in Dublin. My father used to book the cars for American Express. If there was a liner due in, he would have booked between thirty and forty cars for the day. They'd be coming from Killarney and everywhere. It was a good day's pay; ten pounds and ten shillings at one stage. My father was getting ten per cent commission on that. So not only was he getting his own pay, but he was getting commission on the rest as well."

Often, he would have started organising the cars the previous Christmas. "He'd do a lot of legwork. He'd go to Killarney and say, look, we have a liner coming. Are you sure you're going to show up? The last thing you'd want is some fellow from Killarney not showing up on the morning. So my father would always book two or three extra cars, just in case. They'd always be the local guys here, down the end of the line… he'd book them and say, look, you may not be needed for the official tour, but go down the pier anyway, and you might get another job. You'll get your day's pay anyway from American Express, that's no bother, but you might get extra too."

The wealthiest passengers tended to follow a routine of their own. "The ship might have called to Dun Laoghaire the day before; they'd get off there and they'd drive down in a limousine from one of the big outfits in Dublin. Or they might get off in Glengarriff and be driven back to the ship the following day in Dun Laoghaire. I remember my father used have to hire cars from O'Connor's funeral home in Cork. They had the Austin Princesses, and big Cadillacs as well. There'd be two or three of those cars on the day, and the real high rollers might head for Dublin, but they'd stop overnight in some place like Ashford Castle.

"They'd do the same in England. They'd get off in Southampton and be driven to Glasgow. They'd do a trip like that in every country they visited."

In recent years, the liners have favoured the newly developed facilities in Bantry over the harbour at Glengarriff. "There's no security here, is how they put it," says Dónal. "Our pier is a dangerous place to land, apparently. It's not a great excuse."

Maureen O'Hara

One of the most famous visitors to Glengarriff was the Hollywood legend Maureen O'Hara. The star of *The Hunchback of Notre Dame, Miracle on 42ⁿᵈ Street* and *The Quiet Man* first arrived in the village with her third husband, Charles Blair, in 1968. "Blair had an aviation business, and they wanted to buy a place along the west coast of Ireland where they could land their seaplane," says Dónal. "They started in Cork and worked their way west, and when they saw Glengarriff, they said, this is it. Later that year, they dropped the plane in Glengarriff harbour, and they did that every year after. They'd arrive around the end of June or the start of July, and it was a huge occasion, of course; you'd see people lining up to watch them land the plane. They'd put the Irish and American flags on it. It was a great boost to Glengarriff."

Charles Blair's seaplane at Glengarriff

Maureen O'Hara

The couple bought a house on land just outside the village that had previously belonged to the railway mogul and newspaper proprietor William Martin Murphy, a native of Castletownbere who rose to become one of the most successful businessmen in the country.

"Blair had three sons," says Dónal, "and one of them was about my own age. They stayed here in Casey's for about three months while they were having work done on the house, so I got friendly with them. They took me up in the seaplane one time. We flew up around Galway, and landed between Achill Island and the mainland. I was twelve or so, and that was a great buzz."

Dónal became good friends with Maureen when she settled permanently in Glengarriff, after her husband's death in a plane crash in St Thomas in the Caribbean in 1978. "Maureen was very easy to talk to. She came in here to the hotel most Fridays for lunch. She loved to laugh, and as long as she wasn't eating her meal, she was happy to talk away to people, but you could never take her photograph if she had a drink in her hand. That was a Hollywood thing; the stars were never allowed hold a drink when they were being photographed. They could smoke, but no drink.

"Maureen was a lovely lady. She'd always say, 'I'm Irish.' A lot of people don't realise she went to court in America to get the Irish passport recognised by the authorities there. They were mad keen to give her an American passport, but on the form it asked if she had a British passport. And she said, 'I'm not British, I'm Irish.' She wouldn't take the American passport unless her Irish passport was recognised. She went to court over this in Los Angeles, and de Valera thanked her for it when he was in America. The Irish government had been fighting for years trying to achieve the same thing, and she did it in one fell swoop. All Irish passports were recognised after that."

O'Hara had actually been born and reared in Dublin (her real surname was FitzSimons, but it was changed by an early mentor, the actor and producer Charles Leighton). "In Hollywood, she formed what she called the Irish Club, with the likes of Maureen O'Sullivan, Tyrone Power and Anthony Quinn. They were very strong there in the '40s. Maureen was godmother to Tyrone Power's daughter, Stefanie."

Blair objected to O'Hara's continued involvement in films, and she quit acting altogether when they married. "She regretted not fighting that," says Dónal. "She didn't make a movie again for twenty years."

O'Hara's last role was with John Candy in *Only the Lonely* in 1991. She continued to live in Glengarriff until the last few years of her life, when she moved to her grandson's home in Boise, Idaho, where she died in her sleep in 2015, at the age of ninety-five.

10

DÓNAL KELLY

GARNISH AND CASTLETOWNBERE

Dónal Kelly is Managing Director of Fast Fish Ltd, a fish dealing and processing company based in Castletownbere. He grew up in Garnish, where his family were inshore fishermen.

Seining

For generations, the Kellys were involved in seine fishing for mackerel, a practice that involved two boats, the seiner, which cast the net, and the 'foll'er', or follower, which retrieved it. Seine fishing is thought to have been introduced to the south coast of Cork from Cornwall; in Garnish, the system was originally used to catch pilchards.

The seiner and the foll'er were both under the command of a single captain. In Cornwall, he might not go out in the boats at all, but would often direct operations from a nearby clifftop, where he would make such a hue and cry that it gave rise to the term, 'the huer'.

In Garnish, the captain commanded his crews from the seiner, but here too he was known as the huer. Seining for mackerel flourished in the late nineteenth and early twentieth centuries, fell away for a spell in the 1920s, and then underwent another brief boom in the early '40s

before falling away again towards the end of the decade, when the
mackerel seemed to vanish.

Dónal Kelly, 1984

"There were six or eight seines there that time, in the '40s," says Dónal.
"There were six men in each boat, the seiner and the foll'er, and the
one fellow – the huer – would be in charge of both. They always fished
at night, when they could see the *baraois,* or phosphorescence, in the
water. When the fish would come up, the water would go silvery, and
they'd make for them then. You'd still see *baraois,* especially in the full
moon; they used shoot around it. They'd go along under Foilleye,
along by Canalmore, and over as far as Fuhir, I suppose."

There were various rituals associated with the seining. The fishermen
were very superstitious, and all the boats carried a bottle of holy water
in the stem, as well as holy medals, St Christopher – the patron saint of
boatmen - being a favourite. At the end of the season, the nets were
soaked in bark, a pitch-like substance that was added to boiling water,
to prevent them rotting. The barking was done in outdoor pots; there
was one near Dudley's shop at Garnish pier and another at the
entrance to Patie Kelly's lane in Lehanmore.

The end of the season was also when the fishermen were paid. Some of the fish dealers who bought fish out of Garnish were Biggs of Bantry, Dan McCarthy (McCarthy's Bar) and Mrs Lynch in Castletownbere, PJ O'Sullivan, Allihies and Bob Walsh, Scrivogue. Mrs Lynch's drivers were Johnny Sheehan, Barrack Point, and her son-in-law, Neilly Billy of Adrigole. The driver would issue the huer a docket when he collected the fish, but the buyers would not pay until the season was over.

The crews would gather then at the huer's house, and one among them who was good at maths would double-check the huer's accounting before each was paid his share. If they had a good year, there might be a keg of porter; if not, they would make do with a few bottles of stout.

The seine fishing was a boon for rural communities like Garnish. "There was money went into every house," says Dónal. "My father started seining 'the year of the forty pounder'. That was in '43 or '44. Every man made forty pounds that season, which was huge money. There was plenty of shore work that time as well. Everything was salted. There was a river coming down behind the pier, and they'd bring the water down from that to wash the fish before they'd salt them.

"That time, they were different people. Marvellous people. They all helped each other. The *meitheal* went to the bog, the *meitheal* made the haggard cocks. They had a great way of life. There'd be quarter tiers of porter in the house, and that was it. There'd be a barrel of mackerel salted, and a barrel of pollock, and a pig and a heifer. There was no Supervalu. There was nothing bought but flour, to bake the bread."

Even local rivalry, between neighbouring farms, tended to be good-natured. "If you didn't have half your *scoileáns* set for Patrick's Day you were a poor farmer, you weren't up for the thing at all. You'd have to have them finished then for the end of March. Your oats would have to be up and your turf cut for the first of May. It was like clockwork. They were all keeping an eye on each other; if you were going a bit ahead, we'd have to speed up."

Potting

Dónal recalls how the seining at Garnish came to an end when, one season in the late '40s, "the men went out to sea and there wasn't a fish to be seen. Later on, they got into pot fishing for lobsters, and the boats were used for that then. Sonny Sullivan from Schull brought the barrel pots in from France, and Lucey from Waterville was his opposition. Whichever one gave you the pots, you had to bring the fish to him. The ponds are still there, where they stored the lobsters and crayfish, over in Crookhaven and Waterville."

Potting was a new practice, and lobsters were plentiful. "My brother Joe and Jim Mike Jerry (O'Sullivan) went out with my father; they were pulling the two oars and my father was shooting and hauling. They'd put stones in the pots to sink them. Steeping, they called it. First thing, Joe and Jim Mike Jerry baited the pots, and they threw the pots in a straight line south from the pier in Garnish, from the bottom of the slip, and I think they got about a dozen and a half crayfish three days later. The crayfish were walking up the rocks, like. There was a lot of money made on them as well. They were selling them by the score. Or the baker's dozen."

Dónal himself went fishing with John L O'Sullivan from Lehanmore in '67. "We'd be off the Bull Rock that time, and it was a marvellous achievement getting out there, like climbing Mount Everest. We used have an outboard engine on the boat that time, a Seagull, and then there was an inboard engine put into her. That was the next step up. Then Strack (Dave Sheehan) got a contraption, a hauler. Hauling off the Bull was hard work; you'd be pulling away, and next thing the rope would sing out through your fingers.

"But there was plenty of crayfish out there. Next thing, Lucey's divers came over from Kerry. That was heartbreaking. They had onion bags; they'd fill them with crayfish and swing them over the side, and then they'd go down again. They might be there two hours; they'd fill up the boat like a load of turf and then away they'd go. Diving was banned at the time, and Strack went into the barrack in town to complain, but the sergeant told him you'd have to catch the diver putting his hand on top of the fish on the bottom of the sea to get a conviction. And there was no chance that was going to happen."

The fog

On one occasion, Dónal and his companions came close to being lost off the Bull Rock. "I was out with John L and Frank O'Sullivan; their brother Cormac and Noelie David (O'Sullivan) were fishing another boat; and Strack was in another with his brother Vallie and Eugene Michael Owen. It was a lovely evening. We were hauling the pots west of the Bull, west of the *Braonach*. And we turned around and we saw a white wall of fog; it just appeared out of nowhere. The thing was, to get home that time, you took your bearing off the Bull Rock and you pointed her that way, and you put a big long rope out behind the boat, and you kept the rope straight. John L was looking back the whole time, and if he looked ahead he was gone. It was scary enough; we couldn't see twenty yards. Even the birds were lost; they were all sitting in the water, going nowhere.

"The next thing – things look way bigger in the fog, you know - what looked like this big boat came out of the fog… it was Noelie and Cormac, and they heading for America. They were going the opposite to the way we were going, but they were sure they were heading in the right direction. John L slowed down, and once he did, the bow of the boat went every way, and we didn't know where the Bull was any more. We shut off all the engines, and listened for the blast of the foghorn on the Bull. There were five of us, and after it blew, we couldn't agree; we each thought we knew what direction it was coming from, but it was five different directions. Next thing, with the tide, we drifted up against the Bull… we never knew we were there at all."

The five men clambered to safety, up the brass ladder that led to the lighthouse dwellings, but they feared for the lives of the three on the third boat. "We were in an awful way. It was only the previous year the *Seaflower* had gone down. Strack and Vallie Sheehan, and Eugene Michael Owen, who was eighty years old at the time… they were out in the shipping lane, but we didn't know where they'd got to. The lightkeepers phoned the post office in Garnish for us, and we decided we'd say we were all safe on the Bull. So word went out that we were okay, the lot of us, but we didn't know if that was true or not.

"It wasn't till the following morning that we heard Strack's engine, and we put Noelie and Cormac out after him. They caught up with Strack and his crew then, north of the Bull. They'd cut the pots, to anchor the boat, and lit the little gasoline lamp they had, in case a cargo ship would mow them down. They all came back up then, and the lightkeepers looked after us. Top class, they were; we had the best of grub."

The party left for the mainland around midday. "The tower on Dursey Island showed up out of the fog, and we all made for that. We came east the south side of Dursey then, which was beautiful, as clear as that. But when we went through the sound again, east at Garnish, it was black-o. And when we arrived in Garnish, we were all black; whatever was in the fog, it was more like smog. And Mikie Ger O'Neill in Gour was getting married that day, below in Glengarriff, so I tore off up the pier and went away to the wedding.

"Anyway, that wonder didn't last long. It was all back to the grindstone again Monday morning."

Exporting to England

At one point, the fishermen organised to fly the lobsters and crayfish directly to the UK, without the involvement of a middleman. "We had it all arranged; we had the pilot and all. We had the fish on the slip in Garnish, packed, and I was taking them up to Cork airport. The pilot was in Cornwall, and next thing we got a phone call to say there was fog, and the plane couldn't take off. And we said, 'what is going on here?' But we had to do something, or the fish were going to die.

"To cut a long story short, we rang Lucey, the dealer in Kerry, and he said, 'I have no truck, ye'll have to bring them over to me.' So we went over with our tails between our legs and brought the fish down to the pond. We'd done an expert job; we had sawdust and seaweed packed in around them. Lucey saw the packing and said, 'where are ye going with these, lads?' But he knew well, of course.

"It turned there was no fog in Cornwall; the pilot had been got at. No doubt about it. They did not want a crowd like us to start exporting ourselves. So that was another venture gone slightly wrong."

Pre-electricity

Dónal remembers how insular places like Garnish tended to be. "When we were young, the only fellow we knew in the Town minor team was Deccie Wiseman, and we only knew Deccie from the shop.

"We were the first household west to get a radio. Joe Martin Sullivan put it in. It was a massive yoke, with a wet and a dry battery. The wet battery would have to be brought into Peter Murphy's garage to be charged up. In and out in Warner's van. If it didn't come out, and there was a match on Sunday, there'd be total depression. The girls used have Radio Luxembourg and if they didn't put it back to Athlone, my father, God rest his soul, could never find the station and there'd be war!"

There was no electricity in Garnish until the cable car linking Dursey to the mainland was installed in '69. "One time in the early '60s, a gang from Garnish went out to the Bull Rock to watch the All-Ireland on TV; they had a television there before anyone. It was a flat calm day, and Fr Keane, the parish priest, went with them.

"Joe Bán of Urhan had a television that time as well. They'd put the television out on the window, and the yard would be full. They'd be up on the ditches and everything. Downey's pub got it after then. They were getting the reception from Mullaghanish."

The salmon

The fishing at Garnish underwent another boom in the late '60s and '70s as the mackerel returned and, around the same time, the market opened for salmon. "Owenie Séamus O'Sullivan kicked that off," says Dónal. "He was fishing salmon there a long time, and everyone thought he was catching nothing. He kept it close to his chest. Owenie had a net anchored at the point of the island in Garnish for the salmon, and when the salmon was over, he put mackerel nets out there.

"But then, word got out, and more and more of them went at the salmon. Soon they had nets out all the way east, from Canalmore to Foilleye. There must have been over twenty boats. They caught so many fish they'd come in with an inch of boat over the water. It was a miracle no one drowned; thanks be to God there was no accident at all."

Dónal abandoned fishing to take up a secure job as driver of a school bus in '68. "I'd bring the children in to Castletown every morning, and then I'd go to watch the fish auction, at nine o'clock. One morning this fellow – Haulie Driscoll, he worked for Clayton Love - hopped onto the bus after me, and he said, 'there's mackerel west on the pier in Garnish, go out and buy it.' And I said, 'with what?' 'Go out and offer them a pound a box,' he said, 'then ring me, and I'll send trucks west for them.'

"West I went anyway. I turned the school bus down to the pier. Everyone knew down on that pier that I was getting paid a fiver a week. But I said, lads, 'I'll buy all the fish off ye.' They had all these little meetings, to discuss it, but then John L pulled it together. 'We'll do it,' he said. So I made my phone call and Reggie Harrington's two trucks came out and cleaned out the pier. And of course they asked, 'would you take fish tomorrow?' 'No bother,' I said."

Dónal took details of each transaction in a notebook, and met with Haulie to discuss how the fishermen would be paid. "Haulie was staying below in the hotel. Room 40. He asked me then had I a bank account, and I said, no. 'A bank account? What's that?' So we went into the bank, Haulie put in money and I came sailing out the door with a chequebook. My mother never saw a chequebook before that. The only time they'd see a cheque at home was from the creamery, or if they shipped a pig.

"I didn't give the lads the cheques until about half twelve the following Monday. I knew I'd be into the town with the bus around two o'clock. So I stopped in the Square and watched as they all went tearing into the bank. One after the other. And they came out counting the cash. They'd got money. It was real. And off it went from there. There was some mackerel shifted out of Garnish after that."

Most of the market for mackerel was in the Netherlands. "That time the fishermen were using a big mesh, and it was all big mackerel they were catching. The Dutch used smoke them; they were like caviar. Peter Tallon was the agent, and the first truck and trailer that Peter brought to Castletown, I went down to Bantry to meet him, to drive up ahead of him. It was the biggest truck ever came here."

That time, again, income from the fishing was spread around the community. "It was the same thing in Travara and Ballycrovane as it was in Garnish. Everyone who could move was below, taking mackerel off the nets."

A German net factory opened in Castletownbere. "That was going 24/7, and there were eighty-five on the clock. It didn't pay much, but it was money all the same. A girl named Cecilia came to work there from Kealkil. It was like someone landing from Mars… Kealkil was a long way away that time."

Beara was booming; just as there was no shortage of money, there was no shortage of entertainment. "We used never go to pubs, but there was Cametrignane, the Beara Bay and the Wheel Inn, and there was one band better than the next in each one of them. We'd be out Friday, Saturday and Sunday night. Before that then, there'd be a dance in Ardgroom, a dance in Eyeries, and the pictures in town. So we weren't short of a social life at all. The thing was, if you were drunk that time, you hadn't a hope of getting a woman to go out with you. Not a hope. There was a mineral bar in all the halls, and you'd ask a girl if she wanted a bottle of orange."

Dónal married Joan Hanley and moved into Castletownbere in '73. "We were staying in a flat up the top of the town, and Jimmy Murphy

Foilleye was throwing stones up at the window, our first night back, looking for fish boxes, at half past three in the morning."

Most of the young men making money bought new cars. The story is often told of how, one Christmas, ten brand new cars were wrecked going west to Garnish, and were all replaced the morning after.

"I started selling cars myself, for Kavanagh's of Charleville… the brother-in-law was a mechanic there. Joe Somers was the man in Cork; he used to stay west in Terry's every summer, and I knew him pretty well. One Saturday evening he rang me from the showroom in Cork, and he said, 'there's a young fellow here with me. He wants the car for sale in the window. Cash down.' And Joe said, 'this can't be right, he's only a young fellow.' I said, 'what's his name?', and he said, 'Nicky McGuinness.' 'Oh,' I said, 'that fellow's no bother at all.' The car he wanted was a brand new red Ford Escort. Nicky was only seventeen years old, but he put the pound notes up on the counter and sailed off out the Western Road. That's how crazy it was."

The boom lasted for much of the '70s, and only ended when the mackerel vanished again; the circumstances of their appearance and disappearance remain a mystery. "The mackerel seem to come in thirty-year cycles. The gill netting started up in '68, and that went on for about ten years before they vanished again. That time they blamed the trawlers, but they couldn't blame the trawlers in the '40s, could they? And the question I have to this day for the scientists is: how come, when the seine fishing was in Garnish, they went out one year and there was no mackerel? They cannot blame the supertrawlers; they weren't there."

Tank boats

In the '80s, a number of fishermen in Castletownbere invested in larger trawlers, and began venturing further from the traditional grounds. "Larry Murphy was the first man to get a tank boat here. The *Menhaden*. Larry got the boat in 1980, I'd say, and that was another major advance. Kieran O'Driscoll was next, and Frank Downey converted the *Sea Spray* then.

"I was agent that time for Ricky Donnell of Whitehaven, and we brought in a factory ship. She was Russian… she was massive. We went out to meet her, west outside of Blackball. We pulled up beside her. It was a sloppy enough old day, and they put down this bag, down the side of the boat, and there were white gloves in it for everyone. We climbed up the ladder. It was very formal; we were told, 'don't take off the gloves until you shake hands with the captain.' There was a huge crew, hundreds. They had a fully kitted-out hospital on-board; they could perform an appendix operation, there was that much gear on her."

The Castletownbere boats started delivering mackerel directly to the ship. "You could set your clock by the Russians that time. They'd always be back here for Christmas."

Some of the local boats started fishing out of Killybegs in the season, venturing twelve or fourteen miles into Scottish waters. "They'd go a lot further north now, and that'll be the big problem with Brexit. They'll have to wait till the fish come down; they'll have spawned by then, they'll have far less fat and the price will be poor. It's scary stuff."

Fishing now

Dónal believes there is more money than ever being made in fishing today, but the difference is that far fewer people benefit than did in the past. "Fishing is like farming," he says. "When the creamery was going in Castletown, our creamery can number was 810. That time, every house had a creamery can, and the truck would come out in the morning. We'd come up to the stop by Lehanmore school. The lorry wouldn't go west beyond that. That was the big separator lorry; it'd separate out the cream. There'd be a queue of donkeys east past Jerry Kelly's shop, and you took your place. Jack FitzGerald was taking the milk in, and Tommy Shannon was on the other side, after it was separated, giving it back out. And if he didn't like you, if you crossed him at all, he'd drench you with milk.

"But the thing was, if your creamery can didn't turn up, people would know there was something wrong; the bell went off straight away. Later on in the day, the postman arrived, and again, he'd know if there was something wrong. But you could be dead inside now for three weeks, and no one would know. Is there anyone going to the creamery in Beara now? Four or five, maybe, in the whole peninsula."

Fishing, he believes, has gone the same way as that of the small farmer, and the consequences for rural communities have been a disaster. "How many boats are in Garnish now? One or two? It's gone. People think bigger is better, but it's not. The fabric of life is totally changed. We had a great time in my day. Everything was an adventure. We used to get Golden Syrup at Christmas, and it's still the same tin now as it was then. We'd get one tin of it on Christmas Eve, and when that was gone, you didn't taste it again till the next Christmas, and you didn't look for it either. But you couldn't surprise a child these days.

"The whole thing with fishing, and the same with farming, is it kept spreading outwards. They'd go to Dunmore one time; they go to Norway now. And all the tuna's landed into France. Now, from a fishing point of view, to be very blunt about it, it's the most economical way to do it. But it doesn't benefit us so much here."

Dónal believes the EU has impacted badly on the Irish fishing industry. "Our negotiators when we joined did not know what was out there; nobody disclosed what they were getting. But the negotiators from the other EU states did; they knew how important the grounds here were for the industry. I suppose Brian Lenihan, to be fair to the man, his priority was to look after the farmers, and that was it. But our fishing quotas were screwed from the start; whatever they gave us, we took it."

The future of fishing

Dónal acknowledges that the fishing industry in Ireland faces serious challenges today. "The Celtic Sea is ruined, there isn't a fish there anymore. And it's not overfishing this time. It's back to the scientists again; where do the fish disappear to? The questions are still the same, from 1944 to today. The bluefin tuna are jumping up on the shore here; they eat the spawn of the herring, and I reckon they're the problem. Larry Murphy never saw a bluefin tuna here until four years ago. There's no doubt about it, the roe is caviar to them, and they eat herring as well.

"But the scientists will not admit that it's the bluefin are the problem, because they're protected. The same with the seals; nobody will say it. A seal eats its own bodyweight in fish every day; there are any number of them in around the shore, and they're a serious problem."

Dónal expects the industry will survive, in one form or another, but not if decisions on its future are being made without the input of the fishermen themselves. "Just now, I'm not convinced it's going to a good place. It's not being managed as it should. Reality has to dawn as to how important the fishing is for rural Ireland, and control has to be taken away from the pen pushers above in Dublin. They're convinced otherwise, but no fisherman wants to destroy his own livelihood."

11

DECLAN O'SULLIVAN
GARNISH

Declan O'Sullivan from Lehanmore grew up the youngest of five brothers who fished out of Garnish, just as their father and grandfather and all before them had done. His grandfather, Joe O'Sullivan Vallig, famously built a new house on the strength of one particularly bountiful fishing season in 1905. On the night of the 25th of September that year, he captained a seine boat and follower that set a national record by netting seventy-nine thousand mackerel in a single haul.

"Jimmy Mike Jerry was talking to my brother Frank one time," says Declan, "and Jimmy said, 'Joe Vallig was a very cool man. Very cool, he wouldn't get too excited.' The seiners would leave Garnish, rowing at night. They'd head off, and someone would say, 'we'll go east to Foilleye,' and someone else might say, 'we'll go to Fuhir.' But Joe Vallig would say, 'we'll just stay here around the island.' They'd cast the nets a hundred yards out. Just out there by the mooring, or maybe a bit further. And that's where he got the fish that night in 1905. There were so many mackerel in the net, they couldn't bring it into the pier. It was just too heavy. So they brought it in to one of the strands, and hauled it up there.

"They were living down below the road in Canalmore that time, and with the money he made that season, they built the house above."

A new boat at Garnish

From the 1880s, most of the mackerel landed at Garnish was salted and transported to America. Sadly, the market declined in the 1940s, and what had once been a thriving industry was soon reduced to a few boat crews working on a part-time basis.

Old habits die hard, however, and some time in the mid-'50s Declan's father John Joe - a primary teacher in Lehanmore - decided fishing could still be a useful sideline for himself and his sons in the long summer holidays. "My memory of it was that my dad was financed by his brother Pat Joe in England," says Declan. "They got a boat made in Kerry… in 1955/56, I suppose. A wooden boat. The local men rowed it over to Garnish one day. I don't know did money change hands, but three or four of the local men, they rowed it back, and I think my father was with them.

"When they got back, I remember being brought down to Garnish and the boat was on dry land, and the bottle of whiskey was being passed around. It was a big thing at the time; people came down to look at the new boat. It was painted green and yellow, I think; it was very spectacular."

Potting

Crewing the boat was a family affair. "My dad would be there during the summer, and my uncle Denny Joe was second in command, and then you had the lads, my brothers Frank and John L and Tadhg; I suppose they were the main ones at first. They had a Seagull engine on the boat, and it was a curse; it was always breaking down. But they caught fish. They were potting lobsters and crayfish, and I remember John L making the statement once that he got £50 at the end of the summer; that was his share, and it was big money at the time."

L – R: Gerard Harrington, John L O'Sullivan, Denny Joe
O'Sullivan and Noelie O'Sullivan, c. 1960 © Gerdie Harrington)

The fish buyer was a man named Sonny Sullivan. "Sonny had these scales. He'd put the fish on one side and the weights on the other. I was there one day and the scales were at a slant on the slip, and Frank was very unhappy. Frank was saying, 'they're supposed to be on a flat surface.' Your man said, 'okay,' and he put them on the flat surface, and he put the fish in, but he was very reluctant to put on the weight. He used to tip it with his finger, saying, 'it's stiff.' And Frank said, 'you're supposed to put on the weight, not tip it with your finger.' Sonny didn't like that at all!"

Dave Dudley and his son Denis were also fishing out of Garnish, and one day Sonny came to buy their catch, but the two crews had gone on strike. "They said, 'we're not bringing in the fish, we're not getting enough money for it.' The fish – lobster and crayfish – were outside in wooden boxes, floating in the sea. You had to store them like that, to keep them alive. You'd cut the claws so they wouldn't fight each other. And you wouldn't put the crabs in there, you'd throw them out.

"Denis and Frank and John L said, 'we're not bringing in the fish.' So Sonny said, 'I can't do anything about it, I'm not getting enough money either.' So there was an impasse. And Sonny brought the two older men, my father and Dave Dudley, up to the shed there below the Post Office. They had a bottle of whiskey in there, and they were inside for a while. And when they came out, the two men came down and said, 'bring in the fish, everything is sorted out.' But the boys said, 'is there a better price?' 'No, not today,' they were told. 'Sonny's under pressure,' and so on. So the lads still said no. And eventually, Sonny put something on the price, to keep them quiet."

James O'Sullivan and John L O'Sullivan, c. 1960 © Gerdie Harrington)

Declan remembers how one night his brothers had gone fishing around the north side of Cod's Head, and there was no sign of them returning. "Sometimes they came home in the dark, but this was very late, and everyone went down to the pier. It was eleven o'clock, and then it was twelve o'clock. Someone mentioned that it was *Oíche Parthalán*, which was supposed to be bad luck, and people said, 'shhh!' More people arrived down, and they were all there on the slip. It was sort of an emergency. What had happened? But eventually the lads appeared. The famous engine, the Seagull, had collapsed and they had to leave the pots and row home, and it took them hours. But they were grand. Luckily there was no tragedy at all that time."

Cormac O'Sullivan, 1971

The pot fishing continued through the '60s, with the younger brothers, Cormac and Declan, joining the older boys along the way. Declan remembers how they often went potting out around the Bull Rock. "We did a little bit of fishing around the Calf, but it didn't seem to be that good. And we were up on the Cow Rock, all those years ago. Dan Johnny Willie had sheep there at one stage. The Cow is all sea arches. You had this high rock, and these arches, and there's a sort of passageway, and you'd scoot through.

"But the Bull was the thing. There was great fishing at the Bull. It was very shallow. You could see the pots at the bottom, and of course they were barrel pots - the shape of a barrel – and when you looked down, they were rolling around the bottom. Some of the lobsters would get in, and they'd get out again, like something in a comedy. I remember saying to John L, 'did anyone make a rectangular pot? That'd sit in the bottom?' These things were always awkward in the boat. So he said, 'the French have a circular pot, called French pots. They'd be sort of like an oval shape with a flat bottom.' And I said, 'wouldn't they be better?' And he said, 'ah, they would, yeah. Or a rectangular pot... they'd sit on the bottom, and they'd sit in the boat as well.' So these barrel pots, they were completely wrong. But we never did anything about it."

They would sometimes land on the Bull. "That was amazing. Fantastic. There was one time, I went up the brass ladder... there were eighteen steps on the ladder, and another eighty concrete steps with a handrail up to the dwellings. Anyway, I was walking around on top of the rock. I was looking down on the dwellings; there's a little passageway, and two of them were playing hurling back and forth in an alleyway. And they were shouting at each other. I was way up overhead, and I didn't say a thing!"

The mackerel

In the '60s, the fishing provided a subsistence living for a handful, but no more. Even in Garnish, where people remembered the seiners' years of plenty, no one could have foreseen that there would ever again be prosperity in the area. "I was away studying at UCC in Cork, and when I came home after my exams in September '71, my mother said there was a mad fishing boom in Garnish; the mackerel had arrived into the bay. There were always mackerel there, but this was different; the lads were throwing out the nets, and catching loads of fish, and they were selling at a good price. So this was huge.

"The first two boats at the mackerel, as far as I remember, were my brother John L's and Owenie Séamus's. You had these cloth nets; they were always ripping, they were so soft. You'd haul them into the boat, full of fish, and haul them onto the slip, and they'd be ripped to pieces. You'd take the fish off laboriously, and put them into boxes. They were wooden boxes that time. And the fish buyers would come and take them away."

For all the difficulties, fishing would soon provide a substantial living, and more and more young men began acquiring boats. "And then gradually it became more organised. There might have been twenty boats, but each had their own section to fish in. They had their own area out in the sea, staked. You had the buoys; you left them there in wintertime. You had the nets hanging off them. And you went out and cleaned the fish off them every night and brought them in. The fish buyers would provide the boxes, they took them off you, and off you went. And it was John L who said it wasn't fishing at all, it was just sort of industrial… and it was an industry."

The work was nothing if not physical. "The thing was, in the morning, you emptied your net outside. You put your boat in underneath it, and you pulled the head rope up there on top, you pulled the net across the boat. Two men at one end, and two more at the other. You cleared the fish; the mackerel was hanging off like that, and you cleared them off, threw them behind you and so on. When you had that space cleared, you pulled the net across. You kept doing that as long as it took. An hour, six hours, nine hours. And the boat would fill up with fish. But the thing was, then, it was like semi-laziness. Will we get more into the boat? You could have very calm days out. So the boat would be down in the water, full up with fish. It'd sink into the sea. So the sea could be lashing in, but we'd pull in another bit.

"I remember one morning there was this boat, and when they finally threw off the net, the sea was lapping in on both sides. They came in between the islands. You could see these men coming towards you in the distance; they seemed to be standing in the water. And you could see the stem of the boat sticking up, with the water lapping in and out. They made it in all right. Miraculously, there were no serious accidents or drownings at Garnish at that time."

The fish were sold fresh, without needing to be gutted or cleaned. "You had shovels, big scoops, and the boxes were brought down, and you scooped the fish into the box. You made stacks of them, emptied the boat, and went out again. Or you were finished for the day, and that was it. We were getting a very good price, something like £4 a box. Then the fish buyers said, sorry, and they put it down to £3. It went down again and so on. There was a strike at one stage. We started salting the fish. It was very awkward. Very laborious. So you had fish stations then, where you cleaned the fish and put it into the barrels. After all the night fishing outside, you spent the whole time salting. Sure that was murder.

"Fr Keane was the canon in Castletown, and he was brought in as the intermediary. There was a lot of heat, some fellows wanted to break the strike and so on. And eventually, I think, did they move up the price up? They must have done something. This buyer told John L afterwards they could have gone up to £9 a box, but they knew that eventually the strike would break. And eventually it broke, and we went back to fishing again."

The salmon

It was in the early '70s that the salmon fishing took off as well. "Lord Lansdowne had the rights to the Kenmare River, out to the Bull Rock, but as you know, it's not a river at all, it's the sea. My memory is of us going out one night, with a little net a few hundred feet long, and getting salmon in that. A few of the fishermen around had caught salmon before that all right, in trammels, a net that's sunk to the bottom of the sea. You'd get all sorts of things in it, mackerel and crabs and so on. And sometimes they'd get a salmon, but they'd cut it up and put it in the pots for bait. They didn't know what it was.

"So the salmon were in the sea the whole time, but suddenly we were netting them. We started fishing at the beginning of the summer. You didn't fish in the harbour for salmon. We did at first, but it was too tight really, you didn't have the space. You'd go over near Canalmore. You threw out the net and let it drift, you let it float in the water and you followed it. Your eye became used to it; you'd see the fish caught in the net. If it was fishing in a straight line, you might let it go for hours. But generally the net crumpled up, so you'd haul it in. You could get twenty salmon in a single haul, or just one. A shoal could hit it. You could have twenty down at one end, and nothing for the rest of it."

The nets would each be three hundred yards or so, and there'd often be twenty nets, piled up in the boat. "We had an outboard engine, but it was dangerous enough. If anything happened, you couldn't row. You couldn't do anything. These weren't cloth nets; they were some kind of fibre. They were completely illegal, because they were invisible in the water, and you were supposed to give the salmon a fair chance.

"The big thing around here was that the bailiffs and the Navy and the guards were after you always. You were breaking the law. There was always tension. The cut-off point for the salmon was mid-September. If you got caught with salmon in your car, it'd be impounded. And the fish buyers would say, 'I'm not taking any more.'"

Declan, like most in the area, thought it completely unfair that the inshore fishermen were being persecuted. "I was very agitated about it. As Pearse Lyne said, in a little area, where you had high unemployment, depending on small farms and little bits of jobs and so on, you had this huge resource in the sea, the salmon, and they were all down on top of you. And at the same time, you had these big trawlers from Russia and so on, hoovering up fish. And the authorities weren't doing a bit to them, they were concentrating on us."

Declan fished in the holidays as he studied at UCC to become a teacher. "Then I got a job in Dublin, in '76. I think in '79 the fish catch halved, and in 1980 it halved again. Why did this happen? One reason I believe is that the trawlers started fishing for mackerel outside. They were sweeping up and down the coast, hoovering up the fish. And that broke up the shoals. And then eventually the inshore fishing ground to a halt. You might have two boxes of fish or something. Or you'd have only the one. It went down to that from ninety boxes a night."

Declan continued fishing in the summers into the '80s, often with his neighbour, Mitey McNally. "I used to ring Mitey at six in the morning, and by the time I'd arrive over he'd have his breakfast taken, and we'd be off out. Mitey and myself certainly spent the time out in the boat, but I don't know if we were that great at it, as we never made much money."

These days, Declan continues to travel down regularly from Dublin, but the years of fishing are memories now. "The boom that time lasted maybe ten years, and there was huge money involved. Christy Crowley sold some huge amount of cars. He used to send a salesman to Garnish, and young fellows would buy a new car every two years. I'd say you could make the price of a good secondhand car in a few weeks. A good semi-detached house in Cork city might have cost £9,000. In 1974, I had the equivalent of one-seventh of that in twelve weeks. I made £1,400 that autumn; that might be the equivalent of €70,000 today, in terms of its buying power. And it was all cash."

12

ROSARIE O'NEILL
DURSEY ISLAND AND EYERIES

Rosarie O'Neill was born on Dursey Island. She now lives in Eyeries, but returns to the island at least once a week, having built a house near her old family home at Ballynacallagh.

"When I meet people on Dursey, they'd ask, 'do you know anything about the island?' And I'd say, 'of course I do, I was reared here.' They always ask, 'how did ye manage for shopping?' Sure what shopping? We were self-sufficient, we had everything ourselves. We had our own fish and meat, and we grew our own vegetables. Flour, sugar and tea were all we bought in. And when someone came visiting we got the sweets, and we were delighted with that."

Rosarie was the youngest of nine children, the two eldest of whom had already left home when she was growing up. "I was born in Cork hospital, but most of the family were born at home and more of them in town. I don't know why I was born in Cork; people mostly had their babies on the island. The Dennehy woman, Bartley's sister, she was a nurse in the hospital, and when she'd be off, I suppose neighbours came in, and that was it."

Her father, Denis Healy, "was fishing always. He had a 26- or 27-footer, the *Pride of Dursey*. He fished from April till September, depending on the weather. He'd be at the crays and the lobsters, or the mackerel when September came. He'd always salt mackerel and connors in barrels, and they'd be there for the winter."

Rosarie remembers how, in her childhood, crab claws were plentiful, as there was simply no sale for them at the time. "We ate them every night. In the summertime the lads would shoot the pots in the morning, then they'd come home and we'd go at the hay. My mother was in and out of the house, doing everything. I always remember, when she'd come home we'd go away hauling the pots, down west of Kilmichael. We'd go down on the rocks and hop into the boat; we'd haul the pots and we'd bring home our container of crabs' claws.

"My mother would be baking the bread, and she'd have two bastibles going at the one time. There'd be one hanging inside by the fire, and we'd put our crabs' claws in it. She'd run us out of it then, because the water running out of the claws would ruin her bread. So then we'd get a shovel of coal from the fire, and build a fire of our own outside, and we'd boil the claws in a bucket. The water would be sizzling out of them. We'd put a fine dollop of butter on top; the butter was my mother's, and there was no talk of cholesterol in those days."

The island economy

The men of Dursey often worked digging the road for the County Council. "They'd do that for so long and then they'd have their stamp up, and they'd draw the dole for so many months. In May then, they'd go away fishing. Nearly every family had their own boat. There was us and the Sheehans; Bartley Dennehy and the Learys, and John Michael's crowd. There were six boats at least. My aunt would make the phone call to O'Dowd's in Tralee or Lucey's in Waterville that'd buy the crays and the lobsters. She'd send over a note then saying how much they were going to give per pound. It was great income."

Rosarie's family farmed as well, producing milk and sometimes selling cattle. "Dan John Willie used to come in and buy a lot of them. There was the best of grass on Dursey; the animals would be in fine condition coming out. It was the same on Crow Head, with Tadhg Roger; there was fine grazing there too, and the sheep would put on great weight."

The cattle that were sold had to be swum across the Dursey Sound to the mainland. "There were plenty of men for help; you'd have five or six in the boat, and one of them would be holding up the animal. They each had their own rope. You'd often wonder – at the time, we didn't think of the danger – but looking at it now, all you needed was a cow hitting the boat. The leg alone could bust the boat; it'd be done in a shot. But they always managed fine."

Outside the school on Dursey Island

The island population held up for a long time, and there was a great sense of community. "I remember when there was sixty on the island. There were seventeen children when I went to school, all in one room. The teachers were great girls to come into the island. A lot of them would stay with us."

Providing lodging for the teachers brought in another bit of income. "My parents had these extra things; they had the teachers staying, and then my father had a pond, for dipping the sheep. We used to draw all the water for that. Every sheep on the island came to that pond, so there was some buckets of water. My father would be below, cleaning the tank and getting the dip ready. And we'd be up and down all day long with two buckets, as it was easier to bring two than one, and we'd be 'allergic' to it. It would take forty or fifty buckets of water to fill the tank. And when the tank was empty, you'd top it up again. That was done for the three villages, for all the sheep. I don't know how many sheep there were, but it was too many!

"Then we had to take note of how many sheep you had, and my mother had to fill in the book, and send it in, and that came back for the next year. She did the same with the graveyard; she filled the book for that whenever someone died. So they had three extra things, and they were each a bonus."

Helping the neighbours

Over the summer, most of the islanders cut turf for the winter. "That time we'd have scorching weather. My sister Geraldine was snow white; she'd come home at night, and she'd have a fever from being out in the sun, at the turf, with the breeze up on the hill. She'd be burned to the last, and she'd toss and turn from it. Going to the hill, you'd bring away your grub with you. I'll always remember; you'd have my mother's bread, that she baked herself, and that was the main thing. You'd be out to Kelly's shop; we'd always get lovely bacon from there. We'd cut the slice off that for the bread and we'd bring it up to the hill. That was no such thing as you wouldn't eat it, you ate it!"

As well as the turf-cutting, Rosarie remembers how her brothers "would always be down on the shore, picking up wreck for the fire. That was the main firewood, when you think of it. You'd have a big spar inside in the fire and you'd be pushing it in."

In winter, the island was sometimes cut off for as much as five or six weeks; provisions ran low, but the people looked out for each other. "We were never out of milk, for instance. The cattle didn't all calf at the same time; we'd stagger it. And we always gave milk to two neighbours next door. PJ Leary's mother got milk every morning and evening. And so did Mag and Mike up the road. Mag had actually worked in town in the hospital, and she'd worked in Sadler's too, I think. I don't know what happened, but she lost her sight, and ended up blind. So we brought milk to them. Mike used to fish in his younger days, but they never had land or cattle, so we'd bring them the milk morning and evening.

"If you were running late, going on for six o'clock, they'd be saying the Rosary. They had this big long green gate, and when you'd start opening it, it used to make noise. So you were trying to do it as quietly as possible so you could listen to see what part of the Rosary they were at inside, because you'd have to kneel down with them, and it'd be all the saints: St Peter and St Paul and all the rest. Then Mike would come down and put the milk into his bowl, and you'd wash it out and go away home. We'd do that every day; there was no such thing as don't do it."

Mike kept two animals; a donkey named Mick and a dog named Fido. "When he'd go for turf, it was nearly always on Kilmichael hill. He'd be coming home, and when he'd be over near Murphy's, he'd tell the dog to go home. So the dog would jump in over the ditch, and Mag knew then that Mike was on his way with the load of turf. She'd poke her way out and open the two gates, and he'd go in then and put in the turf. Mag died first, then Mike died in hospital. Poor Fido went ballistic altogether. He was so used to the two of them, and he went crazy when they died. He was their pet, sure; he was like family. Germans have that house now."

Change

Dursey would once have had a population of more than two hundred, and three villages - Ballynacallagh, Kilmichael and Tillickafinna - but a number of families were re-settled by the Government in Whitegate in the late 1940s, when the Land Commission allowed them to swap their farms on Dursey for land on Roche's Point. It seemed like a good idea at the time, but many of the families came to regret the move.

"They weren't really wanted there in Whitegate," says Rosarie. "It was tough. There was a fellow down a couple of years ago, a descendant of one of those families; he said they were glad they had their boats, and could go fishing. They'd never have done otherwise. The sea was in their blood. They settled, but I suppose it was a big change from Dursey."

For years, those who remained on the island campaigned for a bridge, and when that failed to materialise, they began campaigning for a cable car instead. Their efforts paid off in 1969, when the then Taoiseach, Jack Lynch, opened the new service. "That was the biggest change in Dursey in my lifetime. That was huge. It's frightening how many people use the cable car now, but in fifty years there was never once an accident."

Sadly, the cable car came too late to save the island community. "It was '79 before we got the electricity. The post office closed in '74, and the school in '75. They were both a big blow to the island. But then, I suppose there were no more children on the island. The school would have closed anyway a few years after, one way or another. There were no more children. There were nine in our house; my sister Bridget died young, so then there was eight of us. There were ten west in Bernie's, and ten in Sheehan's. In my time, those three houses would have kept the school going on their own."

Dursey's future

The population of Dursey is now reduced to a handful, though many who left have kept up their homes on the island and visit regularly. It was, however, a great novelty when Rosarie built her house on Dursey in 2003, as it was the first new dwelling to have been constructed on the island in seventy years.

"It's a small house, with two bedrooms. But we used one thousand, six hundred and eighty blocks, and we brought them in thirty-nine at a time on the cable car. A few years after, we built a little porch. We tried to get a lorry-load of sand into the island, but the morning the boat came, there was too much draw on the tide, and they had to turn back. So they came and dropped it on the mainland, and we had to bag it in on the cable car. I went to everyone in the country to find the bags. I started off fierce brave, with four shovels of sand in each bag, but I wasn't long cutting down to two and a half. I gave a good seven or eight days at it and I got all the sand in to the island eventually. I didn't mind then, because I could carry it west to the house in the car."

A Dream Comes True 2003

My dream was to build my own house on Dursey Island, not a very easy task to wish for. I believe sheer determination and drive will get you anywhere.
First Step was to purchase a site from my brother Denis and his wife Mary.
Second was to apply for planning, which was not easy by any means.
It was the first house to be built on Dursey for over 70 year's.
So work started on the site all hands on deck, all hands were welcome.
The real heavy work was to carry all the blocks on the cable-car. I was dreaming of blocks day and night, when would we ever have them up on the site, time brings everything.
Sometimes I would be asked "was I mad to do such a major job to build on Dursey". I would say "no, I feel great, it's no problem".
To build a house on an island like Dursey, is by no means and easy job, you handle all the materials several times before you even reach the site.
This is proof of real determination, but of course it would be impossible to do such a job only for my wonderful husband Battie, twin sons Barry and Fergus and daughter Kiera. Also for my brother Denis and nephew Gerard always there to give a hand, also not forgetting our neighbours Mickie Joe (Tools supplier) and Martin and all who helped in any way.
So here comes the great day for all, the "Dursey Cottage" opens its doors to Fr Liam Comer to celebrate Mass on 12th of April 2003. A big welcome home for my Mother, who had a misfortunate accident on the 20th of January, spent a week in hospital. So all neighbours and friends, and especially my mother's home help the one and only 'Betty', all celebrated the great occasion. So we had a great day and night in the (Dursey Cottage).
On the 20th of August we hit the headlines "Nationwide" visited the island to interview my Mother re. Island living, it was televised on the 10th of Sept.
What a great show, well done to Marie Mullakey, Martin Cronin and Michael O'Sullivan.
So I achieved my new home on Dursey thanks to all the people who gave gifts and good wishes.
Thanks for the committee for the Parish newsletter every year.
Well done!!

Regards,
Rosarie O'Neill (nee Healy)
& Battie O'Neill.

A dream come true

There may never again be as strong a community on Dursey as there was in the past, but recent years have seen some of the old houses being renovated, the County Council is currently planning improvements to the cable car, and there are more people staying throughout the year. "And when there's a light in the house," says Rosarie, "there's life."

13

MARY AND ANN HANLEY

URHAN AND CASTLETOWNBERE

Mary and Ann Hanley grew up in Knockeen, Urhan, the daughters of Big Mike Hanley, who became one of the most prominent fish dealers in Ireland in the 1960s and '70s.

As it happens, this was but one in a long line of occupations Big Mike undertook. As a young man he had been a builder in Beara, but then, like so many more, he left for England in the late 1930s. During World War II, he took charge of a British Navy construction project in Cosham near Bath. Several of his brothers were less fortunate; they joined the Marines and were sent to sea.

"Uncle Jimmy was killed in action in Singapore. He was on the same ship as Dr Aidan McCarthy," says Mary. "Uncle Paddy was on a different ship, which was torpedoed. He spent hours in the water with two broken legs, and after that he moved to Australia, as he was crippled with arthritis. Dad came back from England around 1947, and he had a boat built then."

The vessel was built by the Healys of Lauragh, in Mike's own farmyard in Urhan. "She was a big boat," says Ann. "And when she was finished, they dragged her on wooden rollers down to Travaud. And do you want to hear a better story? Dad was going out with a girl in England, and when he came back, he was writing to her the same time as he was having the boat built. One time, he wrote her one letter, and he wrote another to some fellow to buy an engine for the boat, but he put them each in the wrong envelope. He reckoned when she received the letter about the boat engine, he never heard from her again!"

Big Mike Hanley

In those days, the Cork County Committee of Agriculture subsidised the use of sea sand as agricultural fertiliser, to the tune of two shillings and three pence a ton, and Big Mike put his boat to use drawing sand from the White Strand, near Cahersiveen in Co Kerry. "He'd leave it in to Urhan or Garnish, and the farmers there would buy it," says Ann.

"He lost two boats at that," says Mary. "In storms."

"And he'd have maybe too much in the loads. There'd be ferocious weight in them."

Mary remembers that he made many friends in Kerry. "He'd do some bit of fishing on the way over, and he'd barter new potatoes from the man in the Black Shop for fish. Himself and Uncle Mike cooked the new spuds and the fish coming back on the boat."

Big Mike was always busy. At one time, in the '50s, he worked planting forestry at Dunboy. "That was after he got married," says Mary. "He worked at the buildings in Bandon for a few years as well. Then he built the television and telecommunication booster here in '64."

It was after that that he started at the mackerel and herrings, out of Travara. "Our brother Jim got his boat in the late '60s, and around the same time Dad started curing and processing the fish in the farmyard," says Ann. It was about then also that he saw an opportunity in free rural school transport, using his bus to drop off and collect local children.

Fish processing and the Beara Bar

Soon, Mike started curing the fish on the pier in Castletownbere, and as he grew more successful as a dealer, he bought a property in Bank Place. It consisted of a public house on the main street, a garden, and a store at the back that opened onto the western end of the pier.

"Dad always said he didn't want the bar at all," says Mary. "All he wanted was the store below for the fish."

"But the bar was going with the store," says Ann. "And Mary came home from England to run it."

"Before me, John and Úna Dennehy were here for years and years. They sold it in 1970, but the people who got it didn't take to it, so they sold it on again. Dad bought it that time; the 23rd of September was the day we opened as the Beara Bar."

Ann remembers that Big Mike "never pulled a pint in his life unless one of us refused to pull it for him after closing. The whole idea was he wanted the store, and the access to the pier."

"He built the slip down there that time as well," says Mary.

"He did. He got permission from the neighbours; John the Buck, Connie Batt, Twomey's... Mary Power wouldn't have been there that time... Donie Dole, I suppose. There was only a walk down there before, where the slip is now."

The store was where the fish was processed. "He had a machine for the filleting," says Ann. "At one stage, there was eighty working down there. There were young fellows then would work for him after school rolling barrels... Christy Collins, Brendan Hanley... Gerry Shea, God rest his soul. All that gang, rolling barrels back and forth. And they were getting pocket money for it, I suppose. They didn't mind. At the height of the fishing, Dad was paying £4.50 or £5 an hour. I mean, convert that now."

"A pint was three shillings that time," says Mary. "They never thought they'd see a poor day again."

"That's right. You'd get six and a half pints for a pound."

The store would be particularly busy in the autumn, and right up until Christmas. The fact that the work was seasonal seemed to suit their workforce fine. "Most of them were farmers anyway," says Ann, "and September would be a quiet time otherwise."

Mary remembers how "there were twenty-three pubs in Castletownbere when we opened the Beara Bar. That time of the year now, when the lads were working below in the store, I'd have twenty-four kegs of Guinness delivered every week; that was the standing order."

"It was the same in the shops," says Ann. "The women would come in September or October and they'd be putting things away for Christmas. They'd be buying curtains and stuff for the house; the money was there, and it was in circulation. The difference then as well was that the trawler crews were local. They were spending locally."

"There was a gang of fellows working in Dinish as well, when the Board of Works started up and they were at the pier… there isn't a sinner around anymore. That whole culture with the fishing has changed. The crews now are all non-nationals. There's still boats fishing, but there isn't that kind of lifestyle anymore. There's a few big boats making money, I suppose. Maybe eight boats in total."

Ann remembers how the fish that didn't sell when it was landed would be cured in the expectation that it would sell later. "There'd be maybe twenty people kept on then, because you'd have to change the brine. They'd go through the barrels, and any fish that weren't right would be taken out. Some of the fish would be there for a year, no problem. The brine would hold it fine."

She can still rattle off the names of the ports the fish were sent out to. "St Vincent. St Lucia. Grenada. I used write them on the barrels. We'd cure the fish in wooden barrels, and then transfer them into white plastic buckets for exporting. You'd get a marker and write on top of them where they were going. They were all islands in the Carribean, but the market came through England. Thomas Archer was the fellow who started that."

"Jamaica was the biggest market for the mackerel," says Mary. "And the herring went to France."

"The fresh fish went direct. If there was a surplus of mackerel, it was frozen in Midleton. They had a massive big freezing plant. Reggie Harrington had his own truck that time. If there was a glut of fish, he used to draw it up there, to be blast frozen. Hennessy's and Murphy's above in Cork did the trucking as well. They'd alternate. Hennessy's are still going today; I'd meet them on the road. Dad would phone them, and they'd send down the trucks."

"Dad would organise the salted fish himself," says Mary. "B&I containers, wasn't it?"

"That's right. They'd drop two or three containers. The crew here would load them up, and they'd be on their way."

Mary remembers the night she and Ann prepared a hundred boxes of mackerel on their own. "To have them ready for the lads when they came in the trucks. But they were disgusted; they'd always have a break for an hour or two, waiting for the fish, and it was all there ready for them. We had the machine for filleting, but I used cut them with the knife. We had years of practice, I suppose. Jim Murphy (Bawn) of Urhan was a dinger as well. He'd cut it clean along the bone."

Inevitably, the traffic in fish generated a considerable amount of paperwork, which Mike generally left to his daughters.

"Compared to nowadays," says Ann, "it wasn't actually that bad. You might have four duplicate forms."

"Micheál Driscoll was the fisheries officer," says Mary. "He was great. He'd come up and stamp the forms. Himself or Dominic Gallagher. That was for BIM."

"The custom officer was here as well."

"That was Michael Carey. You'd get the claims form from him. They were all down on the pier that time, where the old harbour master's office was. There's no custom officer here now."

Big Mike was a director of BIM for eight years, and travelled regularly to Dublin and Brussels, and sometimes to Paris, for meetings.

His own work brought him back and forth to Boulogne. "He'd almost always go over in the hovercraft," says Ann. "He'd be there when the containers arrived, to make sure everything was all right. They'd pay him then when everything was passed. He was there a lot with a Frenchman named Youen Jacob, who was in town for ten or twelve years. He was a way bigger man than our father, and he'd smoke about a hundred cigarettes a day. When the fishing dried up here, he left with his wife and opened a restaurant in Baltimore. His son is running it now."

The downturn

Mike's business had a major setback when Michael Manley's PNP party was voted out of power in Jamaica, and Edward Seaga's JLP party were voted in to replace them. "Seaga wouldn't trade with Europe, and that's when Dad lost the market for the mackerel," says Mary. "He flew out there with our sister Noreen in '82, but he had no luck in getting things going again. He kept the fish he had left in barrels for two years below on the pier, trying to get a market for it."

"And most of it went," says Ann, "bar a few containers. But the market itself kind of dried up at that stage."

Around that time, Mike got a call to meet with an unlikely fish dealer – the former World Champion heavyweight boxer Floyd Patterson – in Dublin, to see if another market could be found for the mackerel.

"I still have that photograph at home," says Ann, "of Dad with Patterson. Dónal Kelly and a man named Christian are in it too. Christian was a marine biologist with BIM, and he used to work at the back of the Beara Bay; there was a building there, with a little office in it. I don't know where Floyd Patterson was importing fish into, but he wanted everything vacuum packed, and I suppose that would have been too much of an investment. So that didn't pan out."

"But that was the time Dad said he shook the hand of the man that shook the world!" says Mary.

Even before Big Mike got out of the fishing business, he had continued as a bus driver, bringing the local children to school and football teams to matches. Later, when he retired, he'd call most days to the Beara Bar. A visiting American writer, Kate Murphy, wrote a vivid account of him reading aloud the headlines from the newspapers, and regaling the customers with tales of his working life.

Mike passed in 2003. His obituary in the Southern Star described him as "one of nature's gentlemen, and everybody's friend."

14

GER LYNCH

DROUMBEG, ARDGROOM

Ger Lynch, a mussel farmer and fifth generation fisherman, lives in Droumbeg, Ardgroom. "My family came down from Glengarriff around 1750," he says. "They rented land from Lansdowne, but it was later split up into three holdings, and we ended up with one of them.

"We built our own house in '93. The first house built when the Lynchs came here was on what's now our lawn, though we didn't know that at the time. The house below here was supposed to have been built sometime between 1792 and '95. That was built out of fishing funds; the Lynchs were always fishing. There were also a lot of terraces of houses at the time, so any individual houses on their own were slightly upmarket. The houses were thatched. I'm not sure when the slates came in, but there again I'd say the fishing community were that bit ahead of the farming community. I'd say most of the slate came from Valentia, though they didn't take too many trips to Valentia, because there was always rivalry between the Cork crowd and the Kerry crowd."

Ger Lynch

The fishing palaces

For a time, in the 19th century, there was a boom in fishing pilchards in Kenmare Bay. "As far as I know, pilchards are half-grown herring. Or very close to them, anyway. And that's the only time I'm aware of that there was seining in here, with the big seine boat and the small boat alongside it. The men did the fishing, but there was plenty of work for the women too, in what they called the fishing palaces."

The remains of one such palace, a stone wall about six metres high, a metre and a half wide and about forty metres long, can still be seen at Cleandra harbour. "I believe there's several of them around the place; apparently they were on the go from around the 1820s up to 1880. There would have been about fifty women employed at Cleandra. The men would bring in the fish, the pilchards, and the women then would gut them. The guts would be thrown away but they'd try and save the oil. The way they did that was they hung the fish up and let them dry out. Across the wall below, there's a series of holes, where they had big long poles where they'd hang the fish, and they'd have a vessel beneath them to collect the oil.

"Apparently they'd trade the fish and the oil with the Spanish. The Spanish would come in, they'd moor offshore with the big boats, and they'd send in the small boats to collect them. I'm told there was no money exchanged, which doesn't make much sense, but they brought timber that our gang would sell to the Mines in Allihies to support the shafts. So there was no money involved in selling the fish, but they still made their few bob out of it."

Ger believes the Spanish left another legacy in the area. "And that was the genes. You'd have thirty or forty women working there and a couple of hundred Spanish men coming in, looking for company and all that. There's four of us in the family, and my sister and one of my brothers look like me; the same hair, face and skin and so on. But my other brother then is totally different; he has sallow skin and pure black hair. It often occurred to me, where did he come from? My answer was found years later, when I did a DNA test, and it came up as 28% Spanish."

Paddy Lynch

Little is known of how the Lynch family fared as fishermen in the 19th century, but in 1904, according to family tradition, Ger's grandfather Paddy Lynch replaced his first boat with a new one he had built in Baltimore.

"They had no engine that time, so six of them would row out to the fishing ground, at the Black Rocks across the bay. They'd shoot the nets, and then they'd go and haul them the next morning. They were cotton nets, and I'm not sure why, but they had to bring them ashore and dry them before they could take them out again. So they had to spread them out in the field, out on the bank below in Cuas, and dry them out, and if it was raining they wouldn't dry, so that was a lot trickier. But they did make a good living out of the fishing, because at the time there was very little way of making a living around here. Or at least they made a better living than if they were sitting at home doing nothing."

Paddy potted lobsters as well, at a time when they could be sold but the crayfish could not. "My own father often told the story of how his father would go out and haul the pots, and when the pot was coming up heavy, it'd often be full of cray. There were so many, he said, that no more could get in, and you might have another one or two sitting up on top of the pot. He said he remembered taking them out and breaking them off the ground because there was no market for them. These days, even one would do you."

Paddy had a market for the lobsters in Billingsgate, London. "He'd ship them directly. He'd wrap them in wet newspaper, and bring them by boat into Kenmare, where he'd put them on the train. They'd go across then on the boat from Rosslare, and on the train again to Billingsgate. It was a long trip, a minimum of two days. There wasn't massive money in it, and he was more or less an organiser rather than a salesman, because he'd have a few fishermen supplying him as well. Billingsgate would only take the lobsters, but it worked out well for him for many years."

Michael Paddy

Paddy Lynch's boat got broken in 1957, "and my father Michael and his brother rebuilt it completely. She was a 26-foot boat, with a square stern and a pointed stem. There'd been a Kelvin engine in it, but they replaced it with a new Lister engine, which was very modern at the time.

"My father would have worked out of Cleandra and Cuas the last thirty years he was fishing. He worked the Kenmare River, mostly on this side, as there was always that bit of rivalry with the Kerry boys. But during Lent, like his father before him, he'd fish cod and pollock on the other side, at the Black Rocks, just east of West Cove. They had the old cotton nets; they'd shoot them one day and then they'd haul them the next. There were three lads on board. My father owned the boat and he owned a third of the nets, and the others had their own nets, or a share in the nets, and that was how they used to get their share of the catch; they'd each get a quarter, and then my father would get an extra quarter because he owned the boat."

They'd shoot the nets and return the next morning, "weather permitting, of course, which was tricky enough that time of the year, as it'd still be winter. They'd haul the nets, and of course there was plenty of fish that time, so they never had an empty haul. They'd get twenty or thirty boxes of fish on a good day. Mixed fish. They threw away the monk, as no one would eat them. In fact, they threw away everything except cod and pollock, because that's all they could sell."

Michael would mostly sell his catch in Sneem, hiring a horse and cart to take the fish up from the pier. "He often said he'd seen fellows heading away with a pollock or a cod over their shoulders and its tail would nearly be touching the ground. There weren't many fishing that time, so there were massive fish, and plenty of them."

Ger reckons he was probably four the first time he was on the boat. "And I would have made a couple of trips to Sneem when I was seven or eight, but only a few. They'd be in Sneem maybe eleven o'clock in the morning, they'd have everything sold out by one, and they'd go down to the pub and have a good meal and a couple of pints. That was their reward. And I'd be hanging around, in and out by the shops. Money would have been kind of *flaithuil* at the time because there was good fishing, so we'd get a bar of chocolate or a bottle of red lemonade. The Cadbury's chocolate with the blue wrapping; I'll never forget that. We wouldn't get too much of it here.

"I wouldn't have made many trips to Sneem. It would have to be a very fine day, and I might have made four or five trips, maximum, but I have very fond memories of those occasions."

Other occupations

Michael worked at a variety of jobs, many of them maritime related, as well as the fishing. "In the early years, he was drawing sand from the White Strand. They found that very good because with the government scheme at the time, you'd get the voucher and they'd redeem it. 'See you Sunday' was gone out the window; you wouldn't be waiting for the money. My father would have two fellows with him. They'd go to the White Strand at low tide, they'd cut the trench, and then at high tide, they'd drive the boat into it; she'd sit up straight, and then they'd load her and they'd wait for the tide again. Then they'd bring back the sand to most of the small piers around the bay - they never went outside it - and they'd shovel it back out again.

"The boat was forty foot, a big-sized boat. She wasn't fully decked, so you wouldn't want to sink her down too much. If you got a sup of water in over the side of her, everything was gone. She had a Kelvin engine as well, but fuel was very scarce during the War and just after; it was rationed. So they used the sails as much as they could, but they used the engine for manoeuvring. My father had the sand boat for maybe twenty-five years; he enjoyed that work, and you were always guaranteed your money."

Michael would occasionally get work piloting boats in the bay. "There'd be a good bit of shipping going up and down, bringing stuff into Kenmare. They'd start blowing the horn off Inishfernard, and whoever got out to them first got the pilot's fee. You had nothing to do but tie your small boat to the big boat and take it into Kenmare. You got your bottle of brandy and your money and you spent a bit of time around Kenmare with them, and then you took them back out again. There was always a fierce dash to get that job. The horn could go off in the middle of the day, or the middle of the night; it could go off any time. You might have five or six racing for the ship; they'd row out, and the first boat that made it got the job."

Michael would sometimes be hired to bring turf out to the lighthouse keepers on the Bull Rock. "You'd have to tender for that as well. He got a couple of those trips, but he found them kind of tricky; you'd go out there and there'd be no swell. He'd have his crew then as well. Bringing up the turf, you'd want to have your hands filled when the swell came up. It was very hard to judge, and you could damage your boat very easily. It was tricky work, but again, it was a little bit of income."

In the summer, Michael provided a water taxi service to Kenmare for his neighbours every Wednesday. "He might have ten or 15 passengers, and they'd all be women. He'd spend a few hours in Kenmare, and have a few pints in the pub; there was no breathalyser to worry about. He'd often tell the story that there was a dolphin used come every morning outside Cuas pier, something like Fungie does in Dingle now, and for about eighteen years, he'd follow the boat all the way into Kenmare and back out again. The journey would take about two and a half hours, weather permitting."

The lobsters

Ger remembers that the fishing petered out at the end of the '60s. "That was when the trawlers started coming into the bay; they just wiped out the stocks. My father took his nets out; he had to give up. There was no point in going to the local politician or anything, because these boys were too strong in Castletownbere. It was the old story; the big guy got his way. My father was getting older that time, he was heading for sixty, but he might have got a couple more years out of it.

"After that he concentrated on potting. That was in the summer time; it had to start no later than the end of May and finish at the end of August. For two reasons: the pots were only timber, and the ropes were only hemp. So you depended on the finest weather, and the season was very short as a result. My father was very good at potting. As children we were often out fishing with him. That time, in the early '70s, he had two dozen pots; he'd have five strings of four, and four singles, and he'd have a special home for each of those. There were plenty of lobsters there, but if he got stuck at all he'd have to break the rope and then he was in trouble. Especially if it was the singles. If it was the strings he could go to the other end and he'd have two chances with it."

Despite the shortness of the season, the potting was often very profitable. "My father would sell the lobsters to Nancy Sheehan in town. I remember going in there one time, in '73. My father had fine big lobsters, and he got £21 for one single lobster, which was serious money. To give you some idea, he got a pound for his weanlings the same year, and a week's wages that time might be ten or eleven pounds. At that time there'd be no bother landing a ten-pound lobster; the gear wasn't there to overfish them, and there weren't too many fishing anyway."

The mackerel

The mackerel boom of the '70s did not really extend up the bay as far as Cleandra. "My own experience of the mackerel was, we were going to secondary school in Castletownbere. I started there at thirteen. There were a lot of fellows fishing mackerel out of Ballycrovane at the time. We used to get off the bus from school and go down and clean the nets on our way home. My father had more or less packed up fishing in the winter then; he was fishing a few pots in the summer, but he got a job working in the water scheme, bringing the water into town from Glenbeg Lake, and he was getting £11 a week. But my brother and myself, we used often have £20 for a couple of evenings' work. It was massive money that time. It was hard work; we started without gloves, we'd have our fingers worn off us, but we soon got used to it and we got the gloves. But that was the only experience I had of the mackerel."

The mussels

Ger remembers going downtown at lunchtime when he was at secondary school in Castletownbere, and witnessing firsthand the prosperity the fishing had brought to the area. "At that time, the fishing was going well. I assume there were quotas, but they were being ignored. So, all we could see was new cars, and fellows drinking in the middle of the day. We didn't realise at the time that those fellows were in for a day or two and they'd be gone again. Anyway, I'd come home and I'd tell my parents, 'I want to do that.' They ignored me till I was leaving school. I did my Inter Cert, and I wanted to go fishing, but they said, 'no, you go back and do your Leaving Cert, or else you do a trade. One of the two.' I went back for one year, but then I got the opportunity to go to Cork to learn a trade. I intended finishing my trade, and then moving home to go fishing. At the time, you did what your parents said, there was no arguing."

Before leaving for Cork, he put four car wheels out in the sea, hoping to grow mussels from them, an activity he'd been reading up on at the time. "That was my first venture, though it didn't last very long; the car wheels sank. But when I started in Cork, around '76, I kept up my interest at the weekends."

He had his first sale of mussels in '78, when a dealer in Scotland agreed to buy three hundred kilos. "We never got paid, of course; it didn't really matter, but we were offended after all the work we'd put into them. After that we got involved with BIM. In the late '70s and early '80s, BIM were offering a 50% grant, and there was 10% more coming from the Whiddy Island disaster fund, so you had 60% overall. We started to get into it more; we threw out a few lines, and of course we made all sorts of mistakes. But eventually we got the hang of it.

"I was still working for a construction company in Cork, learning my trade as a fitter. That was useful for the mussel industry; I'd be down at the weekends, and there were always machines to be maintained, things to be welded and so on. The fishing was still what I wanted to do, and in 1992, I came back here with my wife and two children. I bought a small inshore fishing boat, and between the mussels and the inshore fishing, we were able to make a living. That went on until 2003, when we sold the boat. The effort was too much at that stage; we couldn't make money at it anymore."

Ger concentrated on developing the mussel business, hoping to make a full-time living from it. "I was renting a mussel farm in Ardgroom harbour for six years. So I had my own mussel farm and the one I was renting, and we made quite a good living from the two. In 2009 that lease ended, and then we were looking around the place, saying, 'what'll we do next?' I worked in Norway for a bit, managing a mussel farm. I did that for two years part-time. It was for a school. It started as a six-month contract, but then there was another six months and another. I thoroughly enjoyed it. I learned a lot of new skills; I was supposed to be teaching them, but I learned a lot too."

When that contract finished, Ger came back and applied for a licence to extend his mussel farm. "That was in 2004, and we're still waiting for it. It's not so bad considering we waited twenty-one years for the first licence. We're only waiting sixteen years now."

As it is, Ger's business produces sixty tons of mussels every year. "We were supplying a couple of the local places, Bantry Bay Mussels and all that. But there's very few processing mussels in this country now, so we sell them all to France. We have our own direct link; we cut out the middleman, and that gives us a small bit of an edge. It's not massive money, but it's stable. We're happy enough with it, but we'd need to be producing two hundred and fifty tons a year to make a full-time living out of it. It's difficult to get a licence; it's still up in a heap. We're trying to address that but we don't know where it's going."

The V-notching scheme

Ger was chair of the local fishermen's organisation for several years. The achievement he's most proud of is the V-notching conservation scheme initiated by fishermen to preserve the lobster stock; when female lobsters are caught in the pots, the fishermen cut a V-notch in their tails so they can be identified, and they are then released. The initiative ensures the lobsters can carry on breeding.

"The V-notching has been absolutely brilliant. You'd always have the outlier, but there's 60 – 70% of the fishermen involved, which is a great success. Overall, the scheme is working."

The lobsters stocks came under a fresh threat a few years ago when rising temperatures in the bays began attracting triggerfish, a species with a notorious fondness for shellfish and crustaceans. "They did a fair bit of damage. They were killing small lobsters, but they seem to be gone again. Scientifically, we don't know how many they were taking, but the issue seems to have resolved itself."

Ger observes that the fishing industry is always in flux. "One time, the mussels were seen as a nuisance, and now they're the biggest income from the bay. The inshore fishing is more or less gone; there's no fish, and the regulations still aren't great. But there's 2,000-plus tons of mussels being harvested every year from the three harbours, and that's providing quite a good income for a number of people."

Ger would like to see greater regulation. "Ideally, you'd need a fishing officer for the bay. Someone with a bit of power. They did it in Maine in the '60s, with the lobster fishing. They brought it back big time. If anything, they were too successful, as the price of lobsters dropped. But they showed it could be done, that a conservation scheme could be implemented; you had a fishing officer with teeth, everything was numbered and it worked very well. If we had that here, we'd be flying, but I don't see it happening, because there isn't the political will to do it."

A sanctuary

Ger has kept a keen eye on England, where efforts have been made to set up sanctuaries around the coast. "They're doing it in Grand Banks, with no fishing, and they thought that'd work after twenty years, but it's going into thirty years now. And I suppose it'll take years more."

Despite the difficulties, Ger would like to see a scheme initiated here along similar lines. "It's going to be difficult to do that, obviously. Where do you start, and where do you stop? Personally, to start with, I'd like to see there was only potting, hand lining and shellfish farming in the bay, because you'd have some control over the species, whereas with the dredging and the trawling and the netting, you don't have real control over it at all. I don't think any trawler or dredge should be allowed in. That's going to be very controversial, of course, and very hard to implement, but if we don't do that, the fishing technology has become so efficient that eventually we're going to clean out the stock. And how do you square that up with the guys that are fishing there at the moment? It's very tricky. There's talk of a ban on boats over eighteen metres from next year, but you'd still have smaller trawlers that can do a lot of damage.

"If you don't fish a species for a spell, it has some chance to recover. Ireland is not capable of supervising all its fishery, it's as simple as that. Maybe twenty-five years ago, we proposed closing off an eight hundred square mile box west of Ireland, where no one could fish. Ireland could supervise that. And as the fish come out, you could fish them any way you wanted. I think they'll have to do some sort of system like that. Or you could close off Kenmare Bay, from Dursey across to the Scarriff, and no one gets inside it. If the fish come back then, you could go out and fish them any way you like outside of the closed area. I don't know if that would work in practice or not, but you'd imagine something along those lines would have some chance."

Energy

Ger believes the next big development in the bay will be in the energy sector. "We have up to one and a half knots of water floating up and down out there, except for twenty-eight minutes a day; fourteen minutes each way when the tide stops. Apart from that, it's a guaranteed source of power. The technology isn't there yet, but it will happen, even if it's the next generation that does it."

If and when the technology for wave and/or wind power is employed in the bay, it would mean closing off a proportion of it to fishing. "But that would allow the fish to regenerate. This year, in the French market, thirty thousand tons of mussels showed up from Germany. Germany is more or less landlocked, but they have a small bit of the North Sea. What happened was they went offshore with their wind turbines, and some guy came up with the idea; why not deploy mussel lines between the turbines? They've produced a top quality mussel, a superior mussel. We need to do that; we need to go offshore as well.

We did an experiment offshore back in 2002; the results were brilliant, but the government is slow enough to get interested in it. That would be my dream before I kick the bucket, to get the mussel-growing offshore, but I'd like to look into the energy side of it as well."

Playboy magazine

Asked what his most unusual experience as a fisherman has been, Ger has no hesitation in picking the time he was featured in *Playboy* magazine. "That was maybe twenty years ago. I was fishing lobsters in Coulagh Bay at the time; I came into Ballycrovane one day and there was a film crew on top of the pier. They said they were doing an advertisement for Dubarry shoes, and they asked could they photograph me landing the fish. So I said, 'I don't really want to be in the photographs.' And they said, 'all we're interested in is your catch; if you put a box of fish on the pier and put your hands in and pick up a crab and a lobster, that'd be great.' So I said, 'grand,' and we agreed a fee. I think it was £20, which was probably more than I made fishing that day. So that was that; they took their photographs and off they went.

"I'd say it was six months later that a young fellow said to me, back in Eyeries, 'I see you're in *Playboy*.' And I said, 'no, I'm afraid you've got that wrong.' I didn't know what he was talking about. But as it turned out, I was wearing a fleece that I'd dried on the stove and forgot about, so the sleeves got burned, and they were ten different colours. It was obviously the sleeves of the fleece that your man recognised. But that was the first I knew that the ad was going to be in *Playboy*. The next question was, how would I get a copy of it inside in Supervalu without being seen? But we did get a copy in the end, and yes, the picture was in it. I have it still. And that was the only time I ever bought *Playboy*, by the way!"

15

DECCIE WISEMAN
CASTLETOWNBERE

Wiseman's Drapers and Haberdashery, at the West End of Castletownbere, is one of Beara's longest established businesses, and is now run by the third generation of the family, John and Deccie Wiseman. Like many local outlets, Wiseman's business has often depended on the fortunes of the fishing industry, which has seen both boom and bust.

Deccie remembers how there was widespread poverty in the Beara of his childhood. "Terry Willie O'Sullivan from Allihies came into the shop one time, when I was ten. Terry was talking to my father, and he said, 'you know, from the Barony Bridge (outside Glengarriff) west, there isn't £800 between everybody.'"

People often bought things on credit, and paid when they could. "Where the Buddhist centre is now, in Garranes, the man who lived there was on his own. But his sister came back from America one time and hired a limousine at the airport. She stayed in the hotel below. She went out and told the brother he couldn't live the way he'd been living. So she ordered new beds, new doors, new clothing. The whole lot. He thought she was paying for it, as she was loaded. But in the end she went back to America, and she never told him she was going. He came into my father, and he said, 'I'm in a bit of trouble, Eddie. I owe you a few pounds, and I owe Harrington's and Murphy's as well.' My father paid off the others, and your man paid him back maybe a pound or so a month.

Deccie Wiseman © Anne Marie Cronin

"He signed the land over to my father, but my father and grandfather were never into land. I brought my father out to Garranes one time, when Peter Cornish got it. Where Dzogchen Beara is now. And my father told me, 'this is the place we owned long ago.' I don't know how long it took him, but your man paid the debt off in the end."

On another occasion, a woman whose children were emigrating to America arranged for them to get new clothes on credit. "They all got kitted out before they left. The mother had nothing, but when one of them came home on holidays, she arrived into the shop and said, 'I'm sure my mother has a bill here.' My father didn't recognise her. 'What's your mother's name?' he said. But the mother was dead and gone, of course, and he wasn't pressing the debt. But she said, 'I want to pay it.' And she paid my father in full, and then she took himself and my mother up to the hotel for dinner.

"Another sister came home about three years later, and she came in to me to pay the bill as well. But I said, 'no, your sister has it all paid off already.' And I said how good she was. That time you were only looking for what was owed. They were sad times, tough times."

Some people were not quite so conscientious. "Another fellow came in one time, about four o'clock on Fair Day. 'Hello Eddie,' he said to my father. 'How's it going, boy? You're not looking too bad. I got a letter in an envelope there from you, and you know what you can do; you can wipe your ass with it. And you can do down and tell Arthur Hanley he can do the same.'"

For a long time, businesses in Castletownbere benefitted from the presence of the British Navy on Bere Island. But then, in 1938, Berehaven was restored to the Irish authorities; the British left, and the local economy did not pick up again until the fishing industry kicked off in the 1950s and '60s. "When the fishing boats first came into town, we'd get the odd Frenchman, the odd Spaniard. But the O'Driscolls were the first with the fishing boats locally. They had the one boat between them first, and then Billy O'Driscoll had the *Raingoose*. Then Gerry O'Shea bought the *Ard Bhéara*, and all the other boats came in then. I suppose they were 60-footers. The crew would come in to the shop for the wellingtons and the hip boots and the smocks that time, and most fellows got them on tick. But they'd come in after two or three weeks and they'd have it paid off. In the early '60s, the waders might be £3; they could be €70 now."

As Deccie remembers it, the 1970s were the boom years, when the fishing brought a level of prosperity that had never before been seen in the area, with local boat owners and crews earning large sums of money that went directly into circulation in the local economy. But there were other times, too, when the fortunes of Castletownbere benefitted from the unlikeliest of circumstances, not least the arrival of a fleet of Russian factory ships in the early 1990s.

The Russians

In those years, the Russian factory ships would follow the mackerel down from the west coast of Scotland. "They'd stop in Rathmullan first, and then in Killybegs, and then by the end of February they'd arrive in Castletownbere. They'd stay for March and April, and into May, processing the fish, and the big ship would come down and take the fish away then; that'd be the normal run of things. The Scottish and Killybegs boats used to follow them down with the mackerel, and there'd be five hundred boats in the harbour some years. The local lads were against the Killybegs boats coming down; they had good ships, and our boats were all small that time."

Russian factory ships in Berehaven, early 1990s

It's hard now to imagine the effect the arrival of the Russians had on the local economy. "At one time, there were at least five thousand people in the harbour. One boat alone had maybe eight hundred on board. They were mostly women, working at gutting the fish. One of the guys had good English; he said he'd been on the boat for maybe two years at the time. Those boats were rusty; they were coffin ships. When they got back, I'd say they were never worked again.

"When you think about it, at that time, the population of Beara was maybe four thousand, and you had to feed another five thousand people for two or three months of the year."

In the first few years, the Russian workers were accompanied by a KGB officer whenever they came into town. "He'd walk behind them, eight or ten strides back. He always had a bit of metal – a pistol - in his pocket. He must have had permission to be armed. And they were scared of him, you know."

The Russians spent wisely, investing in anything there might be a market for at home. "This was before the Communist system broke down; they were only given so much money, so they might have a glass of Guinness in the pub. But they'd buy electrical stuff. This was over thirty years ago, and they were probably collecting dollars for the last twenty years before that. They bought in old cars from Bere Island. Anything that looked like a Mercedes, they'd go for, and they were paying big money for them that time. They'd go into the garage and ask for the old Texaco cans, or Shell, that kind of thing. Some of the lads asked, 'what do you want all the empty cans for?', and they said, 'we'll fill them with Russian oil and reseal them, and when we go home, they'll think it's Texaco!'"

Deccie remembers that there were different crews every year. "A lot of them came from Siberia, or Latvia and Estonia, places like that. The first gang that arrived in the shop, there must have been a hundred of them. They were all looking for Wrangler jeans at the time. Wranglers were the in-thing, because they were American. This one woman stood in the middle of the shop and put on one pair of jeans after another. I said, 'they're all different sizes.' But that didn't matter. She went out the door with six pairs of Wranglers on her. She paid for them in dollars, though they weren't supposed to have the dollars at the time."

Another individual was after shoes. "This fellow now, he was about six foot six. He was maybe late fifties or sixty at the time. I probably gave him 10% off or something, because he bought thirty pairs of shoes. He liked the bigger sizes. Size 12, and he worked down from there. The dearer, the better. He must have been taking the money from some of the others for them, or he was buying stuff to sell when he got back to Russia. I brought him up to my house and offered him a drink. Brandy? Vodka? Gin and tonic? I had a bottle of Paddy, that I usually wouldn't drink at all myself, but that was what he wanted. So I got him a glass, and I said, 'you tell me when to stop.' I filled it to the brim, and he threw it back; he drank nearly all of it in one go. Next thing he stopped and said, 'Irish whiskey, good, good!', and then he finished it."

Some of the shoppers were not quite so honest. One bunch asked to see the footwear upstairs, and when Deccie checked the boxes after they'd gone, he realised they'd stolen forty or fifty pairs of shoes. "I totted up what it all cost, and I went up to the sergeant, but he said it was pointless trying to do anything, we'd get nothing out of it. But one of the guards said, 'I can't promise you anything, but leave it with me.' I knew the number of the boat; she was well down the harbour, and there was a big crew on her. So the guard went down and said, 'there's lots of shoes down below not paid for. I'll have to arrest the man who took them.' At first they said, 'no English, no English!' But the guard said, 'that's all right so, I'll lock the boat up, and you cannot leave the port.' They weren't long waking up after that. He got paid for the shoes there and then. But after that, we'd let maybe ten or twelve in at a time, and lock the door while they were shopping."

The Russians' arrival became part of the calendar for businesses in Castletownbere. "You'd know they'd be coming in the spring, and you could get rid of a load of the old stock in the shop. They loved white shoes. I had white ladies' bootees; I got rid of a good load of those. They loved the brand names as well. The USA t-shirts and things like that. I made a fierce mistake one time. This girl came down from Dublin; she was from Trinity. She found out I had old felt hats; they weren't worth much, they were there so long. And I had high-heeled shoes. We were haggling over the price, and we did a deal; she was going to give me a pound a pair for the shoes. But in the end she only paid me 50p a pair. But the Russians would have bought them if I'd waited. They'd have paid more for them."

Deccie remembers that the Russian vessels came for six or seven years before the system changed again. "What happened in the end was that the processors in Scotland and Ireland wanted the mackerel, and they didn't want it going to the Russians. So the EU banned it. But it was very lucrative down here that time; it was a huge plus in those years."

16

PAT FITZGERALD
CASTLETOWNBERE

Pat FitzGerald is a fisherman and artist whose family has had a long association with the sea. His great-grandfather Tom FitzGerald was a boat-builder from Caherdaniel, Co Kerry who married Nancy Dudley from Dursey Island in 1866. They settled at the West End, Castletownbere, where their son Mike carried on the boat-building tradition. Mike married Julia Murphy and they had thirteen children, among them two pairs of twins. One pair died of Spanish Flu; the surviving pair were John and Jim.

John FitzGerald, Pat's father, spent his early childhood being raised by his aunt on their farm in Knockaraud. Later, he and his brothers manned a seine boat they would row out to Dursey and back, setting long lines. When they weren't fishing, he and Jim helped build and repair boats with their father.

Nancy Dudley and Tom FitzGerald on their wedding day in Allihies, 1866. This is believed to be the oldest photograph of Beara people in existence © Mick FitzGerald

Tom FitzGerald in the late 1890s © Mick FitzGerald

"I think my father was a good carpenter," says Pat. "But not as good as Jim, who maybe had more interest too. At any rate, Jim was the one who stayed at home, and my father went to sea. He left Castletownbere in the 1930s. The English trawlers would come in here, and my father went away on one of them. He worked out of Milford, but ended up fishing in 'the Farmyard', as the grounds to the south west of Beara were nicknamed; that's where the Bull, the Cow, the Calf and the Heifer Rocks are. Some nights they would come in to Bantry Bay to clear the deck of fish and he could nearly see his home from the trawler."

Jim and John FitzGerald

After a time, Pat's father quit fishing. "I suppose he didn't like the long trips; they'd go as far as Iceland, the old steam trawlers. He went working instead on the coasters that carried cattle, food and general goods from England to Dublin and Belfast. He married and settled down in London then, simple as that. He was on the coasters all through the Second World War, but he never saw anything of it. He was an ordinary able seaman, though I think he ended as bosun's mate, a few feet up the ladder. I've still got his old discharge books. Sometimes he'd be laid off from the coasters, and he'd sign on for one of the larger ships, so he did a few trips to Canada and New York as well."

Fishing on the Ardent

Pat grew up in London, but his family holidayed in Castletownbere every summer. "We'd be packed off home for six weeks to Clounaglaskin, so this was home from home. My cousin Michael's father, Uncle Christy (the Cooper), was my father's best friend since childhood; they even married two sisters from Kealogue. When Christy died, myself and my father came back for the funeral. And when I came home, I decided not to go back. I said I'd hang on here for the summer."

Pat FitzGerald

Pat had been working in construction in London at that time, and he found work initially helping build the new Eiranova fish processing facility on Dinish Island. "Then one Sunday, I was at Mass, in the naughty boys' corner at the back of the church, and I was talking to Willie Russell. I'd expressed interest in the fishing; they were making good money at the time, compared to the buildings. And Willie tapped Mick Orpen on the shoulder and said, 'you're looking for a fellow, bring Fitzy away with you.' And Mick said, 'all right.' The Orpens and the FitzGeralds went way back."

Pat gave in his notice at work, and on a Monday morning a few weeks later, he packed a bag and left for Howth. "We drove up to Cork and got the train to Dublin, and some fellow picked us up at Heuston Station. That was in '79... I'm over forty years at the racket now."

Mick Orpen's vessel, the *Ardent*, was fishing herring at the time. "That was in July and August. We were landing into the Isle of Man. And it was only a four-day week: four nights fishing. The herrings were making serious money. If you had one hundred cran – four hundred boxes - in one night, that was a week's wages. And if you had four nights like that, that was four weeks' wages. You could build a house for twelve or fourteen thousand pounds at that time. If you were at the herrings, and you had a good season, you had the price of a house. There's no one can do that now, the price of houses is so inflated; you'd have to be on half a million a year."

The *Ardent* had a crew of six. "The way things were done that time, there were twelve shares. They'd take out the diesel and the expenses first, and then it was six shares for the boat, and six for the crew. The last guy on would be the cook, he'd be given the frying pan. That was my job then, to buy the groceries and do all the cooking and keeping the galley clean, but you'd still do the deck work as well. You'd cook two meals a day, or sometimes three. There was always one meal of fish, around teatime. You'd be gutting the fish on deck, and then you'd disappear, to put the dinner on. You weren't losing bunk time or anything. I had it timed so the dinner would be ready for the lads when they were finished. It made life easier for everybody. You'd put the spuds on, but you couldn't be inside sitting on your arse watching them boil; you'd go back out on deck and gut another few boxes of fish, and then you'd come back in and strain them.

"Normally the breakfast was a fry-up; or lamb chops, beans and eggs. Dinner might be bacon and cabbage or a stew. Pretty basic stuff. I used to make a mutton stew and put oxtail soup in it. Then I'd put in different ingredients the day after. I'd put in cornflour to thicken it up, and call it goulash. The next day, you'd make something similar but put curry powder in it. There was no rice, it was all spuds. Sometimes in the evening you might have self-service… cheese and bread and cups of tea. If you had a good cook, dinner was something to look forward to. Normally at that time, you'd be hauling every four hours. You might do a bit longer in the nighttime, you might go up to five. You'd be three or four hours on deck, and you might only have half an hour, or less, before you'd haul again. You'd look forward to food then."

Between hauls, sometimes the crew might get a few hours sleep, "and then you were back on deck again. That's just how things were. Now they'd call it slave labour; the Health and Safety gang nearly want us to have twelve hours on and twelve hours off. But back then, that was the norm; as soon as the fish came in, the net was shot again. You gutted the fish, washed them, put them down, iced them, and then you put them into the boxes and stacked them away. You'd do that as fast as you could; the faster you were at gutting, the better it was for everyone. You'd wash the deck down, and have everything ready for the next haul. You'd have your breakfast or your dinner, you might get to sleep for an hour or two, and then the whole thing would start again. But then, if you were only doing four days fishing, you had the whole weekend to recover. It was hard at the beginning, but soon your body clock got used to it."

The herring trawlers worked in pairs, and took turns shooting the nets. "You made maybe two tows, a tow each. You'd haul the net after three or four hours at the Isle of Man fishery and then take on board whatever you had. You were going for marks; you'd see the little specks on the sounder, and you wouldn't shoot until you saw them. We were fishing just west of the Isle of Man, on the twelve-mile limit.

The British Navy was there the whole time. Denis O'Driscoll - the Sarge - had the *Crystal River*, he'd keep an eye on the land with the radar and plotter… they were the only things we had, there was no GPS tracking that time… and one time the Navy called him up and said, 'you're two cables inside the limit.' The British Navy had it down to a fine art. What was a cable? Two hundred feet, or something. They were strict then."

Every Tuesday, Wednesday and Thursday, the *Ardent* landed her catch on the Isle of Man. "Whatever money you got for the fish, you split between the two boats. You had the day to kill then. You got the grub on board, then you were off to the pub or you hit the bunk, and you went back out that evening." On Friday, the *Ardent* landed back in Howth, "and we'd come home then. We'd be home Friday evening, you had Saturday and Sunday to yourself, and then you left again on Monday morning. So everyone was delighted, you know; you were making a good wage, and you were home every weekend."

When the Isle of Man fishery finished, the Castletownbere herring trawlers moved back to Berehaven. "The Celtic Sea was closed that time, so we'd fish up along the west coast. Everyone would take a turn steering the boat when we were steaming. The skipper would normally do the first shift, but if you left the harbour at nighttime, he'd be straight into bunk. Whoever's turn it was would go up and do four hours. You knew where you were going. If you were going up to Galway, you'd go from here to the Dursey past the Bull Rock, and then you'd follow the lights. You'd keep half a mile to a mile off the Loop, say. In the daytime then, you might take a short cut, through the Blasket Sound or something. The radars then weren't too bad. You'd hug the shore, just to get there faster. You'd have your marks. You'd have your radar, you'd just keep half a mile or so off land."

Certain areas were noted for herring. "Up around the Shannon was a big fishery. We got mighty fishing there, west of the Shannon by Loop Head, but in close to the mouth of the bay. One year we were the first boat on them, and we had maybe three serious nights fishing and short tows. The two boats were loaded. And then the other boats copped on, and they all turned up. The herrings were fetching £80 a cran that time.

That was a lot of money, £20 a box. You wouldn't get that now in a fit. So, that was all well and good, but that might only last a week. And then, when the Shannon quietened down a bit, we'd come down and fish in Dingle Bay, Brandon Bay, Finian's Bay or Ballinskelligs. We got fish one night in the Dursey Sound, towed in from the north and straight through and out by the Cat Rock. We would try in all the holes and corners. You'd end up around Baltimore inside the Stags, but you couldn't go much further east than that as the Celtic Sea was closed for herring fishing.

"Every place seemed to have a time. You'd go there one night, and there wouldn't be a fish. But you'd go the next night, and bang, they'd be there. It'd be as simple as that. You wouldn't tell anyone you'd come on fish, because there'd only be a few nights' fishing in it."

The herring season went on right through late summer, autumn and winter and into the following spring. "And then, when it started to wind down, you could still get two or three more weeks, going after the 'spents', the herring that had spawned. But you didn't get much for those. The fellows who were smoking and salting the herrings wanted them fuller, with the big belly on them. But you might get a week or two at them, around the Blaskets, and when that used finish out, in March, we'd start at the mackerel."

The trawlers that had fished in pairs in the herring season split up for the mackerel; the *Ardent*'s owner and skipper, Mick Orpen, would take a break at that time, and John 'Blackie' Murphy would skipper the vessel instead.

The boats used a three-bridle single boat system. "The three bridles kept the net open. You'd use ordinary whitefish trawl doors, and you'd tow the doors along the bottom, but the net would be up off the bottom. We used to go out here from Castletownbere for the mackerel, and all the Killybegs boats would be down that time too, in the '80s. You'd come in and land every day, because, with that quantity of fish… you might have 200 cran… the boat would be stuffed. You couldn't take on any ice, so you'd have to land them daily. We'd get a month out of the mackerel, maybe more. But the Koreans and Russian and Polish reefers or 'Klondykers' that bought the fish used to stay on. The bigger Killybegs and Scots boats used to chase the fish further south into deeper water, but it wouldn't pay us to do that as the fish wouldn't keep."

When the mackerel season was over, the *Ardent* went whitefishing. "We'd keep the trawl doors on for a couple of months. We'd be working out here, in 'the Farmyard', or off up west off Kerry."

In the early '80s, when much of the country was in recession, the fishing industry in Castletownbere continued to enjoy a level of prosperity barely imaginable today. "There were two auctions a week, on Tuesday night and Thursday night, and the floor used be full of fish. Twenty to twenty-five boats might land on a Tuesday night, and as many on a Thursday night. The pubs and the hotel, the Beara Bay, were all booming. It was like a frontier town; there was no violence or anything, but there was a lot of money around. They were good times. As soon as the auction was over, it was pub time. Or you went home. You'd go home to your family for the night, and head away again in the morning."

As the boats got bigger, and the equipment more sophisticated, the fishing trips grew longer. "We'd go out for a few days first, and then we started doing four-day trips. But even with the four-day trip, you had the weekend off. No boats worked at the weekend then. Nobody did. They'd all tie up Thursday night, and go away again Sunday night or Monday morning. We'd go up to Galway and fish west of the Arans and under the Cliffs of Moher. Up around Mutton Island and Liscannor Bay. We might spend twelve hours steaming up there, and as many steaming back. But we had really good fishing. That time, the big fish would be there; the pollock and the cod. There was a lot of hake that time too, but hake wasn't a popular fish, there was no great money for it. We used to get a lot of black sole and turbot; that was the money fish. Lemon sole and plaice, we'd get them too. We'd take ice for four days, and we'd come back with a fair bit of fish."

The downturn

The first signs of a downturn appeared around '82 or '83, "when the Celtic Sea opened for fishing after a lengthy closure and next thing the price of herring started to drop. The price went down from £20 a box to… you'd be lucky to get a fiver. Everyone thought it was the end of the world back then, but nearly forty years on you'd be glad to get €10 now."

Then the North Sea opened too, "and the price of herring tumbled. They started the fish quotas then; there was so much of a quota for this, so much for that. Everything went down. The EU, who were supposed to be looking after the fishermen, had no problem allowing cheap fish in from South Africa or elsewhere. Then the price of whitefish tumbled as well."

Eventually, the government withdrew funding for new vessels. "In the mid-70s, you could build a boat for £1,000 a foot. You'd have to find £70,000 for a 70-foot boat. The EU had the Fógra grant, and the government would match that. You had support. Then the Fógra grants disappeared because the government wouldn't match them. And if the government won't match the grant, they won't give it to you. A lot of fellows had boats being built, on the strength of the grants, and when the grants were axed, they struggled on or went to the wall."

When the boom times passed, the practice of selling the fish at auction went down in Castletownbere. "I think it was a fellow called Hogg, a Scotsman, came over buying fish that wasn't popular here like hake and megrims. He was exporting to Spain. He used to bring his own boxes and all. Wooden boxes. We'd been using the plastic boxes up till then, the 45-kilo box, or seven stone, as we called it then. Then the Co-Op said, why don't we send it out ourselves? And the Co-Op started to export fish directly to Spain, rather than rely on the buyers. The money was good in Spain, and that brought the price of fish up again. And that was a good thing, of course, but then the auctions got smaller and smaller, and then they went altogether. You were trying to sell the fish by phone instead."

Different vessels

Over the past forty years, Pat has fished on several different vessels, some using different methods of fishing "I was with Mick Orpen three years that time, on the *Ardent*. Then I was with Mick 'Old Road' O'Neill on the *Evening Twilight*, doing exactly the same thing. Then Michael Martin Sullivan, my wife Evelyn's brother, got a 36-footer, and I went with him for a couple of years. You'd be out at the mouth of the bay here, at the prawns, and Dunmanus Bay, then over in Kenmare Bay; between the three places, you'd make a decent living in the spring and summer. But come the wintertime, then the weather was against you if you were in a small boat. You might only get two days out of the week, you wouldn't get much out of that. At the same time, there was no weekend fishing. So you weren't making much money in the winter.

"I had a young family and a mortgage then, and I said, 'flip it, I can't survive on this.' I met John Regan from Schull, he had the *Mulroy Bay*, and I went back to the herrings. I spent twelve years with him. Then a friend of mine, the late Johnny McCarthy, God rest him, told me there was a berth going on the *Menhaden*. They were making a bit more than the regular trawlers. Maybe another grand or so a year, which was a lot. So I gave in my notice, and I started on her, that was twenty-five years ago, and I've been on her since."

The Menhaden

Over twenty years ago, most boat owners had to choose between registering as a whitefish or pelagic trawler. "But then, they had this thing called a polyvalent licence, which was a licence to fish both. Some of the boats still have it. But they don't like you whitefishing if you're at mackerel and herring. Most boats were given the option. They could go whitefishing, or they could be a pelagic boat. The bread and butter for us was on the pelagic side of it. So the *Menhaden* became a strictly pelagic boat.

"September now, that's when we start at the herring; we'll go out east in the Celtic Sea. Back then, the fishery was all in close, but now we have to keep outside twelve miles. If you go in September now, you'll go to the Smalls Bank and the Jones Bank, places like that."

In November, the trawler switches to fishing mackerel, up in the North Sea. "We catch them up there when they're more valuable. By the time they come down here, they're losing their fat content because they're swimming mad and they're burning off their fat. The heavier fish have more oil in them - Omega 3 - before they start travelling."

The *Menhaden* mostly lands its catch in Killybegs, but sometimes it will steam up north as far as Norway, where the price is invariably better. "We'd land into one place called Fosnavaag. It's an old whaling station. You come in a right narrow channel; there's a pier on either side, and it's just wide enough for the boat to get in. Inside there's a big basin, and there used to be all timber buildings around it from the whaling station, but it's all done up now. There's one fish factory, and a net repair place, and there's chandleries. The first time we landed mackerel there, we went to look around the factory, and the freezer room was a cave - a massive cave - and everything was kept in there. We were gobsmacked."

The *Menhaden* usually fishes for about seven months of the year, into March or April. "You'd get issued a new quota in the New Year. And what you'd normally do is, you'd fish so much of your quota in the spring, and keep some for the fall. But in 2019 we caught most of everything in the spring, as no one knew how Brexit was going to pan out. There's no point going up to the North Sea if you've got five hundred tons to catch and then not be allowed to fish there."

Unusual catches

In all his years fishing, Pat recalls that the strangest thing he's ever seen caught in the nets were a few items of crockery. "We'd get cups and mugs and things like that. We got a couple of plates with 'White Star Line' on them. I gave them to my brother over in England; he has them up on the wall. We once got a dead calf. Its belly was open and full of brown crabs; the smell was not too impressive either. But you'd get odd fish too that you wouldn't normally see. Huge skate. Massive. No one wanted them, so you'd throw them back over the side. They're fierce strong, so they'd live. Basking sharks… you'd normally get them over the side alive as well. And catfish. You'd get the odd one of them, and fiddle fish. All those fish are fierce strong, like a dogfish. You'd throw them out and they'd survive. But the cod now, he wouldn't survive. The swim bladder comes out his mouth; the change in pressure is like what it would be for a human."

Other trawlers have dragged up more unusual items, however. "The *Naomh Oilibhéar* hauled up a mine one time. They had it on the deck and they didn't know what to do with it. There was a big hole in it, and there was a nice brass thing inside it, and one of them said, that'd be lovely now on the mantelpiece. He managed to get it out, and then he wanted to open it, so he got it in the vice up under the whaleback. He was beating at it with a lump hammer, and when he eventually opened it, the powder inside it was still dry. It was actually the detonator, and he was hitting it with a hammer!

"A few years later, someone else got a shell. The Navy was called. The boat lost two days' fishing over it. They brought it in, and the experts exploded it across on the strand over on Dinish. I don't think it even blew up. The only thing that exploded was the Navy's own charge. But the boat was stuck inside for two days; I'd say the next time they'd find a shell, they'd fling it back out over the side."

When towing a net in the old days, Pat says, the biggest worry was not so much what they might catch but what it might snag on underwater. "You could be towing for four or five hours, and you might have torn the net in the first ten minutes and not know it. The grounds weren't mapped that well. You'd often come across a wreck, an old transatlantic cable or something. Most wrecks were charted; you had the old Decca plotter, and you'd have your fishing tows and red marks on the graph paper for wrecks, peaks or rough stony ground. Most of the wrecks would be on the plotter; they'd be known wrecks, taken off the charts. But some fellow might get caught on that wreck and he might pull a funnel or a piece of the mast off and tow it a mile beyond the wreck itself, he'd haul up and find a good tear in the net or sometimes very little of it left; that'd set you well back."

Painting

With the *Menhaden* tied up for the summer, Pat sometimes does trips with other boats, fishing for prawns, or cockles, as he's done this year. But more often, he devotes his free time to his other great interest, painting. And it's no surprise to learn that his favourite subjects are fishing-boats and the sea.

"I was always good at art," he says. "In school, I'd win prizes. I was fierce into photography as well; at home in England, I converted the bathroom, so I had my own darkroom. I'd be developing prints in there, in black and white. I used to love the Tate Gallery. There was the Red Bus Rover; you'd get the ticket and you could go on the buses all over London for the day. So we'd go up to London, myself and a couple more, and we'd do the art galleries. We'd see Turners, Constables and everything. Our art teacher, Colin Lythe, was great and would encourage us to do that.

"And then, when I finished school I kind of lost interest. I always had gouache paints and stuff, but I never really used them until some time in the mid-'80s when I was at home in bad weather. I took a picture of a boat, and then I did a painting of it. Gerry O'Shea started doing up the pub, the Marinero, and I said, 'I have a couple of paintings at home, of the boats; do you want to put them up?' And he said, 'sure,' and I sold them. The next thing was, someone asked, 'would you do one for me?' It came on from that then, and soon I was painting all the boats. I must have every boat in Castletownbere painted at some stage. Then I started doing seascapes, I found I enjoyed doing them even more. Now I mainly use oils or watercolours to get the detail in."

Pat FitzGerald with his grandson, Nathan Harrington

17

JIM O'SULLIVAN
CASTLETOWNBERE

Jim O'Sullivan of Beara Tourism has overseen the development of the Beara Way and the Beara-Breifne Way walking routes, and has a particular interest in the history of Berehaven.

"Berehaven can claim to be the second safest natural harbour in the world, after Sydney in Australia," he says. "Cork will dispute that, but Cork harbour has mud three quarters of the way out. You can walk out on it, like our Lord. Whereas the harbour here is seven miles long and it's very deep; it's thirty metres to the east, and roughly about fifteen and a half metres down the centre of the channel, which is as good as any other harbour in the country, and better than 95% of them."

The depth and breadth of Bantry Bay made it a natural choice for the French to anchor their fleet in when Theobald Wolfe Tone urged them to attempt an invasion of Ireland in 1796. "A lot of the French fleet anchored in Berehaven, and even in the late 20th century, there were anchors from those ships being found in the harbour. There's no doubt that a French longboat was captured in Bere Island, and she spent one hundred and four years in Berehaven, and was only ever known as the *Bere Island Longboat* until she was removed to Bantry and renamed the *Bantry Longboat*. That boat is now in the National Museum of Ireland."

*L – R: French Navy officer, Capt Charlie Lunny, John Murphy,
Monica Lynch, Jim O'Sullivan, Michael O'Sullivan, French Navy
Captain, Mary Lotty, French Navy officer and Gerdie Harrington on
the deck of a French Navy vessel at the pier in Castletownbere, 2003*

Among the other notable vessels associated with Berehaven was the
Great Eastern, which anchored there for long periods in 1865/66 during
the laying of the transatlantic telegraphic cable from Valentia Island to
Newfoundland. "The *Great Eastern* was designed by Isambard
Kingdom Brunel and was the biggest ship in the world at the time,
measuring six hundred and ninety-two feet and weighing nearly
nineteen thousand tons. They needed a safe anchorage for a ship of
that size, and Berehaven was perfect."

The British authorities took a greater interest in Berehaven from the
late 19th century, investing heavily in British military fortifications on
Bere Island and commissioning a number of reports on the feasibility
of developing the harbour for pleasure liners. "In 1901, the British
Parliament passed an act allocating £900,000 for the construction of a
railway line between Castletownbere and Cork. The project never
materialised, perhaps because there were objections from other ports,
or because it wasn't the best thought-out plan in the first place; there
was probably a bit of both. But then, in the First World War, the British
based a lot of their fleet here to protect 'the Southern approach', as they
called it, and there were four American naval ships based here too.
Strategically, we were an important location."

Along with Cobh and Lough Swilly, Berehaven was a Treaty Port, initially retained by Britain after Ireland achieved independence; all three were returned in 1938. "But then, in the Second World War, Churchill was seriously thinking of taking Berehaven back again, as Britain was losing so many ships in the Atlantic. The one reason he didn't seize the harbour was that there were so many Irish signing up for Britain in the war, and he didn't want to lose that goodwill. But there was a fair old stand-off between himself and de Valera at the time, and it showed again how strategic a port Berehaven could be."

Harbour authorities

The strategic importance of Bantry Bay for industry and trade was further emphasised in the late 1960s, when Gulf Oil established a large terminal on Whiddy Island. "Around that time, a harbour authority was established to look after all of Bantry Bay, including Berehaven. One result of that was, when the fishing harbour was set up here, it only had powers inside the perch between Cametringane and Dinish; the harbour master had no power beyond that. But another thing was that the Bantry Harbour Authority for many years had no real powers in the bay and the tankers came and went and didn't pay anything. That only changed after the *Betelgeuse* disaster in '79, when there was an inquiry, and one of the recommendations was that, if oil ever again came into Whiddy, there should be a fully-fledged harbour authority in Bantry."

When the Gulf War flared up in 1990, there was major pressure on to get the Whiddy terminal up and running again. "So the Government gave new powers overnight to the Bantry Harbour Authority, which meant they also had powers over Berehaven. At the time, a lot of the Russian fishing ships were anchored in Berehaven, with five thousand crew, and the sub-agent dealing with them was the late Gerard McCarthy. Bantry decided they were owed harbour dues by the Russians, so they sent Gerard the bill. Gerard was surprised at this turn of events, and so too was the harbour master in Castletownbere, a Welshman named Captain Bill Jones. Captain Jones only controlled inside the perch, but he did a small bit of research and discovered there was a relevant harbour act, which stated that a harbour authority could not collect dues unless they had a fully-fledged harbour master in place, and at the time Bantry hadn't. The Revenue Commissioners were dispatched to Castletownbere to impound the Russian boats, but Gerard produced a copy of the harbour act. Revenue went away and checked it out, and realised they couldn't enforce the ruling. So the Russians left without paying Bantry a penny."

The loss to the Bantry Harbour Authority was potentially in the region of tens of thousands of pounds. "So after that, a local committee in Castletownbere wondered, how do we get Berehaven back? At the time, Joe Walsh was Minister for Agriculture and it was a sensitive issue from his perspective. The Government in their wisdom decided to put the whole matter into the Attorney General's office, for his recommendations, with the expectation that the matter could take years.

"This was before the internet, and we didn't know much in Castletownbere about the powers-that-be in Dublin, but I thought I'd take a chance and ring the Attorney General's office one day. I expected to be hung up on, but they put me on to this lady called Sheila. I didn't know who she was, but when I said where I was ringing from, she told me she was Sheila O'Sullivan from Garnish. I gave her the full story, as far as I knew it, and she said, 'ring back in two weeks.' And when I rang back, she said, 'that paperwork is processed here and gone back to the Dept of the Marine.' I think Joe Walsh got a fair shock when he realised it had gone through the Attorney General's office so quickly; he certainly was not expecting that. It must have been a great shock to the whole process at the time. I doubt we'd have got the harbour back only for Sheila's input."

Around that time, a Spanish trawler went on the rocks in Bere Island, "and the press had a field day. They were saying the harbour master in Castletownbere was looking out through his window and had no power to enforce anything over the Spanish trawler. So then the Dept of the Marine accepted in principle that they would put a bill through. A bill would take a long time usually, but there was a short cut where, if you had all party agreement between Fianna Fáil, Fine Gael and Labour, it could jump up the list. And that was what happened. Within the next nine or ten months, Berehaven came back under the jurisdiction of the Castletownbere harbour centre, which meant that any fees from the Russian boats would flow through the coffers of the Dept of the Marine in Castletownbere and not go elsewhere.

"It was a huge blessing to get that back; if we didn't, Cork port would have it now, and we'd be in a sad state. But that shows you... Sheila O'Sullivan, who has since passed, had a major impact on the whole thing, and so did Captain Jones, the harbour master. Basically, you could say that Gerard McCarthy broke the biggest embargo on shipping in Irish history, because there were between sixty and eighty ships in the harbour at the time, that the Revenue wanted to impound. And Gerard proved that they couldn't enforce the law as stated; that was a major coup at the time."

Harbour development

In the late 1960s, five centres around the coast - Castletownbere, Rossaveal, Killybegs, Howth and Dunmore East - were designated as fishery harbours, with Dingle being added later. Work on developing the harbour in Berehaven began in '68, and has continued sporadically ever since.

"In 2010, the new pier on Dinish Island was built, up by Eiranova and in front of the Co-Op, and now they're adding another two hundred metres of pier, which will be a major boost to the port going forward. There must be thirty or forty lads working on the pier in Dinish at the moment; that's a big help around here. The only difficulty we have here now is that the rest of the Beara coastline, on the south side at least, remains under the control of Cork / Bantry Bay Port Company. When the most lucrative part of Berehaven is already under local control, I don't see the point of the coast being under Cork Port's jurisdiction.

"About ten years ago, there was a review of all the harbour authorities in the country, and they deemed that Bantry was a small harbour, and they had a choice of going with Cork Co Council or Cork Port. Bantry decided to go with Cork Port, which means that Cork Port controls Bantry Bay, excluding Berehaven. So, there's free access in and out for Castletownbere, but it means that any policy decisions for a peripheral region in West Cork are now taken by a board in Cork city, which doesn't make sense to me. We'd be better off if the Beara coastline was even under the Council's control, because we'd have the councillors to represent us. But that's how things stand at the moment."

Landings in Castletownbere

Landings in Castletownbere include those from Irish and European fishing vessels, as well as from local fish farms and cargo ships.

"The last official figures posted online by the Sea Fisheries Protection Authority are for 2018. That year, the value of landings in Killybegs, where they'd have much higher tonnage, but lower value, was €98 million, while the value of landings in Castletownbere was €107 million; this makes Castletownbere the top fishing port in Ireland. That figure includes the Irish and foreign fish landings, but not the fish farm landings, which can be between €30 and €40 million a year in Beara. Ballycrovane is probably the third biggest fishing port in the country, with the value of salmon landed there. If I'm correct, the fish farm figures could exceed the value of all fish landed by Irish boats in Castletownbere, but the Dept are very slow when it comes to releasing figures for that.

"The values for Castletownbere have increased substantially over the past ten years. We've gone from €29 million to over €107 million. That's a huge increase. There are about sixty fishing boats in Castletownbere between all the different sizes. Between the tugs and the fish farm boats and all that, there could be another ten or fifteen. Of those sixty boats, maybe forty would have a crew of five, but the smaller ones might have two or three. So there's probably two hundred and fifty fishing, all told. It's a pity that most of the crews are no longer Irish."

Figures for 2018 show that Castletownbere had 59,000 tons of cargo landings. "This is mostly from the sea coral that comes in from Iceland. It's dried here, and used to produce a tablet that's like a Rennie's for cattle. There's roughly about twenty ships come in each year, and each might have two or three thousand tons of sand. One time it was dredged down the harbour, but the Dept put a halt to that many years ago."

The future for Berehaven

The harbour at Berehaven has been put to numerous uses over the past several centuries, and that seems likely to continue. "One time Berehaven was a naval port, and people didn't see beyond that. Now we have a fishing port, a substantial one, and its figures are some of the highest in the country. Hopefully it'll stay the way it is, but that's not likely to create additional jobs going forward, the way it's looking. Fish farming is going to increase in some shape or form, but the servicing of other marine activities, I think, is probably key going forward, from cargo landings to liner visits and leisure boats.

"Hopefully, if things progress, there'll be the need for another pier extension in the next four or five years. The harbour master is under great pressure as it is, with the shortage of berths; he's a bit like the man with the aeroplane slots at Heathrow, it's always a bit tight. The back of Dinish Island looks like the most likely place to develop; there's a depth of between ten and fifteen metres out there. But it all depends on the Dept of the Marine."

The Dept has already agreed in principle to develop a small boat harbour, "a kind of marina in the port. They've put one into the other five fishery harbours, and Castletownbere remains the only one without it. Where it goes all depends on the economics; the cheapest place to put it is in the western slob, but that'll have to be dug out first. The site with the most visual impact would be south beyond the RNLI

Station. But there's contamination in the mud there, so there'd be extra cost. It will be up to the new Minister for the Marine to make that call.

"I think they'd go for a small marina first, at the west end, and then do something bigger and better. The advantage of the western site is that it would lift that end of the town. But that's definitely on their books, a small boat harbour. The Dept are very slow in committing to it, they'll put nothing on paper until a decision is made, but hopefully that'll happen in the next few years."

18

SEÁN O'SULLIVAN

CASTLETOWNBERE

Seán O'Sullivan, along with his brother Joe, owns and skippers the Castletownbere-based trawler the *Cisemair*. Like his father Joe Joe before him, who was one of the pioneers of the fishing industry in Castletownbere, he has worked as a fisherman all his life, and expects to do so until his retirement.

"I started fishing in July '83," he says. "I never worked with my father in my professional career, though I did in my school holidays all right, a couple of times. My father was a few years out of the job, and Ted Harrington Causkey was fishing the boat when I joined."

It was a fortunate time to be starting out in the industry. "Fishing was good, when there wasn't much happening on shore. The lads that I went to school with, some of them went to college, but it was only a shot in the dark in those days; it was another three or four years on the doss if your father could afford it. In hindsight, it worked out well for most of them. But back then, you couldn't get a job, there was nothing here. Or you'd have to go to England to get experience. I remember my Uncle Paddy in Dublin saying he had three qualified engineers labouring for him in the buildings.

"There was a good bunch went to America that time, a few more went to college, and four or five went fishing. As I say, we were very lucky; we made good money and we had a good lifestyle. We didn't have to work terribly hard either; we fished from Sunday to Friday, and we had nearly every weekend off. It's completely different now; it's all about grinding it out these days."

The older generation

Seán believes his father's generation deserves a lot of credit for establishing Castletownbere as a major fishing port. "The boats they had were a heap of rubbish, and they all had a very basic minimum education. It is hard to imagine now, but most of them never got to secondary school, never mind college. A lot of that generation went away and bought boats; for people like that with a modest upbringing it was a fair achievement. They might have had advisors, but still they had to make the decisions. The biggest debt that time would have been for buying a cow or something, and next thing you're talking a bank loan of £10,000. Crazy money to even contemplate, don't mind signing up for it. It didn't work out for some fellows, but to take it on at all was an achievement."

The Estrolita, *1969 Wheelhouse: Joe Joe O'Sullivan (Skipper)*
Standing L - R: Peter Carlton, Mick O'Shea, Unknown and Joe Jack
Harrington Seated on barrel: Nealie Harrington (Mike Dan)

Joe Joe went to Scotland to buy his first trawler, the *Estrolita*. "Most of the fellows here started out with help from local businessmen. My father and Frank Downey started out together, buying a boat with help from Brendan Murphy (Bere Island). Only for the likes of him and other businessmen in the town, many fellows might never have got started. My father went on to buy the *Estrolita*, his first boat on his own. He arrived in Edinburgh with the price of the boat - his whole life - in his pocket. He had no place to stay but eventually he got a room. There was a big rugby match on in the city that weekend and he was walking around with the price of the boat in his pocket, which would be like having £200,000 in your pocket now. They knew very little about banking in those times, I don't know would you even get a loan that time. When Dad went on to buy the first *Cisemair* in the early '70s, I think it was £1,000 a foot for a boat, so if a boat was seventy feet, it cost £70,000. It was massive money. Building a house that time might have cost £5,000.

"But they were the best generation really that came through here. Herring prices were good for a long time. Then they fell, and the stocks got low too. The North Sea fishery completely collapsed. What herring was here then, there was fierce demand for it altogether. All the Dutch buyers were after it, and now it's the other way around again."

Skipper's ticket

Seán was able to study for his skipper's ticket in Castletownbere. "That's how comfortable it was that time, that I could do it here on Saturdays. It was all done through BIM; they had a retired sea captain come over from Wexford to teach us, and I don't think it was for the money he was doing it. We had to go to Greencastle for a spell all right; we were the first class to do that, to learn the navigation systems. You couldn't do that without a proper school. That took three weeks, but that was the longest part of the training."

Young fishermen, mid-1980s Back Row: David Donegan, Eric Murphy, Kevin Downey and Brendan O'Driscoll Front Row: Michael Murphy, Jer Harrington and Séan O'Sullivan

Even the time in Greencastle involved its fair share of socialising. "I remember we were in the pub one evening and in the door walked John Hume with Ray Flynn, the Mayor of Boston. I'd say Flynn thought he was in heaven. He just wanted to mix with ordinary people; there was no FBI with him or anything. And they stayed all night."

The herring

Seán remembers that, when he started, the herring provided the best part of his living. "The rest was only seen as filling in the year. We used to start in August, after the Regatta, and sometimes as early as July, and we'd fish the herring right up to Patrick's Day. We were fishing all along the coast; we were never out of sight of the land. The radars that time weren't great, and navigation was basic enough. They were good boats, but it was all done by knowledge and experience really. The skippers knew all the harbours and bays in their heads. It was second nature to them, you know. All the harbour lights; they could tell you how long they were and so on. These days, I couldn't tell you what the flashes are on Ardnakinna, and there's no need to know. It's a completely different world altogether.

"Before my time, the best herring were got off Dursey in August. It was a short couple of weeks, but that was the best fishing. All the buyers wanted that fish, it was extra pressure. It was a natural phenomenon that the herring were so good out there; it was north of the sound, northwest a bit. The fish were just bigger. I never got the herrings there myself, it was more or less finished before I started. In general, fish on the western side of the country were bigger; it's nature, I suppose."

The Castletownbere boats spent much of the season fishing out of Dunmore East. "The big thing there was the weather; you could fish in Dunmore when you wouldn't get out here for a week. Even when I started, it was packed, and before that, it was jammed altogether. The boats came down from Northern Ireland and everything. It was a lot easier to fish off Dunmore East than the Bull Rock in the winter. The harbour here would have been practically empty. My father might have gone away for six weeks at a time. They had a lot more labour-intensive work than we had, hauling by hand. Landing was a big operation, but everything was in those times. We used to come home practically every weekend."

Seán remembers that there were any number of buyers based in Dunmore in his father's time, "whereas when I started there was none. But the market for herring roe came along then, in the late '80s. The Japanese loved it. I don't know if it's a myth or not, but it's supposed to be that the market only collapsed when their king died and as a mark of respect they stopped eating roe for a year. That's what we were told anyway!

"There were four factories in Castletownbere that time, and every housewife, every kid, anyone you could get, was working at it, cutting the roe out of the fish. It was a great time of year as well, coming up to Christmas. People had spending money, and again, a lot of that was spent in the locality."

The Japanese buyers were a novelty in Castletownbere. "Some of them were staying in Carltons' house. Agnes went out one time to collect the rent, and they were down on their hands and knees with buckets, scrubbing the tiles in the hallway. They were an absolutely spotless people."

In retrospect, Seán thinks the roe "was probably a bad fishery. There was good money made, no doubt about it, but there was a lot of fish killed for that."

Other ports

In October or November, the boats would often land in Cobh. "That was a tough town in those times. We used to land at the pier beside the train station. Unemployment was high and there were long queues for the dole office. We'd have to pass the queues heading up to the town. They'd always be looking for work, and some few of them would get it loading lorries. If they saw anyone double jobbing, they'd lose the plot. Irish Steel was a 24-hour plant even that time, and one fellow working there got a shift on the pier. There was a gang looking for work, and they were all saying, 'where's he going, like?' Cobh was very Republican, and so was Passage West. I never landed fish in Passage, but we'd tie up there in bad weather. They were tough. The hunger strikes were on that time, and there was spray paint all over the place. There were meetings, and they'd march up and down the town.

"You wouldn't see anything like that in Dunmore East. There was good land around there as well as the fishing. There were nice hotels; it was like a different world to Cobh. We loved landing there as young fellas."

One night, returning to the boat after a weekend at home, the car Seán was travelling in was stopped by the Army at Victoria Cross in Cork. "They were looking for someone – was it Dom McGlinchy or the Border Fox? Anyway, there were two fellows in the front of the car, with moustaches, and I was in the back with another fellow, with a beard. And there was a big suitcase between us. And next thing there's a load of soldiers around the car. 'Okay, where are ye going?' 'We're going fishing.' 'Open the boot.' It was full of grub. Your man was stashed somewhere around Cork, and they must have thought we were bringing him grub. Our story must have seemed unbelievable to them. The whole country was on high alert that time, any movement was being watched. And here we were, four fellows in the car with a load of food in the middle of the night… it didn't look good!"

The mackerel

In those days, after the herring season in Dunmore, there was no need for the boats to go north for the mackerel "as we could get them here. We'd fish the mackerel after Patrick's Weekend. They'd be mixed mackerel, but we didn't care, as you'd still be getting good enough money for them. There were ships in the harbour then to buy them. It was better set up for it that time. But there were no quotas then either, you worked as long as the fish were available. They moved on then, and that was the end of that. But now you have only so many tons to catch, and you have to maximise it. The quota went up by 40% in 2019; the stock is taking some hammering, but it's controlled hammering at the same time. And it's only for four or five months of the year.

"The Norwegians and the Scottish are more concerned about controlling the mackerel, they're more concerned about the price holding up. But you'd be half afraid that Iceland would do something radical. They could drop the price into the market. Iceland are like a loose cannon; their economy flopped, and the fishing was what got them out of it. They're still capable of doing something crazy, because they need the money, and their economy is so heavily dependent on fishing."

Norway is famously dynamic in controlling fishing in its waters. "They're probably the most efficient country in the world in that regard. They have healthy stocks, but they take care of them. We were fishing up there, and there was cod going with the herring, so they said they'd close that fishery to preserve the cod. I asked how long it would take to get it closed, and they said, two hours. It would take six months here to do that. By the time you'd get word to Dublin, and they'd get word to Brussels, and everyone would sign off on it, that would take at least six months… and then someone would raise a question, which would delay it again. The Norwegians have fierce control; they can make instantaneous decisions. When they close a fishery, every boat has to be gone out of there in two hours.

"They let other fleets in as well, but like I say, it's heavily controlled. They're as honest as the day is long, but if you screw them over once, that's it, you're gone. There'd be no appeals."

Whitefishing

Before Christmas, Seán was whitefishing, but he planned to head north after mackerel in the New Year. "2019 was not a great year at all for the whitefish. We're only getting the same price now as we did when we got the boat sixteen years ago. It's similar to the beef thing; it's a buyer's market, and the supermarkets control everything. Prices can only go so high, and no matter what happens, they'll go no higher. The supermarkets can fly fish in from Iceland or wherever.

"Monkfish would be €4 a kilo (for a whole fish) in a good month, but if you go into the supermarket, it could be €28-€30 a kilo for fillets. It's crazy. The middlemen are taking a bit all right, but even they're being squeezed. The supermarkets don't want to be hearing stories about bad weather or quotas or anything like that. Mrs Jones with her monkfish on Tuesday evening out in Douglas doesn't know anything about that. Personally, I think those supermarkets have too much control. They're not really worried about a beef farmer in Roscommon or a fisherman in West Cork. They just want good quality cheap food for the city markets. It used to be that they had to source it in the EU, but they've even broken that now; they can bring beef in from South America."

Part of the problem for Irish fishermen is that they're so dependent on exports. "Spanish boats would get at least 20% more for their fish in the Spanish market than we would if we're selling there. We don't have a big enough home market, that's our biggest issue really. We just don't have the population here. Even in Scotland, the chipper market alone is quite lucrative. All those big cities with chippers, they all need fish, whereas here, we're completely export driven. Brexit is going to be very messy for Ireland. England is very often a landbridge for us, so now there'll be one set of rules to get into England, and another set to get out again. They're talking about compensation packages and what have you, but who knows what will happen. Everybody's watching Boris Johnson. He's capable of anything if he thought he'd get away with it."

The EU

Many of the problems with the fishing industry in Ireland date back to when the country joined the European Union. "To be honest, I don't know what happened, but it seems like the Irish government didn't know the value of what they were negotiating with. It's the same with the oil and the gas; they just didn't know what they were talking about. At the end of the day, we're a very small cog in a very big wheel. It's the same in the UK; the Scottish fishermen don't know what way it's going to go, and London couldn't care less.

"Within the EU, there's a thing called 'relative stability'. The rest of the decisions don't matter so much; that's the one that's counted from the beginning. To start with, say, the monk out here, in our own waters, is 40% owned by the French quota, and we have 6%. That's always the way it's going to be, no matter what else happens. You could be arguing about everything else after that, but those are the figures that matter. And that's all down to relative stability. Unless there was a commitment to change that, the rest is just peripheral stuff."

Seán expects to continue fishing, at least for the foreseeable future. "But if my young lad there wanted to follow after me, I'd have a serious chat with him. You'd be better off now with your nine to five job around Cork or somewhere. We're swamped with paperwork, and the returns just aren't in it any more. Some boats are still doing fine, but it's a struggle for a lot of them, to be honest. Quota restrictions and the struggle to get crews are serious problems facing a lot of whitefish boats.

"The Department above in Dublin has no interest. They made no gesture at all that winter there was all the storms, and some of the lads were tied up at the pier for six months. They were all well squeezed that time. There were twenty small boats inside there, and a lot of them were fellows starting off; they had families with young kids. That cut deep with me; it wouldn't have cost much to do something for them.

"I don't know what the future holds. Personally, I'm okay, I'm nearly out the other end of it, but like I say, I wouldn't be advising my young fellow to go fishing. And I'm not proud of it."

19

MARTIN SULLIVAN

INCHES, EYERIES

In May 2020, Martin Sullivan retired after twenty-two years' service as Officer-in-Charge of Castletownbere Coast Guard, a voluntary organisation with its headquarters on Dinish Island, Castletownbere.

Speaking in August 2019, Martin recalled that "as far as I know, it's only since the late '80s that there's been a Coast Guard in Beara. My predecessor as Officer-in-Charge was the harbour master, Captain Bill Jones. He initiated the Coast Guard with a group of volunteers and they got it up and running in '88/'89.

"At the time you didn't have a lifeboat here, you had nothing on the peninsula. The group took it on themselves with a view to doing search and rescue and helping people in the Beara community. They didn't have a boat, only some ex-UK Coast Guard equipment; we still have bits of that in our station store. I think they started off with the breeches buoy, a rescue device for getting someone off a boat."

As the group became involved in cliff-climbing, more and more people got involved. "In the late '80s the Coast Guard was known as the Coast and Cliff Rescue. In 1994, when I came into it, we were just kicking off with the proper cliff equipment and a proper load of rigs. I got involved when I was asked by one of the volunteers at the time if I'd be interested. We're totally voluntary; no one joins for the money, it's just out of the love of doing something for the community. Search and rescue is a serious business, but it's also very rewarding. If you help someone down from the hill, or off the water, it's nice. If you bring back a body to a family, it's a comfort to them."

Martin Sullivan, Officer-in-Charge of Castletownbere Coast Guard
from 1998 to 2020

Premises and equipment

Initially, the Coast Guard was operating out of the old BIM building on the pier, which is now the fishery school. "When they vacated that for the new ice plant in Dinish, we moved in and did a bit of work inside in it. But there was always an understanding with BIM that they'd want it back. After that, we ended up in Portakabins in Dinish Island for a while. Then, out of necessity, this new premises was built. It was opened in 2002 by Joe Walsh TD when he was Minister for Agriculture and Food. At the time, people probably wondered what the building was for. We were criticised for the amount of money that was spent on it, and it was not a big amount of money. But you need a little bit of comfort. There's a kitchen, a training room, a shower and toilets, and then you have the storage room outside. And we have two jeeps and a van. We don't feel bad about this at all. We're not paid, and the least you can have is proper facilities."

The Coast Guard now has two jeeps and a boat. "Equipment-wise, we're not lacking at all; we have a central store in Dublin and they'll send out anything we want. They're very good like that. The days are long gone when you'd go to a rescue in your own car; we have the jeeps for that. There's a 40-horsepower engine on the boat; they're great, you can get into every nook and cranny on a search and rescue. But it takes a lot of manpower, and hours, to exercise with all the gear we've got. We've got a dedicated boat crew, but they have to keep their boat skills up. You have to put so much time in every year, otherwise you fall back. It's the same with the cliff equipment. We're individually assessed and recertified every three years, so you have to keep on top of it all. If you don't, you lose it mighty quick. Everything is certification now, but up to a couple of years ago, we just called in and said, we're off out, and no questions. Now we call in and the first thing we're asked is, 'how's the weather? Is it safe to go out?' It's harder to get out now, they question everything."

The Coast Guard building doubles as a pollutants store. "There are three pollutant stores in the country: one in Dublin, one in Killybegs and this one here. We don't operate the equipment, but it's there for any emergency. They have a private company that services the gear twice a year. Ideally, the harbour crew should have a knowledge of this as well, and in time I think they will. There are skimmers for when there's an oil spill; the blades on top spin around and skim the oil from on top of the water. They work hydraulically. There are baths for cleaning the birds as well, and all the gear is replaced regularly."

Castletownbere Coast Guard covers the entire Beara peninsula. "From Bantry to Kenmare, that'd be our patch. Iveragh Coast Guard is our flank station on one side, and Goleen Coast Guard on the other. We work together; we have the same equipment and if needs be we can call in for help any time. We often go down to Goleen to help out. Last month, we had a woman whose body was picked up in Kenmare; we had the Iveragh coastguard in there for that. We work together very well.

"The whole coast of Ireland is covered by the Coast Guard at this stage. There are forty-nine stations and about one thousand volunteers. The Coast Guard is part of the Dept of Transport, and operates out of headquarters in Leeson Lane in Dublin. The full-time staff are there, co-ordinating the rest of us. They have an office in Cork as well, and we have a fellow in charge of us there."

Martin Sullivan on a medevac exercise on Dursey Island

The Coast Guard trains constantly. "Every two weeks, we do multi-role unit, we do search, we do boat and we do cliff rescue. That is our role within the Coast Guard. We have a small boat, and we do inshore work, while the RNLI do offshore. The advantage would be that our boat is smaller, so if something happens in the neighbouring bays, we can trailer our boat there pretty quickly. We work in conjunction with the RNLI, of course, and on the northern side of the peninsula, we would work very closely with Derrynane Rescue. They're a great asset to the Beara peninsula as well; they can come across to us in fifteen or twenty minutes. We work closely with the helicopter, that's part of our set-up as well."

Call-outs

When the volunteers are notified of a job, as many as possible will turn up. "Generally, out of any call we'd get, twelve or thirteen of our seventeen volunteers might participate. There's a good core crew that we can rely on any time. If people aren't pulling their weight here, they're out. Our response depends on the call. If it's out west, say, most of the volunteers will have their equipment with them. Generally, they'll head straight to the scene, and we'll follow on with the van and the gear. It just makes sense that way. But generally, we'd start from the base on Dinish."

Communications now are a big help to the rescue services. "We use the VHS system and Tetra radio. And the mobile phones are great; most people that are lost would have one on them these times. There's a system in Valentia; if you call in, they'll text you back and pinpoint where you're phoning from, within metres."

Martin estimates that, in the past few years, "we've averaged about thirty calls each year. This year, however, we've been down to about half that, it's been extremely quiet. Maybe people are having more cop-on. Between the RNLI and ourselves, we're educating people all the time. We hope that long-term it pays off. We do school programmes when we can. It's all down to manpower."

Typically, most of the Castletownbere station's call-outs would involve hill work.

"Again, we're Coast Guard, we're cliff rescue, but we're not mountain rescue. But that said, we're surrounded by mountains, and when a person gets in trouble on the hills here, up on Hungry Hill or wherever, it's a great place for us to do a bit of work. Generally, Kerry Mountain Rescue get called for hill work, but with the equipment we have, we'll improvise and we'll do the job. You're waiting two hours for Kerry Mountain Rescue to get down to Beara, and where we can, we'll help out. Someone might slip and break an ankle, or suffer a fracture; you get plenty of that.

"The past couple of years, we've put our cliff equipment into action on a good few occasions. The latest occasion was out in Garranes a couple of months ago; a man got disoriented and tried to get up a hill at the wrong place. There was a steep incline, and he got totally stranded. A couple of years ago, out at Dursey, a fisherman got washed off the rocks. That was a serious one. Luckily, the tide put him back up on the rocks again. When we got out there, the lifeboat couldn't get in to him because it was too dangerous. The helicopter couldn't operate its winch because the downdraft from the helicopter would have blown him off the rock. We were the last option there; we got our ropes down and pulled him up. That's the serious side of it. That's why we train and why we have our equipment here. When the day comes, we'll be ready for it."

Castletownbere Coast Guard, 2019

Castletownbere Coast Guard, 2019

Castletownbere Coast Guard has anywhere between fifteen and twenty volunteers at any one time. "We're all on pager. We're coordinated by Valentia; they call the shots, they radio us and we do our job, and they trust us to do it. I'm the Officer-in-Charge, there's also a deputy Officer-in-Charge, and there's a crew under us then."

There have been many memorable rescues, some of which have had a humorous side. "Four or five years ago, a guy came down from Fermoy and stayed in John Murphy's Restaurant, and went off touring on his bike the next day. He went out towards Ardgroom and in the evening he came back, but he decided he'd go around by Allihies. On the way, he went off-road into Claonach. He was a bit tired, so he lay down on the side of the road, and when he woke up it was dark. So what did he do? He picked up his bike and continued on into Claonach, thinking he was heading for Castletown. When we found him it was maybe two o'clock in the morning; he was on top of the hill, out towards Cod's Head. He was heading down for Reentrisk, and he still had his bike with him, carrying it on his shoulder. He was fine, but it was a funny one."

A more serious rescue occurred three years ago. "At half twelve or one o'clock in the morning, we took three children off a dangerous ledge on the back of Hungry Hill. The family went up there with their father, and the children wandered off. They ended up on a very narrow ledge, with a very serious drop underneath it. We had to come in above them, and go down on ropes and take them up one by one. Everything was done in the dark, and to me, it was great credit due to the crew. In my view, we are never praised enough for what we do. We don't have a great PR machine, compared to the RNLI."

One of the more serious jobs Castletownbere Coast Guard was involved in was the retrieval of material from the *St Gervase*, a local trawler that foundered off Mizen Head in 2000, with the loss of all four of its crew. "We were involved in that big time. A lot of wreckage came across from the Mizen to here. We picked all that up and brought it back down to Schull."

The Coast Guard has been involved many times in retrieving fatalities from the water. "The odd time we've retrieved the body of someone we'd know. But when you do, no matter how well you know them, you feel you've done a good deed for someone. You go into a mode where you just do the job. When you have a group like this, and you've just dealt with a serious incident, it's good to have a place to go and talk about it afterwards. A bit of a debrief."

Martin enjoys the social aspect of his involvement with the Coast Guard. "All my counterparts from around the coast will meet up shortly and we'll discuss how things are done," he says. But he believes the position of Officer-in-Charge should be made full-time and salaried. "There's a massive full-time staff in Dublin, whereas with us, we're juggling this with our jobs. But they don't seem to realise that above in Dublin."

The Castletownbere Coast Guard was invited to participate in the Easter Rising commemorations in Dublin in 2016. "We had to learn to march for that; I never realised there was so much involved in it. We gave Saturday after Saturday going to Cork to train. But that was a great event, and it was nice to be involved."

Martin keeps fit by hillwalking. "I've walked most of the hills in Beara at this stage. I climb Hungry Hill ten or twelve times a month; I must have climbed it at least one hundred times last year. I was up there again yesterday morning. It's amazing, we have all this on our doorstep, but I might meet no one at all on the hill."

20

PAUL STEVENS
CASTLETOWNBERE

Paul Stevens is Lifeboat Operations Manager at Castletownbere Lifeboat Station, and has been involved with the service since it was first established in the area in 1997.

"Castletownbere was unusual for a long time in that it was a major fishing port and didn't have a lifeboat," he says. "The two nearest stations are Baltimore on one side and Valentia on the other, and there's over eighty miles between them. There was a lot of campaigning, led for many years by Sheila O'Driscoll and Dónal O'Driscoll amongst others, to get a lifeboat placed here, with the result that the RNLI eventually agreed to provide one on a trial basis."

The proposal, announced by the RNLI in February 1997, was to place a boat on service in Castletownbere for a period of one year. "That summer about twenty of us went on a lifeboat training course in Poole, in Dorset. We were then given an Arun class lifeboat, the *Roy and Barbara Harding*, that had previously been stationed at the Aran Islands for a decade. The boat arrived in Castletownbere on the 25th of October 1997 amidst much celebration and was placed on a mooring in the harbour."

Arrival of Castletownbere's first lifeboat, the Arun-class Roy and
Barbara Harding

Lifeboat Roy and Barbara Harding *arrives at the pier*

The lifeboat station was initially housed in a metal container at the
western end of the pier, and then moved to a Portakabin on Dinish
Island. "RNLI staff coxswain Mike Storey came over from England.
Sadly, he's passed on since, but he spent six weeks here with the crew,

training us every night. Some people already had maritime experience, but others had none. Currently only about 5% of the RNLI volunteer crew is made up of people with maritime experience; the majority of people who work at sea simply don't have time to be involved. In Castletownbere, we are very lucky to have a significant number of crew who come from a fishing / maritime background which is so valuable in terms of their vast experience and detailed local knowledge."

Arrival Day: Colin Williams, RNLI Inspector of Lifeboats for Ireland, the late Dónal 'Dan' O'Driscoll, Hon Sec of Castletownbere Lifeboat Station, and John Nolan, Chairperson, Castletownbere RNLI

Crew of the Roy and Barbara Harding *L – R: Joe Tim O'Sullivan Sr, Brian O'Driscoll (Coxswain), Paul Stevens, Marney O'Donoghue and Michael Martin Sullivan Sr*

The first mechanic at Castletownbere lifeboat station was Brendan Gonnelly, an ex-Navy engineer. "Brendan was the only one paid a salary at that time. We had a volunteer coxswain, Tony O'Sullivan, who had spent many years fishing and working on tugs; he was there the night of the *Betelgeuse* disaster on Whiddy Island. Tony and the crew were all volunteers."

The lifeboat soon proved its worth, and the RNLI agreed in October 1998 that Castletownbere should keep the service on a permanent basis. "From 1997 to 2004, when we had the *Roy and Barbara Harding*, we had over one hundred call-outs. The RNLI then sold that boat in *Raufarhöfn* in Iceland – they had an arrangement to sell their used old boats on to lifesaving services in Iceland or China – and we got our next vessel, the *Murray Lornie*, from Lochinver in Scotland."

Castletownbere's second lifeboat the Murray Lornie

Crew of the Annette Hutton, 2004 L – R: *Michael Martin Sullivan
Sr, Paul Stevens, Marney O'Donoghue, Mike Murphy, Paddy
O'Conor, Michael Martin Sullivan Jr, Brendan Gonnelly
(Mechanic), Morgan O'Sullivan, Brian O'Driscoll (Coxswain) and
Joe Tim O'Sullivan Jr*

The service of the *Murray Lornie*, from January to June 2004, was a temporary measure until Castletownbere could be provided with a brand new Severn class lifeboat, the *Annette Hutton*. "Annette was one of the Hutton family from Broadstone in Dublin, and she left a legacy to fund the building of a lifeboat. We discovered later that her family were coachbuilders, and had built the coach that the Queen takes to Westminster for the annual opening of Parliament. When we went to collect the boat in Poole, the Queen was there to open the new training college, and we brought her for a spin around the harbour."

The *Annette Hutton* is a 17-metre boat, and the last station-based Severn class lifeboat to be built. "It's an all-weather lifeboat; if it turns over, it'll right itself. When it was being built, I remember going to Berthon's Boatyard in Lymington, and watching them lift it on a crane and drop it down hard, and there was no damage done and she self-righted within seconds."

The crew brought the new lifeboat on passage from Poole to Castletownbere, arriving on the 7th of August 2004. "The night before, we were arriving into Baltimore, only to be tasked on our first mission. With our new lifeboat we were actually faster than the Baltimore boat, reaching the casualty before them."

The lifeboat station

Castletownbere was eventually provided with a new lifeboat station and pontoon, at the eastern end of the pier; the €950,000 two-storey premises was officially opened by marine correspondent Tom McSweeney in May 2013. "The new station was funded by the RNLI and designed by Gordon Philips, an architect from Scotland who was a lifeboat crew member himself, and knew what was needed in terms of design. A number of the new stations that have been built since around the coasts of Ireland and the UK have used a similar design."

There are many advantages to having this dedicated station in Castletownbere, rather than across the harbour on Dinish Island. "For one thing, it's helped us shave five or six minutes off our launching time, which has since proved to save lives," says Paul. "Furthermore, we can now bring casualties from the lifeboat directly to shore, whereas previously we had to transfer them to a smaller boat and then land them at the slip. Sometimes, unfortunately, we have to bring in the remains of people who have been lost at sea, and the new facility ensures that families can come to the station and be afforded privacy.

"There's the whole health and safety side of it as well, which is really important. We now have a lot more room for the storage of equipment, and it's easier to bring it on and off the boat. And the boat can stay plugged in. One of the difficulties we had when she was out on the mooring was that everything was turned off, and then you'd try to turn on the navigation equipment, and the cold or condensation might have got at it and you'd have problems. At the new station, the boat is always ready to go."

The crew

Castletownbere fisherman Brian O'Driscoll eventually succeeded Tony O'Sullivan as coxswain of the lifeboat and Tony became Lifeboat Operations Manager, and then, when Brendan Gonnelly retired, Marney O'Donoghue was appointed full-time mechanic. "Last year, Brian retired from the station to become a regional Area Lifesaving Manager, so he's now manager over the RNLI stations between Ballycotton and Valentia. He was succeeded as coxswain by Dean Hegarty. Dean, at twenty-four, is one of the youngest coxswains in the RNLI.

"In terms of the crew, we have about twenty-five volunteers all the time. As well as our full-time coxswain and mechanic, we have a complement of deputy coxswains and deputy mechanics, so the full-time crew can get time off. I did that myself for a good few years; as second coxswain providing weekend and holiday cover for Brian. Among the crew we have navigators and casualty care responders. When the boat launches, you need seven on the crew but there are times we have gone with only five."

The coxswain's role is similar to that of a skipper, and he manages the boat. "People have this image of the coxswain clinging to the wheel, but that isn't really how it is at all nowadays. His job is to make all the decisions on board, and he has ultimate responsibility for the boat and the crew and making sure the rescue is carried out safely, efficiently and effectively."

The mechanic, meanwhile, is charged with maintaining the engine and all the machinery and equipment. The coxswain and mechanic will always be on board when the lifeboat goes to sea. "The rest of the crew have different roles. You have a navigator, who's in charge of the chart table, the Sat Nav and the radar. And you have someone on the helm, steering the boat. The coxswain is usually in the middle seat, looking out, and checking in with everybody else. Most of the crew will be trained to a high level in casualty care; we've seen some very grisly things, but that's part of the job. Most of the roles are flexible, but you must always have a coxswain in command and a mechanic aboard."

The crew train intensively. "It's all very well structured and well thought out. Crew train every Wednesday evening, mobile training units visit the station from time to time, and volunteers are sent to the Lifeboat College in Poole, which provides a range of certified courses. These include sea survival, seamanship, navigation, boat-handling, command search and rescue, and a variety of other areas. Coxswains are taught how to plan and co-ordinate a search. If the Navy is at the scene of a rescue, say, and you have a large number of fishing boats, how do you set up your search pattern? There are also particular courses for casualty care, as there's quite a high level of First Aid required at sea.

"We also do regular exercises with the local Irish Coastguard unit, the local fire brigade and the Shannon-based Coastguard helicopters *Rescue 115.*"

Tony O'Sullivan, first Coxswain of Castletownbere lifeboat, and Colin Williams, Inspector of Lifeboats for Ireland, on the occasion of Tony's retirement as Lifeboat Operations Manager

Fundraiser Vince Harrington (Gour) and Fundraising Secretary Sheila O'Driscoll

Paul acknowledges that those who go to sea are very often the face of the RNLI. "But the shore crew are equally important," he says. "Without them, the lifeboat station would not function. The Management Committee, led by chairman John Nolan, oversees the general running of the station. The Operations Committee meets monthly and ensures there is adequate coxswain and mechanic cover, that the boat and lifesaving equipment is fully operational and liaises with external agencies. The Fundraising Committee raises those vital funds which keep the boat operational. Over the years there have been many local fundraisers, including Sheila O'Driscoll, Fr Seán O'Shea, Joe Turner, Vincie Harrington (Gour), Anne Finch, Tony O'Sullivan and latterly Peadar Lowney. Over the years the fundraisers have been instrumental in organising and facilitating a wide range of fundraising activities. The people of Beara and further afield have always shown enormous support for Castletownbere lifeboat."

Call-outs

The Castletownbere lifeboat has a range of one hundred and fifty miles offshore, and can achieve a speed of twenty-five knots. "The RNLI's aim is to get to a casualty fifty miles out within two hours of launching. Many call-outs have been fishing boats that experience mechanical failure or get propped. Sometimes we've been called out to a sinking boat, or to search for missing persons. One difficult feature of the job is that it sometimes involves recovering those who have been lost at sea. In a small place like Beara, that can be difficult, as we'd often know the people. We've had a significant number of those types of tragedy, and the circumstances are very challenging for the families in dealing with it. But, in recovering a body, it does make the situation a little easier for the family."

The lifeboat is usually tasked by the Irish Coastguard at the Marine Rescue Co-ordination Centre in Valentia Island. "They usually ring me, as the station's Lifeboat Operations Manager, or if I'm not available, one of the deputy launching authorities; Michael Martin-Sullivan, Paddy O'Conor, Felix O'Donoghue or Brendan O'Neill. As we are a voluntary non-state search and rescue resource, the Coastguard have to request us to launch. They usually give a quick summary of the emergency and ask can they set off the pagers. While the lifeboat is requested to launch, the reality, of course, is that the boat always launches; we've launched over three hundred times by now, and we've saved nearly forty lives."

Once the decision is made to launch, the launching authority rings the coxswain and the crew are informed via pager; all the crew carry one, and it's left on 24/7. "Usually there are two alerts. The first page is to announce the launch, while the follow-up gives more information on the circumstances behind it."

The lifeboat usually launches between six to eight minutes after the first page is transmitted. "If it's not an emergency, if it's someone broken down miles out, and there's no immediate risk to life, we'll take our time, and we'll take people who are maybe training up."

On rare occasions, the lifeboat will no sooner return to shore than it might be called out once more. "It's worth remembering that, even if you come in late at night, the crew and boat have to be absolutely ready to go again. If the crew goes out at three in the morning, they mightn't have eaten since the evening before, and it could be four o'clock in the afternoon before they get back. Although we have very limited supplies aboard, there are times you'd be starving. I remember once, we pulled in alongside the pier after a very long shout. We'd rung ahead and ordered steaks and chips for all the crew, and we were salivating, but as we arrived at the pier we got another shout and we had to go straight back out. We didn't have the grub till we got in much later that night."

Commendations

Most shouts are very straightforward and are undertaken with little difficulty. However, Castletownbere lifeboat has been awarded commendations for a number of call-outs.

"You always think of the lifeboat launching in desperate conditions," says Paul, "but usually the conditions are quite moderate. That said, we've had very difficult shouts in very bad conditions. One was a boat called the *Skellig Dawn*. We went out on a very bad night, with Brian O'Driscoll as coxswain, and three of us managed to get aboard. There was a fisherman in the captain's cabin who had a broken pelvis. We couldn't get a stretcher in, so we had to take the cabin apart and take him out on a board. We got a commendation from the RNLI Chairman for that and another for the rescue of a boat called the *St Gothard*; that was a very long protracted rescue in very difficult conditions, with Michael Martin-Sullivan as coxswain."

Crew of Clodagh O *rescue, 2018 L - R: John Paul Downey, Marney O'Donoghue (Mechanic), Dean Hegarty (Coxswain), Dave Fenton and Séamus Harrington*

The most dramatic rescue in Paul's experience was undoubtedly one that occurred at the harbour's mouth in October 2018. "It was a dreadful night – dark, with gale force 9/10 south-easterly winds, driving rain and a gigantic swell. A fishing vessel, the *Clodagh O*, with six crew on board, lost power and was being swept towards the cliffs near the Piper's Rocks. They issued a Mayday and the lifeboat launched immediately. Such was the urgency that the lifeboat launched with only five crew. Every minute mattered. The lifeboat was on scene within minutes, but the stricken vessel was only twenty metres from the shore at this stage. The crew had just one chance to get a tow rope on board. With superb seamanship, determination and highly effective teamwork, the lifeboat managed to get the casualty under tow. This was a shout where every second mattered. Undoubtedly, if the station had still been based in Dinish Island, our launch time would have been slower and the six fishermen lost.

"In January 2020, the RNLI announced it was awarding the RNLI Bronze Medal for Gallantry, the first in ten years in Ireland, to Dean Hegarty – incidentally, this was Dean's second shout since he was appointed coxswain only a month earlier. Crew members Marney O'Donoghue, John Paul Downey, Dave Fenton, Séamus Harrington and Deputy Launching Authority, Michael Martin-Sullivan, were awarded framed letters from the RNLI Chairperson."

Memorable launches

The most notorious call-out Castletownbere lifeboat has had related to a vessel that got into difficulty in Dunlough Bay in 2007. "That was a bad morning, and the pager message seemed strange – a dinghy fishing got into difficulty. It sounded suspicious but we acted as usual. I was ashore and suddenly I was getting a lot of phone calls. Once on scene, the crew realised very quickly there was something much bigger going on. There was a casualty in the water amidst sixty bales of cocaine. He was recovered by our crew, and later Baltimore lifeboat joined us."

Most of the bales were subsequently recovered by the authorities, and the smugglers were arrested. "There was an amusing newspaper item the next day, when Ryanair had an ad showing a picture of our lifeboat, with one of our crew picking up one of the bales of cocaine, with the caption, 'Dopes? They should have flown Ryanair!'"

There were other memorable call-outs. "Very early on, we went out to a fishing-boat from Dublin. This guy was on his own travelling around the coast with no navigation gear or lights, simply using lighthouses as a means of navigating. When we got to the boat, there was nothing on it at all, but we suspected that its 'cargo' had been dumped. We brought the boat in to the pier, and he jumped off and scarpered as fast as he could.

"Another time we had a call-out to a group who were on one of those inflatable banana boats, rowing from town across to Bere Island. When we came up alongside, they wouldn't get on board the lifeboat at first because they would have had to stop drinking.

Eventually the bottle dropped in the water, and we dragged them on board."

The lifeboat is often called out to medevacs, when people need to be evacuated because of some medical emergency. "We've had some funny ones of those as well. I remember being coxswain one night we went out to a boat. There was a huge lop. One of the difficulties is, you're coming in alongside, you're trying to pace the boat, and get the casualty down on deck. This was about three weeks before Christmas, and we had this guy who'd supposedly had a heart attack. We weren't a minute alongside when he jumped with his suitcase onto the deck. He had no heart attack, of course; he just wanted to go home for Christmas."

The future

The RNLI is not content to rest on its laurels. "The organisation has traditionally been about lifeboats and saving lives at sea. But in recent years there's been a significant shift. In the UK, the RNLI manages lifeguards on the beaches now as well, and a large part of its work is about education and prevention. The RNLI has the strategy to try and reduce the number of drownings. Rather than just be a responsive service, it aims to be proactive. So we have sea safety checks, where the RNLI comes around and advises boat owners on sea safety and helps check equipment. There is also a drive to get the message out to young people, about the importance of water safety and safety at sea."

The RNLI has now established a facility where the boats are built in-house. "Different classes of lifeboat are named after a river. Each boat is then named individually after the person or organisation that bequeathed the funds to build it. So we have the *Tyne*, the *Clyde*, the *Mersey*, and the *Arun*, which is a little river near Southampton. Our own boat is the *Severn* class with the numbers 17-44. The '17' refers to the 17-metre *Severn* class – and the '44' indicates that it's the forty-fourth boat of this type to be built. The boat's name *Annette Hutton* is in memory of the Dublin lady who bequeathed the funding. But this year Clogher Head and Clifden both got a new class of lifeboat, the

Shannon class; this is the first time a type of lifeboat has been called after an Irish river."

Paul sees a positive future for the RNLI in Castletownbere. "We are fortunate to have such a dedicated crew that is committed to training and being as skilled as possible. They are willing to drop everything day or night to respond to the pager. We have a shore crew that ensures everything runs smoothly and a fundraising committee that raises vital funds. Most importantly, we have the support of the local community. With this combination, I think our lifeboat will continue to provide a 24-hour search and rescue service to those who find themselves in distress at sea around our shores for many years to come."